THE FORENSIC EVALUATION OF TRAUMATIC BRAIN INJURY

A HANDBOOK FOR CLINICIANS AND ATTORNEYS

THE FORENSIC EVALUATION OF TRAUMATIC BRAIN INJURY

A HANDBOOK FOR CLINICIANS AND ATTORNEYS

EDITED BY

Gregory J. Murrey

CRC Press

Boca Raton London New York Washington, D.C.

Bay Shore

Library of Congress Cataloging-in-Publication Data

Catalog record is available from the Library of Congress.

Dedication

This book is dedicated to Martha and the boys

BS

6/7/01

Preface

Over the past decade, I have seen a drastic increase in the number of traumatic brain injury (TBI) cases that have ended up in the courtroom. As a clinical neuropsychologist who conducts evaluations of persons with suspected brain injury, I have all too often found myself sitting in a courtroom trying to defend my professional opinion and decisions. I have discovered, along with my colleagues, that to be comfortable or at least confident in such an adversarial system, it is important to be knowledgeable in the entire assessment of TBI and the forensic process involved.

Although there have been a myriad of publications on TBI and forensic neuropsychology, I could not find a text available to provide a medical and legal professional with a concise overview of the forensic assessment process and the issues in TBI. Finding such a need, I felt compelled to draw together a group of experts in the medical, neuropsychological, and legal professions to develop such a text. However, the text was not designed as a comprehensive work on forensic neuropsychology, neuropsychiatry, or even TBI as there are many excellent authoritative texts available on these subjects. Instead, I and my colleagues have designed this text to provide both the clinician involved in forensic examinations and the legal professional involved in personal injury litigation or legal proceedings with a general overview of the issues and assessment process in TBI cases. Accordingly, the text begins with an overview of "key" issues involved in the forensic assessment of TBI including definitions and select medical diagnostic terminology that should be of particular interest to the forensic examiner and legal professional. Subsequent chapters provide an overview of the neurologic, neuropsychological, and psychological forensic assessment process specific to brain injury cases. The final portion of the text provides the reader with an overview of general forensic issues with a particular focus on the forensic examiner as expert witness. In this section, such issues as qualification and credibility of the forensic expert and admissibility of expert testimony in TBI cases are reviewed. This section will, of course, be of particular interest and concern to the forensic examiner in light of new court rulings and possible modifications to the admissibility of a given forensic examiner's testimony.

The contributors to this book have also attempted to provide clinically useful and practical tables and reference pages that can be used by forensic examiners and legal professionals involved in TBI cases. It is my hope as editor that this text will be a useful resource and overview for clinicians and legal professionals alike.

Gregory J. Murrey
Brainerd, Minnesota

Editor

Dr. Gregory J. Murrey, Ph.D., A.B.P.N, received his doctorate in clinical psychology from Washington State University and completed his specialty training in neuropsychology at Duke University Medical Center. He has been awarded a Diplomate in Clinical Neuropsychology from the American Board of Professional Neuropsychology and also holds a Diplomate from the American Board of Forensic Examiners. He is currently the Director of Neuropsychology and Neurobehavioral Services at the Minnesota Neurorehabilitation Hospital in Brainerd, Minnesota. He is also a consulting neuropsychologist at Polinsky Medical Rehabilitation Center in Duluth, Minnesota and holds a faculty appointment at The Fielding Institute.

Contributors

Joseph A. Davis, Ph.D., LL.D., FACFE
Executive Director
Center for Applied Forensic Behavioral
  Sciences
San Diego, California

Gregory J. Murrey, Ph.D., A.B.P.N.
Director of Neuropsychology and
  Neurobehavioral Services
Minnesota Neurorehabilitation Hospital
Brainerd, Minnesota

Donald T. Starzinski, M.D., Ph.D.
Clinical Director
Minnesota Neurorehabilitation Hospital
Brainerd, Minnesota

Joseph Yedid, Ph.D.
Clinical Neuropsychologist
Scripps-Mesa Psychological Services
San Diego, California

Table of Contents

List of Tables and Figures

1 Overview of Traumatic Brain Injury: Issues in the Forensic Assessment

Gregory J. Murrey

CONTENTS

1.1 DEFINITIONS AND CRITERIA FOR TBI

The incidence of brain injury in the United States has been estimated to be in excess of ten million new cases each year (Hartlage, 1990). Approximately 1.5 million Americans sustain head injuries requiring medical attention each year, with roughly half of these requiring hospitalization as a result (Davis, 1990). The etiologies of traumatic brain injury (TBI) are quite varied, but include motor vehicle accidents, falls, on-the-job injuries, and assault. In the forensic evaluation, it is critical for the clinical and legal professional to have a clear set of criteria for and definition of TBI. In the medical, neuropsychological, and legal literature, there is a variety of definitions and criteria set forth on the matter of TBI; however, existence and severity of a TBI are usually established by the following (Evans, 1992; Esselman and Uomoto, 1995):

1. the occurrence and period of loss of consciousness;
2. the degree of loss of memory for events immediately before and/or after the accident;

3. the degree and duration of alteration in mental state at the time of the accident; and/or
4. the degree of focal neurological deficits (which may or may not be transient).

1.1.1 LEVEL OF CONSCIOUSNESS

Level of consciousness is most commonly assessed by medical or emergency personnel using the Glasgow Coma Scale (GCS) soon after the injury (Teasdale and Jennett, 1974; see Table 1.1). The GCS formally and objectively assesses eye, motor, and verbal response to various external stimuli. Total GCS scores range from 3 (no response to stimuli) to 15 (normal response to stimuli), and GCS scores of 13 to 15 are considered to be within the normal range of functioning. The definition and criteria for mild TBI, as established by the American Congress of Rehabilitation Medicine (American Congress of Rehabilitation Medicine, 1993; see Table 1.2), do not require a loss of consciousness. However, loss of or change in level of consciousness post-injury does provide the medical professional or other clinician important information that is helpful in determining the existence and severity of a brain injury.

1.1.2 POST-TRAUMATIC AMNESIA

Another important criteria to be considered in the assessment of TBI is the level of post-traumatic amnesia (PTA) which refers to the loss of memory for events immediately before or after the accident, and typically includes an inability or reduced ability to effectively process information or stimuli (visual or otherwise) post-injury. The level and duration of PTA can certainly correlate with degree of loss of consciousness; however, the existence and duration of PTA can be difficult to determine. A formal, semi-standardized method of assessing PTA is the Galveston Orientation and Amnesia Test (GOAT) (Levin et al., 1979; see Table 1.3). The GOAT quickly screens a patient's orientation to self, place, and time as well as assesses existence and degree of anterograde (post-injury) and retrograde (prior to the injury) amnesia (memory loss or memory processing deficit). Scores on the GOAT range from 0 to 100, with 76 to 100 being within the normal range and 65 or lower being in the impaired range. Although the GOAT is a commonly known and utilized instrument among neuropsychologists who work in acute rehabilitation settings, it is not commonly used by medical professionals. Thus, the forensic examiner must often rely on somewhat subjective reports (after the fact) of family members and observers or even the injured person. When it is used, the GOAT is typically administered in the emergency room or other acute medical setting to individuals suspected of having suffered a brain injury. It is important for the examiner to determine if there was any indication of PTA and to arrive at a gross estimate of the period of PTA. It is not so critical nor typically possible to determine the exact number of minutes or hours of PTA. Rather, it is important for the examiner to determine if: (1) there was a period of PTA; and (2) if the duration was less or more than 24 hours.

TABLE 1.1
Glasgow Coma Scale (Recommended for ages 4 to adult)

EYES	SCORE
Open	
Spontaneously	4
To verbal command	3
To pain	2
No response	1

BEST MOTOR RESPONSE	
To Verbal Command	
Obeys	6
To Painful Stimulus	
Localizes pain	5
Flexion-withdrawal	4
Flexion-abnorma	3
Extension	2
No response	1

BEST VERBAL RESPONSE	
Oriented and converses	5
Disoriented and converses	4
Inappropriate words	3
Incomprehensible sounds	2
No response	1

GCS TOTAL	3–15

Source: Adopted from Teasdale and Jennett (1974).

TABLE 1.2
Definition of Mild TBI — Head Injury Special Interest Group of the American Congress of Rehabilitation Medicine

A patient with mild brain injury is a person who has had a traumatically induced physiological disruption of brain function as manifested by at least one of the following:

- Any period of loss of consciousness.

- A loss of memory for events immediately before or after the accident.

- Any alteration in mental status at the time of the accident (e.g., feeling dazed, disoriented, or confused).

- Focal neurological deficit(s) which may or may not be transient, but where the severity of the injury does not exceed the following:

    (a) loss of consciousness of approximately 30 minutes or less;

    (b) after 30 minutes and initial Glasgow Coma Scale of 13–15; and

    (c) post-traumatic amnesia not greater than 24 hours.

Source: Adapted from American Congress of Rehabilitation Medicine (1993).

TABLE 1.3
Galveston Orientation and Amnesia Test (GOAT)

1. What is your name?
   Where do you live?

2. Where are you now? City _____ Hospital _____
   (unnecessary to state name of hospital)

3. On what date were you admitted to this hospital?
   How did you get here?

4. What is the first event you remember **after** the injury?
   Can you describe in detail (i.e., date, time, companions) the first event you can recall after the injury?

5. Can you describe the last event you recall **before** the accident? Can you describe in detail (i.e., date, time, companions) the first event you can recall **before** the injury?

6. What time is it now?

7. What day of the week is it?

8. What day of the month is it?

9. What is the month?

10. What is the year?

Source: Adapted from Levin et al. (1979).

1.1.3   ALTERATION IN MENTAL STATUS

Alteration in mental status, often described by the injured party as feeling "dazed," disoriented, or confused at the time of the accident, can at times be formally observed and documented by emergency or medical personnel at the scene of the accident or in the emergency room. Assessment of alteration in mental status is particularly important in mild TBI cases. Yet, such alterations are most commonly reported only by the patient/injured person after the fact. Even though an alteration in mental status has not been formally documented by an outside observer, the forensic examiner should not and cannot conclude that it did not occur. The alteration or transient change in mental status could be momentary and may have resolved (at least to some degree) before the arrival of a reliable observer or examiner (e.g., law enforcement or emergency medical personnel). However, duration and extent of alteration in a person's mental state post-injury certainly should be considered by the forensic examiner and typically correlates with severity of injury.

Focal neurological deficits, typically assessed by technical neuroimaging studies such as MRIs, CT scans, EEG studies, and on rare occasions, PET scans (see Chapters 2 and 3 for further discussion on these technologies), need to be considered in determining the existence and severity of a TBI. Medically documented neurological deficits are not a required criterion for the existence or occurrence of TBI, although such technologies as MRI and CT scans are invaluable in its assessment. However, both of these technologies are limited and may be insensitive to abnormalities and/or functional deficits after brain injury (Wilson and Wyper, 1992). In fact, it is not uncommon for persons who have suffered a mild brain injury to have normal CT and MRI scans, which argues for the importance of the functional (neuropsychological) assessment in such cases. A prime example of the limitations of CT and MRI scans as well as the often lack of correlation between such neuroimaging studies and neuropsychological results is the research data in the area of persons with Alzheimer's disease. The majority of persons diagnosed with mild to moderate Alzheimer's disease who present with clear neurobehavioral and neuropsychological dysfunctions and deficits often have normal CT or MRI scans; whereas many "normal" functioning (neuropsychologically and neurobehaviorally speaking) elderly persons have abnormal CT or MRI scans (Thatcher et al., 1997; Gonzales et al., 1978; Eslinger et al., 1984; Hatazawa, 1981; De Leon, 1997; Bird et al., 1986).

Newer and more sophisticated technologies and procedures such as Positron Emission Tomography (PET) and functional fMRI are proving to be more sensitive to neuropsychological changes following TBI and are more highly correlated with neuropsychological findings (Ruff et al., 1989; Gale et al., 1995). In fact, it was once commonly believed and accepted within the medical field that once a TBI person is out of the acute recovery stage, there should be no further decline in cognitive functioning nor adverse change in neuroanatomical or neurophysiological systems; however, more recent research using PET studies has actually demonstrated that cerebral atrophy (shrinkage) may occur as a result of cellular damage, but may not be able to be observed clinically until at least six to nine months post-injury. Newer research also suggests that mildly brain injured persons with evidence of neurological deficits or documented focal lesions (e.g., more complicated mild head injuries), may actually have poorer functional outcomes (Williams et al., 1990) than those without such deficits or lesions.

The term *concussion* is a common term used by medical professionals which often corresponds with the diagnosis of mild or moderate brain injury. According to the International Classification of Disease — 9th Revision (ICD-9, Medicode, Inc., 1998), a concussion is a "transient impairment of function as a result of a blow to the brain" which can include brief, moderate, or prolonged loss of consciousness, "with or without return to pre-existing conscious level."

Another term that would be important for the legal and medical professional to understand is *post-concussional* syndrome or disorder. This is a term commonly used by treating and consulting physicians and is typically seen in the medical documentation of persons who have suffered or are suspected of having suffered a mild TBI. The term infers the existence of chronic or ongoing cognitive, physical, and social/functional impairment as a result of a TBI (or more specifically, a significant cerebral concussion). Table 1.4 outlines the research criteria found in Appendix B of the *Diagnostic and Statistical Manual of Mental Disorders, Fourth Edition* (DSM-IV, American Psychiatric Association, 1994). Note that this is labeled as "research criteria" as the task force reviewing these specific criteria at that time determined that "there was insufficient information to warrant inclusion (of the proposals) as official categories or axes in the DSM-IV." DSM-IV diagnoses that can be used for persons presenting with post-injury cognitive or emotional impairment (transient or permanent) include: dementia due to head trauma, amnestic disorder, cognitive disorder not otherwise specified, delirium due to a general med-

TABLE 1.4
DSM-IV Research Criteria for Post-Concussional Disorder

A. The history of head trauma that has caused significant cerebral concussion.
   NOTE: The manifestations of concussion include loss of consciousness, post-traumatic amnesia, and, less commonly, post-traumatic onset of seizures. The specific method of defining this criterion needs to be established by further research.

B. Evidence from neuropsychological testing or quantified cognitive assessment of difficulty in attention (concentrating, shifting focus of attention, performing simultaneous cognitive tasks) or memory (learning or recalling information).

C. Three (3), or more, of the following occur shortly after the trauma and last at least 3 months:

   1. Becoming fatigued easily.
   2. Disordered sleep.
   3. Headache.
   4. Vertigo or dizziness.
   5. Irritability or aggression on little or no provocation.
   6. Anxiety, depression, or affective lability.
   7. Changes in personality (e.g., social or sexual inappropriateness)
   8. Apathy or lack of spontaneity.

D. The symptoms in criteria B and C have their onset following head trauma, or else represent a substantial worsening of pre-existing symptoms.

E. The disturbance causes significant impairment in social or occupational functioning and represents a significant decline from a previous level of functioning. In school-aged children, the impairment may be manifested by a significant worsening in school or academic performance dating from the trauma.

F. The symptoms do not meet criteria for Dementia due to Head Trauma and are not better accounted for by another mental disorder (e.g., Amnesic Disorder due to Head Trauma, Personality Change due to Head Trauma).

Source: Diagnostic and Statistical Manual of Mental Disorders — Fourth Edition (1994).

ical condition (TBI), personality change due to TBI, mood disorder due to a general medical disorder, and anxiety disorder due to a general medical disorder. (See also Table 1.5 for a listing of the DSM-IV diagnostic criteria for each of these diagnoses.)

A final term that should be reviewed here is that of *closed head injury* (CHI) and how it is similar and how it differs from the term *traumatic brain injury*. According to the *International Classification of Disease — 9th Revision* (ICD-9, Medicode, Inc., 1998), Section 907, closed head injury is defined as "late effects of inter-cranial injury without mention of skull fracture." Thus, the terms closed head injury and TBI are standardly used interchangeably in the field of neuropsychology. It would also be important for the medical and legal professional to be aware of any definitions of TBI within his or her respective state statutes that may be applicable to a given case. For example, the State of Minnesota has a statutory definition of mild TBI (see Minnesota Statute 144.661).

In summary, it is important for a professional conducting the forensic assessment to be knowledgeable in the varied and often conflicting definitions and criteria applied to a TBI (particularly mild TBI). The examiner should also be clear on the definition or criteria that he or she is applying to determine the existence and/or severity of a TBI and should be able to defend the decision to use that particular definition. It is also necessary for the examiner to address the definition and criteria applied by other medical professionals involved in a particular brain injury case.

1.2 ESTIMATION OF PREMORBID INTELLIGENCE AND FUNCTIONING

Obviously, a key issue in the forensic assessment of persons with TBI is the determination if, and to what extent, cognitive or functional change has occurred. In such a determination, an ideal situation of course would be to have available to the examiner results of neuropsychological and/or intelligence tests administered prior to the injury. However, such data are rarely available to the examiner as these tests are not routinely administered to "normal functioning" individuals in academic or other settings. When such pre-injury data are not available, the forensic examiner (specifically the neuropsychologist) must estimate the premorbid IQ and cognitive functioning level of the examinee so as to be able to make a comparison with the current evaluation data and/or test results. Four methods typically used by neuropsychologists to estimate premorbid functioning include the following:

1. *Review of pre-injury academic and occupational records and history* (including military records, if available). Evaluation of school records including secondary and post-secondary transcripts and grade reports can aid the neuropsychologist in making a professional opinion regarding the examinee's pre-injury gross intellectual and cognitive functioning level. Such information, combined with occupational history, such as type of positions held, (e.g., technical or management-level positions) educational level achieved (including post-secondary training, courses, or degrees completed), and military training in specialized technical or professional areas, can provide the examiner with important data with which to support a given opinion of the examinee's general abilities prior to the injury. Of course, an exact IQ level cannot be ascertained from such history, but an opinion as to whether the examinee was at, above, or below the normal (average) functioning level can be typically established.

2. *Use of reading and vocabulary test scores.* Certain intellectual and cognitive function tests have been found to have a high sensitivity to brain injury or neurological impairment (see Chapter 3 for an in-depth review of such tests); whereas other tests, namely certain reading or vocabulary-type tasks have been found to have a very low sensitivity to brain impairment (Blair and Spreen, 1989; Crawford, 1992; Wines et al., 1993) — particularly when speech/language functions have not been significantly impaired as a result of the injury. For example, the vocabulary subtest on the Wechsler Intelligence Scales (Psychological Corporation, 1997) has little to no correlation with neurological impairment; thus, persons with brain injury or other neurological insult (including Alzheimer's dementia)

TABLE 1.5
DSM-IV Diagnoses and Criteria Commonly Used in TBI Cases

DSM-IV Criteria for Dementia Due to Head Trauma

A.   Disturbance of consciousness (i.e., reduced clarity of awareness of the environment) with reduced ability to focus, sustain, or shift attention.

B.   A change in cognition (such as memory deficit, disorientation, language disturbance) or the development of a perceptual disturbance that is not better accounted for by a pre-existing, established, or evolving dementia.

C.   The disturbance develops over a short period of time (usually hours to days) and tends to fluctuate during the course of the day.

D.   There is evidence from the history, physical examination, or the laboratory findings that the disturbance is caused by the direct physiological consequences of a general medical condition (TBI).

DSM-IV Criteria for Dementia Due to Other General Medical Conditions

A.   The development of multiple cognitive deficits manifested by both
  (1) memory impairment (impaired ability to learn new information or to recall previously learned information)
  (2) one (or more) of the following cognitive disturbances:
    (a) aphasia (language disturbance)
    (b) apraxia (impaired ability to carry out motor activities despite intact motor function)
    (c) agnosia (failure to recognize reality or identify objects despite intact sensory function)
    (d) disturbance in executive functioning (e.g., planning, organizing, sequencing, and abstracting)

B.   The cognitive deficits in criteria A1 and A2 each cause significant impairment in social or occupational functioning and represent significant decline from a previous level of functioning.

C.   There is evidence from the history, physical examination, or laboratory findings that the disturbance is the direct physiological consequence of one of the general medical conditions listed below (dementia due to HIV disease, head trauma, Parkinson's disease, Huntington's disease, Pick's disease, Creutzfeldt-Jakob disease, or TBI).

D.   The deficits do not occur exclusively during the course of a delirium.

DSM-IV Criteria for Amnestic Disorder Due to (Indicate General Medical Condition)

A.   The development of memory impairment is manifested by impairment in the ability to learn new information or the inability to recall previously learned information.

B.   The memory disturbance causes significant impairment in social or occupational functioning and represents a significant decline from a previous level of functioning.

C.   The memory disturbance does not occur exclusively during the course of a delirium or a dementia.

D.   There is evidence from the history, physical examination, or laboratory findings that the disturbance is the direct physiological consequence of a general medical condition (including physical trauma).

TABLE 1.5

DSM-IV Diagnoses and Criteria Commonly Used in TBI Cases (Continued)

DSM-IV Criteria for Cognitive Disorder Not Otherwise Specified

This category is for disorders that are characterized by cognitive dysfunction presumed to be due to the direct physiological effect of a general medical condition that do not meet criteria for any of the specific deliriums, dementia, or amnestic disorders listed in this section that are not better classified as Delirium Not Otherwise Specified, Dementia Not Otherwise Specified, or Amnestic Disorder Not Otherwise Specified. For cognitive dysfunction due to a specific or unknown substance, the specific Substance-Related Disorder Not Otherwise Specified category should be used.

    Examples include

        (1) Mild neurocognitive disorder: impairment in cognitive functioning as evidenced by neuropsychological testing or quantified clinical assessment, accompanied by objective evidence or a systemic general medical condition or central nervous system dysfunction

        (2) Post-concussional disorder: following a head trauma, impairment in memory, or attention with associated symptoms.

DSM-IV Criteria for Personality Change Due to TBI

A.   A persistent personality disturbance that represents a change from the individual's previous characteristic personality pattern. (In children, the disturbance involves a marked deviation from normal development or a significant change in the child's usual behavior patterns lasting at least 1 year).

B.   There is evidence from the history, physical examination, or laboratory findings that the disturbance is the direct physiological consequence of a general medical condition.

C.   The disturbance is not better accounted for by another mental disorder (including Mental Disorders Due to a General Medical Condition).

D.   The disturbance does not occur exclusively during the course of a delirium and does not meet criteria for a dementia.

E.   The disturbance causes clinically significant distress or impairment in social, occupational, or other important areas of functioning.

DSM-IV Criteria for Mood Disorder Due to TBI

A.   A prominent and persistent disturbance in mood predominates in the clinical picture and is characterized by either (or both) of the following:

        (1) depressed mood or markedly diminished interest or pleasure in all, or almost all, activities

        (2) elevated, expansive, or irritable mood

B.   There is evidence from the history, physical examination, or laboratory findings that the disturbance is the direct physiological consequence of a general medical condition.

C.   The disturbance is not better accounted for by another mental disorder (e.g., Adjustment Disorder with Depressed Mood in response to the stress of having a general medical condition).

D.   The disturbance does not occur exclusively during the course of a delirium.

E.   The symptoms cause clinically significant distress or impairment in social, occupational, or other important areas of functioning.

Source: Diagnostic and Statistical Manual of Mental Disorders — Fourth Edition (1994).

will typically show little to no significant decline in performance on this test. Likewise, normal aging with the associated (expected) cognitive decline will have little effect on a given individual's performance on this type of test. Therefore, performance on these tests can be used to estimate pre-injury verbal intellectual abilities. Two additional tests which have been effectively used to estimate premorbid intelligence in neurologically impaired patients are the Wide Range Achievement Test — Revised (WRAT-R) (Jastak and Wilkenson, 1984) and the North American Adult Reading Test (NAART) (Blair and Spreen, 1989). Both are considered reading screening tests but, more accurately, are tests of word pronunciation. Although reading comprehension and memory can decline significantly after neuropsychological impairment, word pronunciation and vocabulary abilities are much less sensitive to brain injury. Both the NAART and the WRAT-R can be useful to the examiner in estimating premorbid intellectual functioning, although the WRAT-R has been found to provide a slightly more accurate estimate and is a "preferred measure of premorbid verbal intelligence." (Johnstone et al., 1996). It should be noted, however, that both the WRAT-R and the NAART may tend to underestimate higher intelligence ranges and overestimate lower intelligence ranges (Wines et al., 1993; Johnstone et al., 1996; Barry et al., 1994).

3. *Use of a demographic-based indexes.* Statistical formulas based on intelligence test scores, education, and occupational history have been used to develop demographic-based indexes for estimating pre-injury IQ level. The Barona Index (Barona et al., 1994) for the Wechsler Adult Intelligence Scales has been used quite frequently by neuropsychologists in the past. However, with the revision of the Wechsler scales, there is currently no prediction formula for the new instrument and, thus, such an approach is now less likely to be used by an examiner. Additionally, with the new research on the efficacy and utility of the WRAT-R or NAART approaches in estimating premorbid IQ, such demographic-based approaches are, in general, being used less (Karaken et al., 1995).

4. *Use of highest test scores of current neuropsychological evaluation.* In this approach, the professional examiner uses the highest or average of the highest scores on the neuropsychological and/or intelligence tests (that are assumed to represent relatively intact or unaffected functions) as a gross estimate of premorbid or pre-injury functioning (even though such an approach is not based on a statistical formula per se). One common example of use of this method is to compare the performance IQ and verbal IQ subtest scores on the Wechsler Intelligence Test (see Chapter 3 for a complete discussion of the WAIS-III). The logic behind such an approach is quite obvious in that: (1) normative data used in standardized neuropsychological testing take into account individualized strengths and weaknesses; thus, for an individual to perform outside of the normal range and/or to have a significant difference between test scores is statistically and often clinically quite rare (suggesting a decline

and/or impairment in that selected functional area); and (2) the highest scores from tests are often viewed as a reflection of the examinee's actual or highest attained cognitive abilities. Typically, the examiner should and does use a combination of these various approaches to estimate pre-injury functioning.

1.3 POST-INJURY EMOTIONAL FUNCTIONING AND PERSONALITY ASSESSMENT ISSUES

Emotional disturbance and "personality changes" following or secondary to the brain injury can often complicate the forensic assessment process in TBI cases. The medical and psychological examiners need to assess for the presence of any psychological sequelae such as post-traumatic depressive or anxiety symptoms. Such an assessment can be quite complicated as many symptoms related to depression can mimic or even confound post-concussional symptoms (Rosenthal et al., 1998; Busch and Alpern, 1998; Klonoff et al., 1993). Additionally, post-injury depression, anxiety, and/or stress disorder can adversely affect a person's cognitive functioning (at least in a transient manner) in such areas as attention, concentration, speed of processing, memory and learning performance, and psychomotor functioning. Thus, it is often difficult for the examiner to reliably determine if specific symptoms or symptom profiles are due to an actual brain injury or resulting from an emotional disturbance (see Chapter 4 for a more complete discussion of psychological symptoms and assessment). Certainly, such symptoms could be related to both an actual post-concussional syndrome and an emotional disturbance secondary to the injury — which is often the case (Rosenthal et al., 1998). Rosenthal's recent review of the literature on depression and brain injury suggests a high incidence of depression following brain injury (much higher than is found in the general population). These research studies have found incidence rates of post-TBI depression anywhere between 33% and 66%. In fact, onset of the depressive symptoms often may not occur until several months post-injury, which may be due (in part) to increased insight or awareness of the deficit and/or losses or changes in the person's support system such as family members, work, or financial status (Prigatano and Attman, 1990, Sherer et al., 1998; Rosenthal et al., 1998; Prigatano and Klonoff, 1997).

At any rate, it is often quite difficult for the examiner to determine if a particular cognitive or emotional presentation is a direct or indirect symptom of the injury. In regard to depression, for example, injury to the brain may damage or affect the neurophysiology of the brain, resulting in an "organic-based" mood or depressive disorder (associated with neurochemical changes that affect emotional modulation) which would be a direct symptom of TBI; conversely, an individual may suffer a reactive or post-traumatic type of depression which is not a direct effect of injury to the brain, but a reaction to suffering a trauma and/or experiencing loss or change in one's life. This latter condition would be an indirect symptom of the injury. Of further complication is the issue of pre-existing emotional or psychological disturbance. The examiner needs to review and consider any history of pre-existing psychological disturbance and determine if, and to what extent, the injury may have influenced or exacerbated the pre-existing condition. Legal and medical professionals need to understand that TBI typically exacerbates (worsens) pre-existing affective and cognitive conditions. For example, a person may have had a pre-disposition for clinical depression or an anxiety disorder, which then becomes more pronounced or problematic and even less responsive to traditional treatments (such as antidepressant or antianxiety medications) after TBI. An additional issue that must be addressed by the medical and legal examiner is the effect of litigation on affective, cognitive, and somatic complaint or symptom presentation. Some research suggests that persons claiming to have suffered a mild TBI, and who are going through litigation report more affective and physical symptoms than persons not involved in litigation (Sherer, 1998; Lees-Haley and Brown, 1993; Lees-Haley, 1989; Lees-Haley, 1990; Lees-Haley and Fox, 1990). Researchers, as well as clinicians, often conclude from such data that persons going through litigation typically exaggerate their symptoms and thus, may actually be malingering. However, professionals should be cautious in making such a conclusion as this research is correlational and not causal; that is, a cause and effect relationship cannot be concluded from such research — the medical or legal professional could equally argue that persons in litigation may actually have severe cognitive or emotional impairment as a result of the injury which has resulted in their seeking compensation for such injuries. Interestingly, many researchers have not found differences in symptom presentation between litigants and non-litigants (Dikman, 1995). A corresponding issue, of course, is assessment of malingering, which will be further elaborated on in Chapters 3 and 4. Assessment of malingering or secondary gain can be quite problematic in that the definition of malingering is "the intentional production of false or grossly exaggerated symptoms" (DSM-IV, 1999, p. 683), and to truly be able to determine a given individual's intentions, the legal or medical professional would have to be able to read that person's mind. An additional problem in the assessment of "malingering" or "incomplete effort" (Denney, 1999; Binder, 1993; Bernard et al., 1993) is that a majority of the research conducted thus far was: (1) with college students or other subjects who are coached or instructed to attempt to feign particular symptoms (Binder, 1993; Franzen, 1990; Iverson et al., 1990); or (2) comparing symptom profiles or neuopsychological test performances of litigants and non-litigants in personal injury cases (Franzen et al., 1990; Frederick et al., 1995; Scott et al., 1999; Mittenberg et al., 1993). From this latter research, researchers have often made assumptions regarding the causality between involvement with litigation and increased symptom report/presentation (as earlier discussed within this chapter). This author is not aware of any reputable or replicated study in which "known post-injury malingerers" were studied.

Although the Minnesota Multiphasic Personality Inventory — Second Revision (MMPI-2) (Butcher et al., 1989) will be discussed at length in Chapter 4, a brief discussion here of this instrument is in order, particularly regarding the issues of psychological assessment of post-injury emotional status and "malingering." Clearly, the MMPI-2 is not designed as an instrument to assess brain injury or any type of injury for that matter (although some researchers have attempted to assess its utility as such). It is important to emphasize that the normative sample for the MMPI-2 included normal, ("healthy") controlled subjects and mentally ill subjects. Thus, the validity of such a test with medical patients, particularly traumatic brain injured persons, should be of concern for the medical and legal professional involved in such cases. Unfortunately, many clinicians (namely psychiatrists and psychologists) quite commonly apply the standard "textbook" interpretations to the results and data which may clearly not be relevant to this specific medical population. This, of course, becomes problematic in a forensic (legal) setting as two or more psychiatric professionals may actually come to the same or similar conclusions based on the textbook interpretations — both of which may not in fact be valid. Perhaps the best word to describe the research on the use of the MMPI with persons with neurological disorders (including TBI) is "inconclusive." For example, several researchers have suggested the use of a "neurocorrection factor" (Levin et al., 1997; Alphona et al., 1990; Gass, 1991) with profiles of persons with (or suspected of having) neurologic impairment; whereas other researchers argue against such an approach, supporting the standard scoring and interpretation of the MMPI-2 with such populations (Scott, 1999; Lees-Haley, 1991). Several reputable studies have consistently demonstrated elevations on specific MMPI-2 clinical scales and profiles in traumatically brain injured persons. For both the mildly and severely brain injured populations, the "depression" and "schizophrenia" scales are often elevated (Paniak and Miller, 1993; Bachna et al., 1998; Peck et al., 1993). Thus, this "abnormal" profile may possibly be the norm for this particular population (which is analogous and in some ways similar to other medical populations such as chronic pain patient populations; see Butcher et al., 1989). Nevertheless, clinicians should be very cautious in applying "textbook interpretations" of the MMPI-2 with persons with suspected brain injury.

Clearly, there is research, although *inconsistent* in the literature, that suggests that persons going through personal injury litigation show higher elevations on the MMPI-2 profiles than "non-litigants" (Lees-Haley, 1991; Scott et al., 1999; Youngjohn et al., 1997). It would, however, be absurd for the clinician to either conclude (though some have done so) that such elevations are evidence of a particular pre-morbid personality, or (as discussed previously in this chapter) conclude solely from the MMPI-2 profile (even if the MMPI-2 profile is found to be invalid) that the examinee is malingering, although such information can certainly be valuable when considered with all the historical and testing data. An exhaustive discussion of the MMPI-2 is beyond the scope of this section, but it is important to note that although the MMPI-2 is titled a personality (trait) assessment inventory, the profile/results are clearly influenced by the state (medical and emotional) of the examinee at the time of the testing.

1.4   ASSESSMENT OF EXECUTIVE CONTROL DYSFUNCTIONS AND IMPAIRED AWARENESS FOLLOWING BRAIN INJURY

Although a comprehensive and technical discussion of the executive functions of the brain is beyond the scope of this text, an overview of this issue is certainly important for the clinician and legal professional involved in brain injury cases. Over the past decade, there has been a fair amount of research on the executive functions and of the impairment of such following TBI (Stuss and Gall, 1992; Varney and Menefee, 1993; Sherer et al., 1998). According to Lezak (1993), executive functions can be classified into the following four major areas:

1. volition, which includes the capacity for awareness of one's self and surroundings as well as motivational state;
2. planning, which includes the ability to conceptualize potential change, to be objective, to conceive alternatives in decision-making, and the ability to conceptually or mentally develop a plan;
3. purposeful action, including the ability to be productive when using self-regulation; and,
4. performance effectiveness, which is basically "quality control" or the ability to review, and as needed, modify one's performance (i.e., an ability to learn from one's own mistakes).

Understanding disorders in executive functioning, which are typically attributed to and/or associated with damage to the frontal lobes and/or regions of the brain (in particular the orbital frontal cortex), is critical for the forensic examiner and legal professional in TBI cases. Injury to this particular region of the brain is quite common following TBI (Varney and Menefee, 1993; Stuss and Benson, 1984; Stuss and Gall, 1992) — particularly as a result of a motor vehicle accident. Perhaps one of the least understood (by both medical professionals and lay persons) and more problematic symptoms associated with executive dysfunction is impaired awareness known as anosognosia (Giacino, 1998; Crisp, 1992; Prigatano and Schacter 1991). Disorders of awareness following brain injury can be quite problematic as they are typically not well understood, (particularly by family members and caregivers) and they can often significantly impair a person's functioning — psychosocial, emotional, and behavioral (Prigatano and Fordyce, 1986; Varney and Menefee, 1993). Disordered awareness symptomatology is often described by friends and family members as a "change in personality" in the injured person. These disorders of awareness following TBI can be acute or transient, that is, they may improve or resolve within the first several months following the injury, or they may be more chronic or permanent in nature (Prigatano et al., 1998). Indeed, disorders of awareness post-TBI often can be misdiagnosed as a psychiatric denial state by even experienced psychologists or medical professionals. Although both could certainly occur following a TBI, denial is a psychiatric condition defined by Freud as an "ego-defense mechanism" and would be an indirect symptom of an injury, whereas a true anosognosia or awareness disorder is a neurological condition and a direct symptom from the brain injury. Chronic or more permanent anosognosia most often occurs in more severe brain injuries and has been found to significantly and adversely affect the individual's recovery and rehabilitation therapy outcome (Sherer et al., 1998a; Fleming et al., 1998; Godfrey et al., 1993; Lamb et al., 1988; Willer et al., 1993).

The assessment of executive dysfunction and, in particular, anosognosia can be quite complex and very difficult for the forensic examiner as there are no assessment tools or standardized tests available that are highly sensitive in evaluating these disorders. (Prigatano, 1999; Lezak, 1993). Although there are several neuropsychological or cognitive tests that, in part, tap into some of the executive functions, current research on assessment techniques in this area focus more on functional and behavioral measures such as self or significant other reports (Malec and Thompson, 1994; Prigatano and Klonoff 1997; Solberg et al., 1998; Heart and Jacobs 1993).

Some common quasi-objective approaches used by neuropsychologists in evaluating frontal lobe dysfunction and anosognosia include the following:

1. Observation by the professional or caregiver of the subject while performing specific cognitive tasks.
2. Comparison of caregiver ratings of the patient's abilities with self (examinee) report ratings (Malec and Thompson, 1994; Solberg et al., 1998, Lezak, 1987). Using this approach, the clinician reviews the specific and global difference scores or ratings between the family/caregiver and those of the TBI client. The larger the difference in ratings of cognitive and psychosocial functioning areas the more likely the existence of an anosognosia or awareness disorder. Researchers are still collecting normative data to standardize such instruments and to improve the clinical utility of such measures.
3. Comparison of self (examinee) report ratings with ratings by the professional (Malec and Thompson, 1994; Lezak, 1987, Prigatano et al., 1990, Prigatano and Klonoff 1997). With this approach, a similar analysis process is used by the clinician as described in #2 above.
4. Comparison of self (examinee) report scales of cognitive functioning with actual neuropsychological tests results. In this method, the objective test results from the neuropsychological evaluation are compared to the patient's evaluation of his or her own performance or functional ability in those areas tested. Higher levels of discrepancy would again argue for higher probability of the existence of an anosognosia.
5. Comparison of the TBI client's prediction of performance (prior to testing) on specific neuropsychological or cognitive tests with the actual test results. In this approach, the examinees are asked to predict how well they will perform on selected neuropsychological tests or tasks; these predictions are then compared to their actual test performance. Higher discrepancy scores would suggest the existence of an anosognosia.

In summary, the assessment of executive functions and awareness disorders following TBI is quite complicated and can be quite difficult. However, assessment of these functions by the clinician is critical, particularly in forensic cases, as executive dysfunction can significantly influence vocational, psychosocial, and functional outcome or recovery post-injury.

1.5 SPECIAL ASSESSMENT CONSIDERATIONS IN MILD TBI CASES

An authoritative definition of mild TBI, as developed by the Mild TBI Committee of the Head Injury Interdisciplinary Special Interest Group of the American Congress of Rehabilitation Medicine (American Congress of Rehabilitation Medicine, 1993) has already been reviewed at length earlier in this chapter. However, there are some specific issues that need to be considered by the professional when conducting an assessment in a mild TBI case. This brief discussion on the issues particular to mild TBI cases may be beneficial to the reader. It is again important to emphasize that neither loss of consciousness nor a strike to the head is a required criterion for a TBI. Symptoms associated with mild TBI typically fall into three categories: (1) physical symptoms; (2) cognitive deficits; and (3) behavioral changes or alterations in "emotional responsivity." Mild TBI has previously been referred to as post-concussion syndrome, minor head injury, traumatic head syndrome, traumatic cephalgia, post-brain injury syndrome, and post-traumatic syndrome.

Over the past decade, there has been an enormous amount of research focused on the assessment of mild TBI (Dikman and Levin, 1983; McCaffrey et al., 1993; Larrabee, 1997; Williams et al., 1990; Binder, 1986; Bohnen and Jolles, 1992). The most common symptoms or complaints of persons who have suffered mild TBI are outlined in Table 1.6. Clearly, such symptoms can be direct (physiogenic) or indirect (psychogenic). Obviously, the issue of malingering discussed elsewhere in this and other chapters is most applicable to mild TBI cases. As has been discussed previously, some studies have shown a "correlation" between involvement in litigation and increased symptom presentation. However, such has not been consistently shown throughout the research; for example, in a study of the outcome one year post-injury, litigation did not appear to have systematic effects on the neuropsychological outcome of 436 head injured participants (Dikman et al., 1995). In considering the complexities and variables involved in trying to determine the existence and severity of a TBI in such cases, it is essential for the examiner to research the data on "base rates" as part of the assessment process. Base rates simply refer to the frequency of occurrence of a particular symptom, impairment, etc., within a given population. For example, it is clear from the research (Dikman et al., 1995) that significant neuropsychological impairment at one year follow-up in mild TBI cases is as unlikely as escaping such impairment in severe TBI. Additionally, a clear majority of well-designed outcome studies have demonstrated good long-term neuropsychological recovery for most cases of mild TBI (Dikman, 1995). Thus, it is extremely rare, per the base rate data (1.9% - 5.8%), for persons with mild TBI to experience extended post-concussive symptoms one year post-injury (Alves et al., 1993; Nemeth, 1996; Dikman et al., 1995; Larrabee, 1997). Further complicating the data are the base rate studies which showed a high frequency of reported post-concussive symptoms in a person going through litigation for emotional distress or industrial stress without report of "central nervous system" (brain) injuries or claims (Larrabee, 1997; Lees-Haley and Brown, 1993; Putnam and Millis, 1994). Base rate research in mild TBI is not only focused on frequency of symptoms and recovery rates, but is also now being included in the normative data for specific neuropsychological tests (Heaton et al., 1993; Palmer et al., 1998) Such base rate information for specific neuropsychological tests provides the examiner with critical information; for example, when analyzing test result performance of a person claiming to have suffered a mild TBI, the examiner can determine not only the statistical significance (e.g., how reliable that difference is) of a given score or set of scores, but the clinical significance as well. A common example is when comparing the difference in scores between the verbal and performance IQ subtests on the Wechsler Adult Intelligence Scale — Third Revision (WAIS-III) (Psychological Corporation, 1997), with base rate data, the examiner can determine if the difference between the two tests is statistically significant, and

---

TABLE 1.6
Complaints and Symptoms in Mild TBI by Category

PHYSICAL

Headache
Dizziness
Nausea
Positional vertigo
Noise intolerance
Sleep disturbance
Blurred or double vision
Mental and physical fatigue
Poor coordination
Reduced alcohol tolerance

COGNITIVE

Forgetfulness
Slow mental processing
Excessive mental and physical fatigue
Loses train of thought
Poor concentration or distractibility
Increased distractibility

EMOTIONAL/BEHAVIORAL

Low frustration tolerance
Emotional lability
Depression
Diminished libido
Anxiety
Sleep disturbance

Source: Adapted from Nemeth, A.J. (1996) and Larrabee, G. (1997).

---

if this difference is clinically significant, as well. Thus, a score difference between the performance and verbal IQ on the WAIS-III may be statistically significant, but using base rate data for a given population (based on age, educational level, and Full Scale IQ) such a difference in score may occur in 25% of the population, which is in no way clinically significant.

Appendix A provides an outline of a model assessment approach for the medical and legal professional involved in mild TBI cases. Also, Appendix B provides a list of important articles and references by key issues or categories related to the forensic assessment of mild TBI. Clearly, the assessment of mild TBI is a complicated and difficult task for the medical professional, and, therefore, an in-depth knowledge of base rate research on mild TBI and neuropsychological assessment is critical in the assessment process.

REFERENCES

Alphona, D.P, Finlayson, A.J., Stearns, G.M., and Elison, P.M., (1990). The MMPI in neurologic dysfunction: profile configuration and analysis. *The Clinical Neuropsychologist,* 4, 69–79.

Alves, W., Macciocchi, S., and Barth, J.T., (1993). Post-concussive symptoms after uncomplicated mild head injury. *Journal of Head Trauma Rehabilitation,* 8, (3) 48–59.

American Psychiatric Association (1994). *Diagnostic and Statistical Manual of Mental Disorders - Fourth Edition,* American Psychiatric Association, Washington, D.C.

American Congress of Rehabilitation Medicine (1993). Definition of mild traumatic brain injury. *Journal of Head Trauma Rehabilitation,* 8(3), 86–87.

Anderson, C.V., Wood, D.M., Bigler, E.D., and Blatter, D.D., (1996). Lesion volume, injury severity, and thalamic integrity following head injury. *Journal of Neurotrauma,* 12(1), 35–40.

Bachna, K., Sieggreen, M.A., Cermak, L., Penk, W., and O'Connor, M. (1998). MMPI/MMPI-2: Comparisons of amnesic patients. *Archives of Clinical Neuropsychology,* 13(6), 535–542.

Barona, A., Reynolds, C.R., and Chastani, R. (1994). A demographically based index of premorbid intelligence for the WAIS-R. *Journal of Consulting in Clinical Psychology,* 52, 885–887.

Barry, D.T., Carpenter, G.S., Campbell, D.A., Schmitt, F.A., Helton, K., and Lipka-Molby, J.N., (1994). The New Adult Reading Test — Revised: Accuracy in estimating WAIS-R IQ scores obtained 3.5 years earlier from normal older persons. *Archives of Clinical Neuropsychology,* 9, 239–250.

Bernard, L.C., McGrath, M.J., and Houston, W., (1993). Discriminating between simulated malingering and closed head injury on the Wechsler Memory Scale — Revised. *Archives of Clinical Neuropsychology,* 8, 529–551.

Binder, L.M., (1993). Assessment of malingering after mild head trauma with the Portland Digit Recognition Test. *Journal of Clinical and Experimental Neuropsychology,* 15, 170–82.

Binder, L.M., (1986). Persisting symptoms after mild head injury: A review of the post-concussive syndrome. *Journal of Clinical and Experimental Neuropsychology,* 8, 323–346.

Bird, J.M., Levy, R., and Jacoby, R.J., (1986). Computer tomography in the elderly. Changes over time in a normal population. *British Journal of Psychiatry,* 148, 80–85.

Blair, J.R. and Spreen, O., (1989). Predicting premorbid IQ: a revision of the national adult reading test, *The Clinical Neuropsychologist,* 3, 129–136.

Bohnen, N. and Jolles, J., (1992). Neurobehavioral aspects of post-concussive symptoms after mild head injury. *Journal of Nervous and Mental Disorders,* 180, 683–692.

Busch, C.R. and Alpern, H.P., (1998). Depression after mild traumatic brain injury: a review of current research. *Neuropsychology Review,* 8(2), 95–108.

Butcher, J.N., Dahlstrom, W.G., Graham, J.R., Tellegen, A., and Kaemmer, B. (1989). *Manual for Administrating and Scoring the Minnesota Multiphasic Personality Inventory — II.* University of Minnesota Press, Minneapolis, MN.

Crawford, J., (1992). Current and premorbid intelligence measures in neuropsychological assessment, in *A Handbook of Neuropsychological Assessment,* Crawford, J.R., Parker, D.M., and McKinlay, W.W., Eds., Lawrence Erblom Associates, Englewood Cliffs, NJ.

Crisp, R., (1992). Awareness of deficit after traumatic brain injury: a literature review. Australia. *Occupational Therapy Journal,* 39, 15–21.

Davis, E.M., (1990). Mild to moderate brain injury. *Trial,* Nov., 109–114.

De Leon, M.J., George, A.E., Golomb, J., Tarshish, C. et al., (1997). Frequency of hippocampal formation atrophy in normal aging in Alzheimer's disease. *Neurobiology of Aging*, 18(1), 1–11.

Denney, R., (1999). A brief symptom validity testing procedure for logical memory or the Wechsler Memory Scale - Revised, which can demonstrate verbal memory in the face of claimed disability. *Journal of Forensic Neuropsychology*, 1(1), 5–26.

Dikman, S., Machamer, J., Winn, H.R., and Temkin, N., (1995). Neuropsychological outcome at one year post head injury. *Neuropsychology*, 9(1), 80–90.

Dikman, S. and Levin, H., (1993). Methodological issues in the study of mild head injury. *Journal of Head Trauma Rehabilitation*, 8(3), 30–37.

Eslinger, P.J., Damasio, H., Radford, N.D., and Damasio, A.R., (1984). Examining the relationship between computer tomography and neuropsychological measures in normal and demented elderly. *Journal of Neurology, Neurosurgery and Psychiatry*, (12), 1319–1325.

Esselman, P.C. and Uomoto, J.M., (1995). Classification of the spectrum of mild traumatic brain injury. *Brain Injury*, 9, 417–424.

Evans, R.W., (1992). Mild traumatic brain injury. *Physical Medicine and Rehabilitation Clinics of North American*, 3(2), 427–439.

Fleming, J., Strong, J., and Ashton, R. (1998). Cluster analysis of self-awareness levels in adults with traumatic brain injury in relationship to outcome. *Journal of Head Trauma Rehabilitation*, 13(5), 39–51.

Franzen, M.D., Iverson, G.L., and McCracken, L.M., (1990). Detection of malingering in neuropsychological assessment. *Neuropsychology Review*, 1(3), 247–279.

Frederick, R.I., Carter, M., and Powel, J. (1995). Adapting symptom validity testing to evaluate suspicious complaints of amnesia in medicolegal evaluations. *The Bulletin of American Academy of Psychiatry and the Law*, 23(2), 227–233.

Gale, S.D., Johnson, S.C., Bigler, E.D., and Blatter, D.D., (1995). Trauma-induced degenerative changes in brain injury: a morphometric analysis of three patients with pre-injury and post-injury MR scans, *Journal of Neurotrauma*, 12(12), 151–8.

Gass, C.S., (1991). MMPI-II - Interpretation of closed-head trauma: A correction factor. *Psychological Assessment*, 3, 27–31.

Giacino, J.T. and Cicerone, K.D. (1998). Varieties of deficit unawareness after brain injury. *Journal of Head Trauma Rehabilitation*, 13(5), 1–15.

Godfrey, H.P., Partridge, F.M., Knight, R.J., and Bishara, S., (1993). Course of insight disorder in emotion and dysfunction following closed head injury: a controlled cross sectional follow up study. *Journal of Clinical and Experimental Neuropsychology*, 15, 503–515.

Gonzales, C.F., Lentieri, R.L., and Nathan, R.J. (1978). CT scan appearance of the brain in the normal elderly population: a correlative study. *Neuroradiology*, 16, 120–122.

Hartlage, L.C., (1990). *Neuropsychological Evaluation of Head Injury*. Professional Resource Exchange, Sarasota, FL.

Hatazawa, I., Wamaura, H., and Matsuzawa, T., (1981). Age-related brain atrophy and mental deterioration — a study with computer tomography. *British Journal of Radiology*, 54(641), 384–390.

Heart, T. and Jacobs, H., (1993). Rehabilitation management of behavioral disturbances following frontal lobe injury. *Journal of Head Trauma Rehabilitation*, 8(1), 1–12.

Heaton, R., Chelune, G., Talley, J., Kay, G., and Curtiss, G., (1993). *Wisconsin Card Sorting Test Manual: Revised and Expanded*. Psychological Assessment Resources, FL.

Iverson, G., Franzen, M., and McCracken, L., (1990). *Standardization of an Objective Assessment Technique for the Detection of Malingering Memory Deficits*. Poster presented at the National Academy of Neuropsychologists. Fall, 1990.

Jastak, S. and Wilkenson, G.S., (1984). *Wide Range Achievement Test - Revised Administration Manual*. Western Psychological Services, Los Angeles.

Johnstone, B., Callahan, C.D., Kapila, C., and Bounan, D., (1996). The comparability of the WRAT-R reading test and NAART as estimates of premorbid intelligence in neurologically impaired patients. *Archives of Clinical Neuropsychology*, 11(6), 513–519.

Karaken, D.A., Gur, R.C., and Saykain, A.J., (1995). Reading on the Wide Range Achievement Test - Revised and parental education as predictors of IQ: comparison with the Barona Equation. *Archives of Clinical Neuropsychology*, 10, 147–157.

Klonoff, P., Gustavo, L., and Chiapello, D., (1993). Varieties of the catastrophic reaction of brain injury: a self-psychology perspective. *Bulletin of the Menninger Clinic*, 57(2), 227–241.

Lamb, C.S., McMahon, V.T., Proddy, D.A., and Gehred-Schultz, M.A., (1988). Deficit awareness in treatment of performance among traumatic brain injury adults. *Brain Injury*, 2, 235–242.

Larrabee, G., (1997). Neuropsychological outcome, post-concussion symptoms and forensic considerations in mild closed head trauma. *Seminars in Clinical Neuropsychiatry*, 2(3), 196–206.

Lees-Haley, P.R., (1991). MMPI-II F and F -K. Scores of personal injury malingerers in vocational neuropsychological and emotional distress claims. *American Journal of Forensic Psychology*, 9(3), 5–14.

Lees-Haley, P.R., (1990). Contamination of neuropsychological testing by litigation. *Forensic Reports*, 3(4), 421–426.

Lees-Haley, P.R., (1989). Litigation response syndrome: how the stress of litigation confuses the issues of personal injury: family and criminal litigation. *Defense Counsel Journal*, 56(1), 110–114.

Lees-Haley, P.R., and Brown, R.S., (1993). Neuropsychological complaint base rates of 170 personal injury claimants. *Archives of Clinical Neuropsychology*, 8, 203–209.

Lees-Haley, P.R. and Fox, D., (1990). Neurological false positives in litigation: trailmaking test findings. *Perceptual and Motor Skills*, 70, 1379–1382.

Levin, H.S., Gass, C., and Wold, H., (1997). MMPI-II interpretation in closed-head trauma. Crossed validation of a correction factor. *Archives of Clinical Neuropsychology*, 12(3), 199–205.

Levin, H.S., O'Donnell, V.M., and Grossman, R.G., (1979). The Galveston Orientation and Amnesia Test: a practical scale to assess cognition after head injury. *Journal of Nervous and Mental Disorders*, 167, 675–684.

Lezak, M., (1987). Relationships between personality disorders, social disturbances and physical disability following traumatic brain injury. *Journal of Head Trauma Rehabilitation*, 2, 57–69.

Lezak, M., (1993). Newer contributions to neuropsychological assessment of executive functions. *Journal of Head Trauma Rehabilitation*, 8(1), 24–31.

Malec, J. and Thompson, J., (1994). Relationship of the Mayo-Portland adaptability inventory to functional outcome and cognitive performance measures. *Journal of Head Trauma Rehabilitation*, 9(4), 1–15.

McCaffrey, R., Williams, A., Fisher, J., and Ling, L., (1993). Forensic issues in mild head injury. *Journal of Head Trauma Rehabilitation*, 8(3), 38–47.

Medicode, Inc. (1998). *International Classification of Disease — 9th Revision*. Medicode, Inc., Salt Lake City, UT, Section 850.

Mittenberg, W., Azrin, R., Millsaps, C., and Agilbronner, R., (1993). Identification of malingered head injury on the Wechsler Memory Scale - Revised. *Psychological Assessment*, 5(1), 34–40.

Nemeth, A.J., (1996). Behavior-descriptive data on cognitive, personality and somatic residua after relatively mild brain trauma: studying the syndrome as a whole. *Archives of Clinical Neuropsychology*, 11(8), 677–695.

Palmer, B., Boone, K., Lesser, I., and Wohl, M. (1998). Base rates of "impaired" neuropsychological test performance among healthy older adults. *Archives of Clinical Neuropsychology*, 13(6), 503–511.

Paniak, C.E. and Miller, H.B., (1993). Utility of MMPI-2 validity scales with brain injury survivors. Paper presented at the meeting of the National *Academy of Neuropsychology*, October 28-30, 1993, Phoenix, AZ.

Peck, E., Mitchell, S., Burke, E., Baber, C., and Schwartz, S., (1993). Normative data for 463 head injury patients for the MMPI, BDI, and SCL-90 tests across three time periods post-injury. Poster presented at the 21st Annual Meeting of the International Neuropsychological Society, February 24, 1993, Galveston, TX.

Prigatano, G.P., (1999). Impaired awareness, finger tapping and rehabilitation outcome after brain injury. *Rehabilitation Psychology*, 44(2), 145–159.

Prigatano, G.P. and Fordyce, D.J., (1986). Cognitive dysfunction and psychosocial adjustment after brain injury, in *Neuropsychological Rehabilitation after Brain Injury*, Prigatano, G.P. and Fordyce, D.J., and Zeiner, H.K., Eds., Johns Hopkins University Press, Baltimore, MD.

Prigatano, G.P. and Klonoff, P.S., (1997). A clinician's rating scale for evaluating impaired self-awareness in denial of disability after brain injury. *Clinical Neuropsychologist*, 11, 1–12.

Prigatano, G.P. and Schacter, D.L., Eds., (1991). *Awareness of Deficit After Brain Injury: Clinical and Theoretical Issues*. Oxford University Press, New York.

Prigatano, G.P. and Altman, I.M., (1990). Impaired awareness of behavioral limitations after traumatic brain injury. *Archives of Physical Medicine and Rehabilitations*, 71, 1058–1064.

Prigatano, G.P., Bruna, O., Mataro, M., Munoz, J.M., Fernandez, S., and Junque, C., (1998). Initial disturbances of consciousness and result in impaired awareness in Spanish patients with traumatic brain injury. *Journal of Head Trauma Rehabilitation*, 13(5), 29–38.

Prigatano, G.P. and Klonoff, P.S., (1997). A clinician's rating scale for evaluating impaired self-awareness and denial of disability after brain injury. *Clinical Neuropsychologist*, 11, 1–12.

Prigatano, G.P., Altman, I.M., and O'Brien, K.P., (1990). Behavioral limitations that traumatic brain injured patients tend to underestimate. *Clinical Neuropsychologist*, 4, 163–179.

Psychological Corporation, (1997). *Wechsler Adult Intelligence Scale — Third Revision* (WAIS-III/WMS-III, Technical Manual). The Psychological Corporation, San Antonio, TX.

Putnam, S.H. and Millis, S.R., (1994). Psychosocial factors in the development and maintenance of chronic somatic and functional symptoms following mild traumatic brain injury. *Advances in Medical Psychotherapy*, 7, 1–22.

Rosenthal, M., Christenson, B.K., and Ross, T.P., (1998). Depression following traumatic brain injury. *Archives of Physical Medicine and Rehabilitation*, 79, 90–103.

Ruff, R.M. et al., (1989) Computerized tomography, neuropsychology and positron emission tomography and evaluation of head injury. *Neuropsychiatry, Neuropsychology and Behavioral Neurology*, 2(2), 103–123.

Scott, J., Emick, M., and Adams, R., (1999). The MMPI-II and closed head injury: effects of litigation and head injury severity. *Journal of Forensic Neuropsychology*, 1(2), 3–13.

Sherer, M., Berglof, P., Levin, E., High, W.M. Jr., Oden, K.E., and Nick, T.G. (1998a). Impaired awareness in employment outcome after traumatic brain injury. *Journal of Head Trauma Rehabilitation*, 13(5), 52–61.

Sherer, M., Boake, C., Levin, E. et al., (1998b). Characteristics of impaired awareness after brain injury. *Journal of the International Neuropsychological Society*, 4, 380–387.

Solberg, M., Mater, C., Penkman, L., Gleng, A., and Todis, B (1998). Awareness intervention: who needs it? *Journal of Head Trauma Rehabilitation*, 13(5), 62–78.

Stuss, D. and Gall, C., (1992). Frontal dysfunction" after traumatic brain injury. Neuropsychiatry, *Neuropsychology and Behavioral Neurology*, 5, 272–282.

Stuss, D. and Benson, D. (1984). Neuropsychological studies of frontal lobes. *Psychological Bulletin*, 95, 3 - 28.

Stuss, D.T., Gow, C.A., and Hetherington, C.R., (1992). "No longer gage": frontal lobe dysfunction and emotional changes. *Journal of Consulting in Clinical Psychology*, 60(3), 349–359.

Teasdale, G. and Jennett, B., (1974). Assessment of coma and impaired consciousness: a practical scale. *Lancet*, 2, 81–84.

Thatcher, R.W., Camacho, M., Salazar, A., Linden, C., Biver, C., and Clarke, I., (1997). Quantitative MRI of the gray-white matter distribution in traumatic brain injury. *Journal of Neurotrauma*, 14(1), 1–14.

Varney, N.R. and Menefee, L., (1993). Psychosocial and executive deficits following closed head injury: Implications for Orbital Frontal Cortex. *Journal of Head Trauma Rehabilitation*, 8(1), 32–44.

Willer, B., Rosenthal, M., Kreutzer, J.S., Gordon, W.A., and Rempel, R., (1993). Assessment of community integration following rehabilitation for traumatic brain injury. *Journal of Head Trauma Rehabilitation*, 8(2), 75–87.

Williams, D., Levin, H., and Eisenberg, H., (1990). Mild head injury classification. *Neurosurgery*, 27(3), 422–428.

Wilson, J. and Wyper, D., (1992). Neuroimaging and neuropsychological functioning following closed head injury: CT, MRI and SPECT. *Journal of Head Trauma Rehabilitation*, 7(2), 29–39.

Wines, A.N., Bryan, J.E., and Crossen, J.R., (1993). Estimating WAIS-R FS IQ from The National Adult Reading Test — Revised in normal subjects. *The Clinical Neuropsychologist*, 7, 70–84.

Youngjohn, J., Davis, D., and Wolfe, I., (1997). Head injury and the MMPI-II: Paradoxical severity effects and the influence of litigation. *Psychological Assessment*, 9(3), 177–184.

2 TheForensicNeurological Assessment of Traumatic Brain Injury

Donald T. Starzinski

CONTENTS

2.1 ELEMENTS OF FORENSIC NEUROLOGIC DIAGNOSIS OF TBI

Within the realm of medical practice, the subspecialty of neurology is traditionally thought of as a rather complex endeavor. The nervous system is implicated in a multitude of human functions, playing a central role in most of what the body does. In order to arrive at an understanding of a person's neurologic functioning, and specifically whether it deviates from normal patterns, a systematic approach to neurologic diagnosis is undertaken (DeJong and Haerer, 1998; Mayo Clinic, 1991).

    The basic elements of neurologic diagnosis consist of a comprehensive history, thorough examination, and various diagnostic testing. Neurologic diagnosis is a deductive process attained by a synthesis of all of these elements. The physician

TABLE 2.1
Elements of the Neurologic Diagnosis

- History
- Neurologic examination
- Diagnostic studies
- Assessment

must make observations of these elements, correlate and interpret them, and articulate the conclusions in an assessment (see Table 2.1).

2.1.1 HISTORY

It may come as a surprise to many that it is generally not the sophisticated imaging studies of the brain nor the complicated neurophysiological testing (bioelectrical testing) that typically leads to the most information about a neurologic condition. Rather, it is the history which actually gives the practitioner the most diagnostic information.

A thorough history includes thoughtful review of an individual's symptoms which are quite revealing in portraying neurologic syndromes or neurologic abnormalities in general. Such a history can reveal specific disease processes as revealed in syndromes (constellations of symptoms). A thoughtful history can also lead to localization of a problem within the orderly neuroanatomy of the human body. Specifically, the neurologic history can determine whether a problem is focal (localized) or diffuse and also what the etiology (cause) of the neurologic dysfunction may be (see Table 2.2).

Specific clues from a person's medical history such as their habits, including for example, occupational toxin exposure or chemical dependency, can lead to important data that further guide neurologic examination and testing. Other examples of historic elements that may be quite helpful in guiding a diagnosis would be family history, which of course would provide explanations for genetic tendencies such as psychiatric illness, headache predilection, arthritic conditions, or disease processes such as diabetes that may have important implications for neurologic involvement (Popkin, 1997).

2.1.2 EXAMINATION

The neurologic examination, which is actually one of the most involved subspeciality physical examinations, can lead to valuable diagnostic clues with regard to nervous system abnormalities that may have value in leading to conclusions regarding localization of dysfunction in the nervous system and hence, further clues about etiology. As suggested previously, the neurologic examination may be quite useful, but is more often a confirmatory process with suspicions already being raised by the thoughtful neurologic history. The neurologic examination consists of specific tests to assess functioning of a person's mental status, cranial nerve function, motor function, sensory function, and coordination capabilities (see Table 2.3). A thorough and skillful performance of the neurologic examination can, in some cases, localize

TABLE 2.2
Elements of the Medical/Neurological History

- History of present illness
- Review of neurologic systems
- Review of medical systems
- Past medical history
- Medications
- Habits, including substance abuse
- Family history
- Social history, including occupational/ADL's

(Activities of Daily Living)

TABLE 2.3
Elements of the Neurologic Examination

- Mental status
- Cranial nerves
- Motor
- Sensory
- Coordination

neuropathology within the axis of the nervous system (that is, whether the problem involves the brain, spinal cord, peripheral nerves, or muscles) and in some cases, very specifically identify the precise locale of the neurologic dysfunction. In some instances, the careful neurologic examination can reveal abnormalities of the nervous system which had previously been unsuspected and could guide further inquiry regarding "subclinical" symptoms. Such subtle abnormalities could be elucidated by more detailed testing such as imaging studies and neurophysiologic testing as maneuvers to further refine the neurologic diagnosis.

2.1.3 LABORATORY STUDIES

The third tier of neurologic investigation includes sophisticated studies (see Table 2.4) such as imaging of the brain with computerized axial tomography (CT) scans and magnetic resonance imaging (MRI). Also, investigations of nervous system function with physiological screens such as the electroencephalogram (EEG) and electromyelogram (EMG) which study the electrical activity of the brain and peripheral nerves and muscle, respectively, are available (Aminoff, 1986). An even broader spectrum of neurologic tests include such high tech analyses as the metabolic functioning of the brain via investigation of energy utilization (PET and SPECT scans). Functional MRI imaging (fMRI) is yet another modality being developed to study the dynamic changes that occur with brain activity (Hammeke, 1999; Thatcher et al., 1997; Gale et al., 1995; Cecil et al., 1998). Still, other testing includes "brain mapping" using an array of electrical recording devices to study the distribution of electrical activity of the brain. Many of these later strategies are primarily experimental in nature, but have been used in forensic settings (Restale, 1996). It should be stressed that these sophisticated tests can be invaluable in confirming diagnoses but are generally confirmatory maneuvers. Justification has to be given to use of

---

TABLE 2.4
Diagnostic Studies by Type

I Imaging studies
- X-rays
- CT scans
- MRI scans

II Neurophysiologic studies
- EEG
- Evoked potential studies
- Brain mapping

III Functional imaging studes
- PET
- SPECT
- Functional MRI

---

these various studies, particularly because of cost concerns and also the invasive risks of some of these studies.

Hence, neurologic diagnosis involves a quite sophisticated synthesis of historical and physical examination findings and laboratory testing.

2.2   THE NEUROLOGIC EXAMINATION IN FORENSIC ANALYSIS

The various elements of neurologic diagnosis will be systematically examined, particularly as they relate to their value in the independent medical examination for purposes of forensic examination.

2.2.1   NEUROLOGIC HISTORY

Every neurologic evaluation must be accompanied by as accurate a history as possible. As implied above, a skillfully taken history with careful analysis and interpretation of the chief complaint and the course of the problem frequently indicates a probable diagnosis even before any of the other elements of the evaluation, namely the physical and neurologic examination as well as laboratory investigations, are performed.

The history of present illness should include clear descriptions of the onset of the problem with symptoms at the time of the traumatic injury being particularly important in the analysis of the severity of traumatic brain injury (TBI) (Malec, 1998; Restale, 1997). For example, the presence of altered consciousness and the duration of such altered consciousness is quite important. Other historic features at the time of an injury, such as altered cognition in the form of memory difficulties or confusion, is again very important to inquire about. As with all details of medical symptoms, their onset, duration, magnitude, and course or trend are important to characterize.

A specific review of neurologic symptomatology that relates to dysfunction of the nervous system must be inquired about in order to thoroughly cover the range of possible problems that may result from injury to the brain and nervous system more generally. The review of neurologic systems actually mirrors the elements of the neurologic examination, namely mental status, cranial nerve, motor, sensory, and coordination functions, as well as their related conditions.

Inquiries into a person's past medical history is also quite important in placing the presumed new process in its proper context. For example, previous history of head injury may predispose a person to more severe brain damage, even with a relatively minor trauma. Other historic features such as previous seizure disorder history, developmental disabilities, or psychiatric conditions, including chronic pain syndromes are vital to inquire about.

Examples of problems in a past medical history that may impact on sequelae of TBI include history of cognitive or neurobehavioral problems in the past such as confusional episodes related to epilepsy or migrainous headaches. History of psychiatric illness is particularly relevant in that various syndromes, especially in stages of acute exacerbation, may present with confusional episodes and delirium. Also, various psychiatric conditions may significantly influence cognitive testing and hence, the "appearance" of organic neuropathology.

Other general medical problems such as diabetes and hypertension are quite relevant as such medical conditions may strongly predispose a person toward a cerebrovascular disease and related cognitive difficulties which may mimic sequelae of TBI. Cerebrovascular disease, related to a number of etiologies including atherosclerosis and various rheumatologic conditions, may also predispose a person to certain vascular dementias.

A medication history is also quite relevant in that medications used around the time of a traumatic injury may mimic or mask symptoms that could be indicative of TBI. Also, many medications used to treat chronic medical conditions have cognitive changes as part of their common side effect profile.

Furthermore, the patient's habits are also part of a thorough medical history and may lead to revelations about significant exposure to chemicals which may have either transient or long-term effects on neurocognitive functioning. This would include alcohol exposure, which over time can lead to not only a dementing process, but also rather striking focal amnestic syndromes in the setting of vitamin deficiencies, namely the Wernicke-Korsakoff's syndrome. Certainly other drugs of abuse, including from the stimulant, opiate, and benzodiazepine classes, have clearly associated neurocognitive changes, which again may impact on brain abnormalities attributed to traumatic injury.

Family history is important in identifying genetic and familial tendencies toward certain conditions which may present as neurocognitive syndromes which may, in turn, mimic traumatic injury. This would include such entities as Huntington's Chorea, Alzheimer's disease, and other chromosomal syndromes which can present with subtle neurological abnormalities, particularly in their early stages and could confuse the issue of causal manifestations of a TBI.

Social history is important in identifying factors which may lead to organic neurologic conditions that have TBI-like manifestations. A person's socioeconomic status may predispose him or her toward nutritional deficiencies or even other traumatic injuries which again may mimic or impact on sequelae of a subsequent

TBI. Other factors such as toxin exposure from certain environmental settings and occupational situations may have implications for neurologic pathology as well.

2.2.2 PHYSICAL EXAMINATION

Prior to the neurologic examination itself, it is useful to observe and comment on a person's general appearance, including their willingness to participate in the examination process. Such factors as impulsiveness or inappropriate comments along with observations of emotional lability and general mood are invaluable in fitting the neurologic observations in their proper perspective. A musculoskeletal examination which would include observations of range of motion of the spine and elicitation of any tenderness or paraspinous musculature abnormalities may be particularly important in individuals with TBI who have complaints and neurologic findings relative to pathology of the spine. (These observations relate to the sensory-motor components of the neurologic examination.)

Having completed the general observations, including musculoskeletal functions, the neurologic examination is accomplished with examination of the five elements discussed previously, namely the mental status examination, cranial nerve examination, motor examination, sensory examination, and coordination testing.

The mental status examination, as performed in the neurologic examination, would represent a screening examination as contrasted to the very detailed testing done by the neuropsychologist. A neurologist would perform a mental status screening using elements of a "Mini Mental Status Examination" which although somewhat general in nature, is quite useful in identifying cognitive abnormalities which may lead to suggestion of focal neurologic dysfunction (Folstein, 1997). This survey includes the testing of attention, memory, and language, as well as some abstract cognitive functioning. Additionally, the mental status examination includes observations regarding thought process, lability, and affect to detect such psychiatric concerns as psychotic thought or mood disorder. Care should be taken to make note of any internal inconsistencies which would suggest functional (nonorganic) manifestations of a person's mental status abnormalities. This latter observation is particularly relevant in forensic examinations.

The second element of the neurologic examination is cranial nerve testing which assesses the integrity of the motor and sensory function in the head and neck. Cranial nerve abnormalities which are particularly common in the setting of traumatic injury, include visual and oculomotor abnormalities as well as articulation difficulties from disruption of the bulbar (mouth and throat) functions. Subtle hearing abnormalities and subjective symptoms such as tinnitus can be sequelae of TBI as well. Impairments in sensory functions such as vision and hearing can, in turn, influence various neuropsychological testing that is used to investigate cognitive deficits related to brain injury.

Motor examination includes the testing of musculature throughout the extremities and trunk, particularly with regard to strength, tone, gross motor movements, and reflexes. Such testing can discover subtle focal abnormalities which may be part of TBI and may have implications in the overall abilities of an individual. For example, motor abnormalities may have significant impact on activities of daily living (ADLs) including occupational activities. Again, functional (nonorganic) features may be seen with motor testing including the feigning of paralysis or at least gross motor weakness, but exam inconsistencies elicited by a skilled examiner can detect such a functional process.

Sensory examination assesses the ability of the individual to perceive various sensory modalities including light touch, sharp sensation, position sensation, vibratory sensation, and some higher cortical perceptions of sensation such as the detection of writing on the hand and perception of simultaneous presentations of stimuli symptoms to both sides of the body. These more complex perceptions are disrupted in subtle parietal lobe injuries. Hence, sensory testing is also quite useful in localizing neurologic dysfunction and assessing functional sensory loss as well. There is a very defined "wiring system" of the central (brain and spinal cord) and peripheral (outside the spinal cord) nervous systems that make it possible for the neurologist to detect whether an individual has organic pathology in the central and/or peripheral nervous system or if there is a "nonanatomic" pattern of sensory abnormalities to suggest a functional process.

The final element of the neurologic examination is testing of coordination. This is done by assessing coordination and fine motor movements of the extremities, both arms and legs, as well as the assessment of a person's balance and ambulation abilities. The testing of coordination is quite useful in detecting damage to specific anatomic structures including the cerebellum and basal ganglion areas which give rise to characteristic coordination difficulties with regard to fine finger movements, rapid alternating movements, and other coordinated motor activities with standing and walking, etc. Again, functional abnormalities of the coordination examination may include a phenomenon of "astasia abasia" which is a characteristic balance difficulty that is present in nonorganic neurologic conditions and essentially consists of highly inconsistent balance difficulties. Hence, virtually all the elements of the neurologic examination not only lend themselves to identification of focal central or peripheral nervous system problems, but also can be quite helpful in identification of organic and nonorganic (functional) abnormalities. This is critical in forensic evaluations which have as their question whether a neurologic abnormality relates to traumatic injury or not.

2.2.3 DIAGNOSTIC TESTING/LABORATORY STUDIES

After obtaining a thorough neurologic history and supporting clinical suspicions with neuroexamination findings, further testing can be warranted in the form of any number of ancillary tests which act to confirm neurologic diagnoses and sometimes indicate etiologies of a neurologic process, as well (Garada et al., 1997).

Imaging studies have become quite sophisticated in detecting very small structural abnormalities, but even the most sophisticated imaging studies, including advanced generation MRI scans, cannot always detect subtle areas of neurologic dysfunction by virtue of the subtlety. The abnormalities may be electrical and biochemical in nature rather than related to anatomic changes. In the setting of TBI, a vast spectrum of neuroimaging abnormalities can be detected depending on the degree of damage. For example, intracranial bleeding can be quite obvious at times and is typically detectable by standard CT scan studies. Edema (swelling of the brain) is also evident at times as a result of head injury. More subtle abnormalities can sometimes be detected by MRI scans which can, for example, reveal even more subtle areas of edema (disruptions in the blood-brain barrier).

Neurophysiological studies of the brain may be useful in cases where there has been new onset of epilepsy or other focal neurologic abnormalities as a result of TBI. Again, these studies are primarily confirmatory and guided by clinical symptoms and neurologic examination findings.

EMG, or electromyogram, is a study of primarily peripheral nerve and muscle function and would not necessarily be indicated or abnormal unless there was additional damage to the peripheral nerves or muscle disease process, concomitant with, or independent of the suspected brain injury. Other more advanced neurologic screening such as PET and SPECT scans, fMRI, and brain mapping techniques can reveal subtle metabolic abnormalities of the brain and also very subtle changes in electrical patterns of the brain, respectively. However, such studies are largely experimental with regard to detecting or elucidating patterns of brain injury after trauma. Certainly these more advanced studies are not standards of care with regard to the proof of brain injury or localization (Weiss, 1996; Mayberg, 1996).

It should be noted that these type of studies may not only confirm evidence of traumatic injury, but may reveal other neurologic conditions which actually prove to be alternative etiologies for neurologic dysfunction such as neoplastic diseases, degenerative diseases, infections, cerebrovascular abnormalities, or even congential abnormalities.

2.3   THE NEUROLOGICAL EXAMINATION vs. INDEPENDENT MEDICAL EXAMINATION

Having discussed elements of the neurologic examination, it should be recognized that the forensic use of the neurologic examination requires some modification of the traditional exam, at least with regard to emphasis, and also with regard to the focus of such an examination, specifically not being meant to establish a physician/patient relationship. In fact, an interview with the client should take place before the examination, specifically clarifying the issue of the examination not being meant to establish traditional medical advice and/or treatment.

With regard to the interview in such an encounter, unless there is significant evidence to the contrary, it is best to accept a client's history at face value and portray it as stated during the interview. Data from medical records which are reviewed allow comparisons and contrasts to the stated history in order to corroborate or dispute interview evidence being offered.

A meticulous review of previous medical records, particularly important in the IME process, establishes the presence or absence of previous medical conditions or injuries which may impact a person's current neurologic functioning. Such medical records could, of course, include prior medical or therapeutic efforts to address injuries including TBI as well as psychiatric issues and any number of medical conditions and medical therapies, which may impact brain functioning.

The actual neurologic examination, as part of an IME process, should be prefaced by clear intention that the examination is being done as a standard medical examination, not meant to extend a person beyond their capabilities, that is, not to cause any injury which may be a remote potential in some elements of examination that are done to test extremes of function such as passive range of motion, particularly if performed incorrectly. Generally, a neurologic examination should not pose any significant risk of harm. As alluded to in the description of elements of neurologic examination above, there are particular maneuvers and observations which are useful in eliciting functional abnormalities (Weintraub, 1997). At this point, it would be important to clarify the terminology used to describe nonorganic neurologic problems, that is, problems that have a nonphysical basis. Terms with somewhat subtle nuances of meaning include: hysterical, malingering, factitious, nonphysiologic, functional, and psychogenic. Many of these terms have rather extended implications and are probably best avoided. For example, hysterical has some specific psychiatric implications and an implicit gender bias. The term malingering imputes motivation to cause some disruption in function and is difficult to demonstrate objectively. Factitious implies conditions that are actively caused by the patient themselves and again implies a more specific psychiatric diagnosis such as Munchausen's. The term functional, in my opinion, is a preferred term to describe a person's actual ability to perform a certain act, but not demonstrate that ability on examination. The term functional (psychogenic) is used by some authors to more definitively imply that the patient's inability to perform an act that they have the capability to perform has a psychological component.

The demonstration of functional abnormalities essentially cuts across all of the aspects of the neurologic examination as demonstrated in some of the examples given above. Particular emphasis should be given to various aspects of the neurologic examination that are important to focus on when issues of TBI are being examined (McAllister and Green 1998; Weintraub, 1999). Specifically, certain patterns of functioning with regard to neurocognitive abilities can be a means of identifying functional patterns of neuropsychological functioning. Such issues are dealt with in detail in other areas of this text. False memory syndromes are, for example, a rather important possible forensic outcome to such investigations.

In the realm of cranial nerve functioning, ophthalmologic (eye findings) can be particularly important in identifying functional processes. Both the area of visual loss and other ophthalmologic abnormalities relating to eye movements, etc., can be elegantly detected by skillful neuro-ophthalmologic maneuvers. Also, the issues relating to psychogenic movement disorders are quite prominent in the area of forensic neurology, particularly as implicated in instances where head injury has been postulated as the etiology (Nora and Nora, 1999). In such cases, it is very important to have a global understanding of a person's medical history and genetic predispositions, as many of these movement disorders can readily be demonstrated to have other definite identifiable causes. In the realm of cortical functioning, a person's ability to perform some higher cortical functions such as recognition of deficits, computational abilities, writing abilities, etc., are screened by the routine neurologic examination and again interface very directly with neuropsychological testing to identify convincing organic deficits. There is, hence, a close interplay between what is screened by the neurologic examination and confirmed and better characterized by detailed neuropsychological testing.

Some syndromes may be a direct result of acquired brain injury. A specific neurologic process, namely epilepsy, is a sometimes subtle, but important entity to demonstrate as potentially related to TBI. Usually, post-traumatic epilepsy is quite dramatic and can easily be identified by subsequent intermittent generalized seizures and related electroencephalogram abnormalities which, in turn, can be effectively treated with appropriate anticonvulsant medications. In the more subtle aspects of epilepsy, certain neurobehavioral problems and even neurocognitive difficulties have been definitively ascribed to epileptic events. Conversely, there are events termed pseudoseizures which typically consist of some elements of "true" epilepsy, but are psychological in nature and do not have an organic basis for their occurrence. The area of forensic neurology has dealt prominently with issues of epilepsy as a potential cause of aggressive behavior (Treiman,1999). Significant implications relate to the culpability of an individual who performs an aggressive act in the context of an epileptic condition. These types of clinical questions have varying degrees of subtlety and recognition of epilepsy as a potential factor in a person's behaviors can be quite important. The convincing demonstration of pseudoseizures as a diagnosis can be quite involved, oftentimes requiring very extensive electroencephalographic monitoring in the setting of a comprehensive epilepsy treatment program. However, such a process is very important to clarify in that it not only may explain a person's paroxysmal neurocognitive and neurobehavioral difficulties as functional in nature, but may also obviate the treatment of seizures with any number of medications which have inherent side effect risks. The demonstration of pseudoseizures, in my opinion, can be one of the more difficult diagnoses to make with regard to a person's neurocognitive and neurobehavioral functioning in that pseudoseizures can often coexist with an organic seizure disorder. Hence, one must be sophisticated enough to be able to discriminate epileptic from nonepileptic events on an ongoing basis in such an individual.

The problem of language dysfunction (aphasias) can be quite important to recognize and characterize as a neurologic entity that may have profound implications for a person's cognitive and even behavioral abilities. A wide spectrum of language dysfunction is possible as a result of disruption in the "language centers' in an individual's "dominant cerebral hemisphere." The basic subtypes of aphasias include receptive aphasias which primarily affect a person's ability to receive language information from their environment, either by written or verbal input. Such an individual may still be able to produce some fluent language, but the speech typically deals with well learned phrases and there are obvious problems with the processing of new information presented to such an individual. A second major type of aphasia is an expressive aphasia in which an individual may understand language input by way of various verbal and/or written materials. However, such an individual has difficulty expressing thoughts and ideas and sometimes can only produce very over-learned and stereotyped words. Such an individual has extensive problems with language expressions of anything but the most basic ideas. The third, and most severe type of aphasia, is one of a global type of aphasia where a person may have impairment in both reception and production of language. Such an individual is relatively devoid of the ability to use language and is quite significantly impaired. Individuals who have language dysfunction to this degree oftentimes have other motor deficit such as hemiparesis because of the relatively large area of cortex that would be damaged in order to produce these problems. Deficits related to aphasia, of course, would tie in with neurobehavioral functioning in that individuals with aphasia characteristically have a good deal of frustration with their language abilities and oftentimes exhibit agitation and sometimes other problems with impulse control as a result of a secondary effect of the aphasia. Certainly, other areas of cortical damage such as frontal lobe damage correlated with some of the language dysfunctions may also predispose toward disinhibition by virtue of other areas ("control centers") of the brain being affected as well.

Discussion of epilepsy, aphasia, and concerns about functional disorders bring up the issue of how psychiatric diagnoses could enter into the context of brain injury. Certainly, various aspects of neurocognitive and especially neurobehavioral problems due to brain damage mimic various aspects of psychiatric disorders. For example, disinhibitions from certain anterior frontal lesions may closely resemble disorders of impulse control, and on the other end of the spectrum, abulia (disinterest), which is due to deep midfrontal lesions, could closely mimic some of the vegetative symptoms of depression or psychotic disorders (McAllister and Green, 1998). There are, of course, clearly defined psychiatric syndromes as outlined in the DSM-IV (Diagnostic and Statistical Manual of Mental Disorders) and there are certainly biological bases for these psychiatric syndromes, although some are more clearly characterized than others (APA, 1994). For example, the biochemical bases of schizophrenia and depression have been extensively delineated, particularly on a neuropharmacological level, by virtue of medications that have been found to be effective in their treatment. The actual overlap of psychiatric syndromes as per DSM-IV criteria and sequelae from brain injury are sometimes disputed, although evidence does suggest that fairly typical psychiatric syndromes can be produced after TBI. It is debatable as to whether a head injury actually causes the biochemical condition that produces the psychiatric syndrome vs. the psychiatric syndrome simply being a "reaction." For example, a reactive depression can be on the basis of deficits from a brain injury engendering a grief reaction. In any case, various accounts have demonstrated neuropsychiatric illness after TBI, which would not be accountable by factors such as reaction to an event. In some cases, psychiatric syndromes are suggested even after the syndrome of "mild" TBI.

Hence, in the setting of the neurological forensic examination in the context of brain injury, a very thorough focus has to be placed on these various cognitive and neurobehavioral issues including a cognizance of psychiatric symptomatology as possible sequelae of the brain injury. Such screenings ideally should be done by a neurologist skilled in neurobehavioral issues as the subtle cognitive and behavioral manifestations of brain injury may not be as apparent to a neurology practitioner who does not have experience in this area.

With regard to the conclusions of an Independent Medical Examination (IME), specific interrogatives are frequently requested of the neurologist pertaining to diagnoses as well as correlations to any particular accident in question. The key to an effective IME is an accurate identification of causal factors which contribute to an individual's neurocognitive and neurobehavioral functioning as well as any other sequelae from the TBI such as motor deficits, sensory deficits, or other aspects of neurologic functioning as outlined previously. The determination of an accurate cause hinges on a careful history, examination, and interpretation of diagnostic studies as discussed. As part of the analysis of a person's neurologic functioning, requests are made to determine an apportionment of causality to specific injuries, particularly if there is more than one event implicated in the cause of a person's deficits. Such apportionment may certainly have quite important implications for legal responsibility pertaining to a certain neurologic condition. Nevertheless, further opinion may be requested with regard to a period of healing following such an event. Again, knowledge of the natural history of a brain injury is quite critical in being able to predict clinical improvement or not in a certain condition and a time frame in which such improvement can be expected.

In summary, it is apparent that a forensic neurologic examination would closely mirror a traditional neurologic examination, but would focus on certain elements of the examination that are particularly important in legal settings, such as issues related to causality of a certain condition and its implications for an individual's abilities and general lifestyle over time. This, of course, includes the focus on neurocognitive and neurobehavioral functioning as well as other higher cortical functions and psychiatric symptoms which are also important neurologic concerns in a forensic setting. Adherence to standard neurologic principles engenders the highest quality to such an analysis. Furthermore, awareness and experience in the neurobehavioral aspects of medicine provides the strongest position for scientific and, specifically, medical credibility in this area.

TBI has a rather varied spectrum of manifestations, but these manifestations are identifiable and manageable in a forensic sense if there is thoughtful adherence to the scientific body of neurological knowledge in this setting.

2.4   SPECIFIC ISSUES IN THE INDEPENDENT MEDICAL
EXAMINATION (IME)

Having outlined elements of the neurologic examination and how Independent Medical Examinations (IMEs) require emphasis in various aspects of the neurologic examination, it would be useful to explicitly discuss how an IME report can be optimized with regard to its effectiveness as a medical analysis.

Various aspects of the IME from its inception as an IME request to a specialist, all the way through the writing of clinical summaries and interrogatives, can influence the IME quality. Elements of IME that should be particularly focused on include: type of subspecialist, medical record issues, X-ray and diagnostic information, clinical summaries, and specific interrogatives.

Specifically, there are certain technical aspects of IMEs that may offer stronger evidentiary credibility to establish a position.

2.4.1 IME REQUESTS

A very basic issue relates to the type of subspecialist requested to perform an IME. Obviously, in the setting of TBI, both the opinions of neurologists and neuropsychologists may be useful. Which subspecialist is chosen would depend on the exact question being asked (Tsushima and Nakano,1998). For example, if the question pertains very specifically to neuropsychological functioning such as detailed analysis of neurocognitive and neurobehavioral factors, the neuropsychologist would certainly be critical in producing the most optimal report. However, if a more global look at a TBI is desired (such as various medical aspects including technical details of the mechanism of injury, medication management, epilepsy issues, and other more general medical concerns), then obviously the neurologist would be more appropriate as an independent medical examiner. It should be recognized that at times, both subspecialists may be required to lend the strongest analysis to a particular case. Again, the role of the neurologist and neuropsychologist are complimentary in the setting of TBI and choice of one or the other, or both, may be a matter of the emphasis needed.

Efficient and comprehensive gathering of medical records can strongly influence the quality of an IME. A thoroughly organized set of records in chronological order and indexed by subspecialty provider can more efficiently and clearly disseminate medical information. The more comprehensive and clear the medical records, the more possible it is to gather information regarding preexisting factors, including both medical conditions and other activities of daily living which may influence a person's deficits following a TBI. Again, comprehensive history of medical problems can be invaluable as strongly suggested in the points made concerning neurologic diagnosis. Particular attention should be given to details in medical records relating to medical conditions, both before and after a particular traumatic event. This would include not only records relating to previous traumatic events, but indeed any medical condition which may directly or indirectly impact on neuropsychological functioning.

For example, medical documentation of a cognitive or behavioral limitation prior to a traumatic event may indicate a pre-existing problem that could progress with or without the traumatic event in question. As discussed previously, any number of causes for such neurobehavioral or neurocognitive difficulties should be carefully noted as they may impact substantially on subsequent neuropsychological developments after an injury.

The course of events after a traumatic injury may also be quite critical in analyzing a person's ongoing neurologic functioning. For example, the development of other new problems such as medical conditions may either delay, or in and of themselves, cause neurologic problems that would otherwise have resolved during the natural history of healing after the traumatic event itself. Hence, it is important to note new medical diagnoses such as cerebrovascular disease, rheumatologic conditions, infections, neoplastic processes, or other medical conditions which may impact on a person's apparent recovery or not after traumatic injury.

Psychiatric conditions are also, again, very important to note. If a psychiatric problem is noted following an injury, even if it was not present before the injury, causality is not necessarily implied. Such other factors as reactive depression (depression caused by physical or emotional loss following an event) can cause marked disability in an individual, and it may have only a very indirect relationship to the traumatic injury itself. In fact, there is a fairly high spontaneous occurrence of such problems as depression, either with or without injuries, which should be taken into account in analysis of a person's functioning after a traumatic event. The recurring theme of distinguishing causality from correlation is, of course, quite important in a careful scrutiny of medical records.

Pharmacologic interventions via chart records may give a clue as to other etiologies for a person's apparent neurocognitive or neurobehavioral problems. If a person develops need for ongoing pain treatment, such analgesic medications may, in and of themselves, cause significant side effects with related neuropsychological limitations. Also, there may be need for pharmacologic therapies which have no relationship to a traumatic event such as treatment for high blood pressure or other unrelated conditions which occur after an injury. The side effects from such pharmacologic interventions may mimic neurocognitive and neurobehavioral problems seen after traumatic injury, but have no relationship to a particular traumatic event. Hence, astute recognition of both medical and pharmacologic issues are invaluable in better elucidating causality of a traumatic neurologic process.

2.4.2 DIAGNOSTIC STUDIES

X-rays and other diagnostics are also quite useful in better delineating the extent of neurologic involvement, including important corroborative evidence for neuropsychological testing. Other neurophysiological testing, such as electroencephalograms, etc. may, again, lend confirmatory evidence toward diagnoses such as epilepsy or other organic cortical processes.

Proof of structural and functional neurologic abnormalities may be quite useful in strengthening evidence of a neurologic condition. It is more convincing to have subjective symptomatology, physical examination findings and diagnostic studies such as X-rays all supportive of the same neurologic process. Conversely, if an individual's symptoms are somewhat equivocal and the examination findings are subjective in nature, inconclusive radiographic studies can further cast doubt on the validity of a postulated disability. This can relate not only to radiographic studies, but also to constellations of neuropsychological deficits and detailed neurologic examination findings which can be quite specific and difficult to contrive. Personal review of diagnostic studies can also strengthen the nature of a medical record review. For example, personal review of imaging studies by an independent medical examiner qualified to view such studies can lend an increment of confirmatory evidence to objective physical findings as well. Along these lines, the degree of expertise of an individual would certainly impact on how credible the interpretation of diagnostic studies would be in any given setting. For example, a practitioner's experience with review of radiographic or electrophysiologic studies would certainly influence the quality of the medical evidence.

2.4.3 SUMMARY/INTERROGATIVES

Perhaps the most important aspect of the mechanics of an IME request would be a summary of the legal concerns of a case and related, clearly stated legal questions. As medical practitioners oftentimes have limited or at least unsophisticated knowledge of legal technicalities, interrogatives posed in direct language can obviate the educing of medical opinions which do not really address the legal perspective desired. It would certainly be useful for the attorney or legal representative to define what degree of certainty to ascribe to a medical opinion. Explanation of such phrases as "within a reasonable degree of medical certainty" can be useful, particularly to medical practitioners who are not versed in the legal process. Other aspects of the interrogatives on a request for IME which may be ambiguous to the relatively legally unsophisticated medical practitioner would include such phrases as "reasonable" or "necessary." Such phrases may not have the precise meaning to a medical practitioner as they do to the legal expert and hence, explanation of such questions may be necessary to optimize the IME document.

Hence, it is the clear understanding of the neurologic diagnosis process and how this process interfaces with the legal questions posed that can best lead to effective IME reports.

2.5 INDICATIONS FOR NEUROREHABILITATION

Based on the previous discussion regarding the spectrum of disability that can result from TBI, it is evident that rehabilitation is quite a broad topic. Some basic principles regarding recommendations/indications for neurorehabilitation can be useful. One must first consider the natural history of a TBI, specifically recognizing that some degree of natural healing would be expected without intervention, but that certain interventions would be vital to assure optimal and timely recovery from a TBI. Certainly, the severity and extent of brain injury would dictate needed interventions. After a severe injury, prompt and thorough interventions may limit the extent of brain damage and optimize the recovery of areas of the brain which may be partially damaged and more amenable to "healing" when supportive interventions have been accomplished. With milder degrees of injury, there may be lack of recognition of any particular difficulties for some time and only with various environmental challenges will they be made evident. As indicated with severe brain injury, there would be an expected "healing process" from the physical damage done to the brain. With mild TBI, there is optimism of good and sometimes complete recovery, although such recovery may take many months to accomplish. Hence, physical changes of structural and biochemical "healing" may take place over many months to a few years after brain injury, again depending on the extent and severity of the process. Neurorehabilitation is useful both during and after such physical changes have occurred, again with the intention of optimizing the degree and rate of recovery to afford the best outcome. As implied previously, the spectrum of rehabilitation is even broader than the wide spectrum of injuries that may manifest after trauma to the brain. The range of interventions include medical and pharmacologic strategies to address the physiologic and biochemical needs of a healing nervous system in conjunction with neuropsychological and neurobehavioral interventions to serve cognitive, behavior, and social issues which present after brain injury.

The physiologic support to the brain after acute injury includes such interventions as control of edema, oxygenation of brain tissue, and support of other bodily functions such as the circulatory and respiratory systems during vital times of early brain repair. Also, pharmacologic interventions to improve the balance of altered neurochemistry in the setting of brain damage can optimize recovery of the damaged brain tissue.

Pharmacologic interventions beyond the acute phase to address biochemical imbalances that persist even beyond the time course of normal healing may be up to several months to a few years after brain injury. Hence, rehabilitation efforts in the form of pharmacologic interventions may extend well beyond the time course of "physical healing."

Rehabilitation in the form of neurocognitive and neurobehavioral therapies also apply to both acute brain injury situations and in a more chronic context. There is certainly controversy and conflicting data regarding the extent of benefit from neurocognitive interventions with regard to the ultimate functional result after brain injury. An argument certainly can be made that at least the rate of improvement is better for individuals receiving the benefit of neurocognitive retraining following brain injury. A body of literature also supports the argument that the extent of recovery is better when neurocognitive interventions are applied during the "healing process" after brain injury. Even in the subacute and chronic time frames after brain injury, neurocognitive interventions certainly have been demonstrated to be beneficial, at least with regard to compensatory strategies which aid in an individual's functional status.

In situations where an individual lacks adequate social controls due to disinhibition, etc., neurobehavioral strategies can also be quite useful (both acutely and chronically). Such strategies as increased environmental structure and behavioral programming can often optimize that individual's functioning, particularly conditions related to agnosia (significant impairment in judgement and insight).

Therefore, when considering issues of appropriate neurorehabilitation after brain injury, the natural history (physical recovery) must be taken into account as should the severity of the brain injury in dictating neurorehabilitation needs. The spectrum of neurologic deficits is an integral part of the analysis of neurorehabilitation as well. It should be mentioned that within such categories as pharmacologic interventions, neurocognitive therapies, and behavioral therapies, there are many modalities offered as options to address this broad spectrum of manifestation post brain injury.

2.6 CONCLUSION

It is evident from the previous discussion, that the realm of the neurologic diagnosis is quite a complex endeavor. The interface between neurologic diagnosis and forensic concerns adds yet another level of complexity. This topic is manageable only with a basic understanding of some of the standard principles of neurologic diagnosis previously portrayed.

Certainly, this treatment is not intended to be a comprehensive examination of neurologic concerns that may enter into the forensic arena. Rather, established standard diagnostic processes pertaining to neurologic conditions, including TBI, will engender a method of logically approaching such problems.

Hence, a firm methodology of approaching the neurologic issues of TBI will serve as a solid foundation even as some of the exciting technologies aiding neurologic diagnoses are advanced. Again, it is the established standard methodology of neurologic diagnosis as presented above that will stand the test of time and lead to the most credible forensic analyses of neurologic concerns, including TBI.

REFERENCES

American Psychiatric Association, (1994). *Diagnostic and Statistical Manual of Mental Disorders — Fourth Edition*, American Psychiatric Association, Washington, D.C.

Aminoff, M.J., (1986). *Electrodiagnosis in Clinical Neurology*, Churchill Livingston, New York.

Anderson, C.V., Wood, D.M., Bigler, E.D, and Blatter, D.D., (1996). Lesion volume, injury severity, and thalamic integrity following head injury. *Journal of Neurotrauma,* 12(1), 35–40.

Cecil, K.M., Hills, E.C., Sandel, M.E., Smith, D.E., McIntosh, T.K., Mannon, L.J., Sinson, G.P., Bagley, L.J., Grossman, R.I., and Lenkinski, R.E., (1998). Proton magnetic resonsance spectroscopy for detection of axonal injury in the splenium of the corpus callosum of brain-injured patients. *Journal of Neurosurgery,* 88(5), 795–801.

Deb, S., Lyons, I., Koutzoukis, C., Ali, I., and McCarthy, G., (1999). Rate of psychiatric illness 1 year after traumatic brain injury. *American Journal of Psychiatry,* 156(3) 374–378.

DeJong, R.N. and Haerer, A.F., (1998). Case taking and the neurologic examination, in *Clinical Neurology*, Joint, R.J. and Griggs, R.C., Eds., Lippincott Williams & Wilkins, Philadelphia.

Folstein, M.F., (1975). Mini-mental state. *Journal of Psychiatry Research,* 12, 189–198.

Gale, S.D., Johnson, S.C., Bigler, E.D., and Blatter, D.D., (1995). Trauma-induced degenerative changes in brain injury: a morphometric analysis of three patients with pre-injury and post-injury MR scans. *Journal of Neurotrauma,* 12(12), 151–158.

Garada, B., Klufas, R.A., and Schwartz, R.B., (1997). Neuroimaging in closed head injury seminars. *Clinical Neuropsychiatry,* 2(3), 188–195.

Hammeke, T.A., (1999). Clinical applications of functional magnetic resonance imaging, in *Current Topics in Brain Injury Rehabilitation*. Mayo Clinic Center, Rochester, MN.

Malec, J.F., (1998). Mild traumatic brain injury: concepts and controversies, *1998 Brain Injury Conference,* Mayo Medical Center, Rochester, MN.

Mayberg, H.S., (1996). Medical-Legal Inferences from Functional Neuroimaging Evidence. *Seminars in Clinical Neuropsychiatry,* 1(3), 195–201.

Mayo Clinic, (1991). *Clinical Examinations in Neurology.* Mayo Clinic and Mayo Foundation for Medical Education and Research, Mosby Year Book, St. Louis, MO.

McAllister, T.W. and Green, R., (1998). Neurobehavioral consequences of traumatic brain injury, *Seminars in Neuropsychiatry,* 3(3) 157-241.

McAllister, W.W. and Green, R.L., (1998). Guest Eds., Neurobehavioral consequences of traumatic brain injury, *Seminars in Clinical Neuropsychiatry,* 3(3).

Nora, L.M. and Nora, R.E., (1999). Selected legal issues in movement disorders, in *Neurologic Clinics*, Weintraub, M.I., Guest Ed., Medical-Legal Issues Facing Neurologists, W.B. Saunders Co., Philadelphia, 17(2).

Popkin, M.K., (1997). Guest Ed., Neurobehavioral Aspects of Diabetes Mellitus. *Seminars in Clinical Neuropsychiatry,* 2(1), 1–98.

Restale, R.M., Guest Ed., (1996). Brain damage and legal responsibility, *Seminars in Clinical Neuropsychiatry,* 1(3).

Restale, R.M., Guest Ed., (1997). Neuropsychiatry of minor head injury. *Seminars in Clinical Neuropsychiatry: 2* (3).

Thatcher, R.W., Camacho, M., Salazar, A., Linden, C., Biver, C., and Clarke, I., (1997). Quantitative MRI of the gray-white matter distribution in traumatic brain injury. *Journal of Neurotrauma,* 14(1), 1–14.

Treiman, D.M., (1999). Violence and the epilepsy defense, in *Neurologic Clinics*, Weintraub, M.I., Guest Ed., Medical-Legal Issues Facing Neurologists, W.B. Saunders Co., Philadelphia, 17(2).

Tsushima, W.T. and Nakano, K.K., (1998). *Effective medical testifying, A Handbook for Physicians,* Butterworth-Heinemann, Boston, MA.

Weintraub, M.I., (1999). Guest Ed., Medical — legal issues facing neurologists, *Neurologic Clinics,* 17(2).

Weintraub, M.I., (1997). Malingering and conversion reactions, *American Academy of Neurology 49th Annual Meeting,* Boston, MA.

Weiss, Z., (1996). The legal admissibility of positron emission tomography scans in criminal cases, in *Seminars in Clinical Neuropsychiatry, People vs. Spyder Cystkopf,* 1(3), 202–210.

3 The Forensic Neuropsychological Evaluation

Joseph Yedid

CONTENTS

0-8493-2035-6/00/$0.00+$.50

The complexity, different definitions, and various approaches to the assessment of brain-behavior interactions are probably correlated with the fact that neuropsychology as a specialty is a relatively emerging field. Indeed, the initial construct of neuropsychology was proposed approximately 50 years ago by Donald O. Hebb, in his well-known book, *Organization of Behavior*, published in 1949. The term neuropsychology was formulated by Hebb as a part of the sub-title of this pioneer publication, which includes Hebb's proposed hypotheses regarding the functioning of the brain. Since 1949, neuropsychology has become an integral and prominent field within clinical psychology. Indeed, this statement is clearly supported by Muriel D. Lezak in the preface section of the well-known compendium entitled: *Neuropsychological Assessment — Third Edition* (1995).

Lezak (1995) stated that when she first decided to compile a review of tests to assess brain damage, clinical neuropsychology was in its infancy, with only a handful of clinicians utilizing a few structured tests. Additional tests constructed for other purposes were integrated into the existing neuropsychological armamentarium.

The initial growth and development of the field of clinical neuropsychology was a direct outcome of the urgent need to formulate a clinical paradigm for the assessment of how brain-behavior correlates due to gun shot wounds and impaired neurological functioning. In his well-known publication entitled, *Brain and Intelligence*, Halstead (1947) proposed several unique and ingenious assessment techniques. Among Halstead's students was Ralph Reitan who significantly contributed to the further development of the clinical neuropsychology field (Reitan and Davidson, 1974; Reitan and Wolfson, 1993). A partial list of some of the other prominent clinical neuropsychologists in the Western Hemisphere and United States includes the following names: N.M. Adams; Nelson Butters; M.J. Ball; D.F. Benson; A.L. Benton; R.J. Boll; R.A. Bornstein; Geshwind; L.R. Goldberg; Golden, C.J.; R. Heaton; E.F. Kaplan; B.E. Levine; M. Lezak; B. Milner; F. Newcombe; G. Prigatano; E.W. Russell; and D. Wechsler. The multitude of original contributions facilitated the foundation, development, and formation of the field of clinical neuropsychology and its applicability to various other specialties, i.e., neurology, psychiatry, rehabilitation medicine, endocrinology, and internal medicine.

3.1 THE DEFINITION OF THE NEUROPSYCHOLOGICAL EXAMINATION: GOALS, COMPONENTS, AND APPLICABILITY

The specific components of the comprehensive neuropsychological evaluation usually depend on the clinician's training, methods of information gathering, and the specific domain (i.e., location) of the evaluation. In the context of the present manuscript, the definition of clinical neuropsychology is: "comprehensive approaches to applied problems concerning the psychological effects of brain damage in humans" (Reitan and Davison, 1974).

The four most popular neuropsychological batteries are:

1. The Halstead-Reitan Neuropsychological Evaluation.
2. The Luria-Nebraska Neuropsychological Evaluation.
3. The IOWA–Benton Neuropsychological Approach.
4. The Process Approach to Neuropsychological Assessment.

The main differences and similarities among the various approaches previously indicated will be elaborated upon in the following section. However, regardless of the specific components (i.e., screening methods, specific tests utilized, etc.) the following descriptions of the neuropsychological examination are probably the most direct and parsimonious:

1. The determination of appropriate tests and assessment techniques is based on the patient's capacities, and the questions the examiner asks the patient. The examiner usually relies upon a solid base of several assessment tools and customizes the evaluation to suit the individual patient's circumstances. The expert neuropsychologist should start with a basic battery that appraises the patient's cognitive, emotional, and behavioral functions. Hypotheses are made in regard to possible diagnoses, areas of cognitive dysfunctions, and various psychosocial and/or emotional contributions to the total behavioral presentation. The potential diagnostic impression is therefore based on a comprehensive appraisal of the patient's overall functioning.
2. A comprehensive neuropsychological evaluation must encompass the assessment of a broad spectrum of functions: from sensory input and perceptual integration, to motor output and certain cognitive functions such as memory, concept formation, and problem solving.

The goal of the neuropsychological examination is the assessment of the various domains of brain-behavior relationship. Therefore, the clinical objectives of the examination should entail the qualitative and quantitative appraisal of the examinee's observed behavior. The process should include: the behavioral observations; clinical interview; and structured quantifiable tests which are valid, reliable, and accepted on the basis of normative data and base rates. The following specific functions should be evaluated by the neuropsychological examination: concentration, attention, and information processing; sensory-perceptual functions; fine and gross motor strength and coordination; memory, learning, concept formation, and concept utilization; verbal/language functions and academic skills; central auditory and visual processing; construction and assembling; and emotional status and personality attributes.

3.1.1 THE SPECIFIC COMPONENTS AND ASSESSMENT STRATEGIES INCLUDED IN THE NEUROPSYCHOLOGICAL EXAMINATION

In order to successfully accomplish the goals and objectives of the neuropsychological examination, various data and objective parameters must be accumulated, analyzed, and interpreted by the examining neuropsychologist. One is then able to derive a valid and reliable appraisal of the examinee's true level of functioning. Therefore, the following sources of information must be included in the comprehensive process of the neuropsychological examination.

A thorough review of the medical history and background of the examinee, including retrospective data dating to early childhood, adolescence, and adulthood. Physical developmental and/or chronic medical conditions, pre-existing or coexisting, should be part of this review.

A comprehensive review of the examinee's social-developmental history and background. The components of this section should include:

a. psychosocial and intrafamilial background and major life events, with history of any form of abuse or traumata; interpersonal, intimate relationships with significant others, including ages, durations and quality of life
b. educational history based on school records, certificates, diplomas, etc.
c. occupational history, including specific durations, places and types of employment, written work-performance evaluations, periods of unemployment, dependency on welfare or other resources
d. past or present juvenile delinquency, probation, criminal behavior, arrests, imprisonment, and DUI (driving under the influence)
e. history of any prior brain injuries and/or personal or familial neurological condition.

3.1.2   CLINICAL INTERVIEW

The neuropsychologist should obtain the examinee's subjective description of the alleged injury, complaints, symptoms, and alleged dysfunctions that interfere with the present functioning and result in any form of physical, cognitive, or emotional impairment. Verbatim recording and/or note taking provide relevant information with emphasis placed on the examinee's emotional composure, eye-contact, tone of voice, cooperation, compliance, and the content of the answers provided.

3.1.3   THE STRUCTURED NEUROPSYCHOLOGICAL ASSESSMENT

Several approaches to direct assessment of the individual's neuropsychological status have been indicated above and include four batteries. However, prior to elaborating on information regarding the theoretical and actuarial foundations of the various approaches, it is essential to indicate that each has ethical, legal, and scientific aspects. In the context of the neuropsychological examination the primary responsibility of the clinical neuropsychologist is to insure strict and consistent adherence to specific guidelines. The resources for these guidelines are included in the following references:

1. Standards for Educational and Psychological Testing, (1985). The American Psychological Association, Washington, D.C.
2. Impara, J.C. and Plake, B.S., (1998). *Mental Measurement Yearbook*, Buros Institute of Mental Measurements. University of Nebraska–Lincoln, NE.

3. Law and Human Behavior.
4. Spreen, O. and Strauss, E., (1991). *A Compendium for Neuropsychological Tests,* Oxford University Press, New York.
5. Specialty guidelines for forensic psychologists, (1990). American Psychology-Law Society News, II, 8–11.
6. Snyder, P.J. and Nussbaum, P.D., Eds., (1998). *Clinical Neuropsychology: A Pocket Handbook for Assessment,* American Psychological Association, Washington, D.C.

Although each one of the various approaches to the neuropsychological examination is characterized by somewhat unique attributes, these aspects are not elaborated upon in this chapter. The interested clinician and/or attorney would benefit from reviewing the most recent and comprehensive handbook by Muriel D. Lezak titled: *Neuropsychological Assessment* (1995).

The tests recommended for inclusion in the neuropsychological examination meet the criteria of reliability, validity, and the robust structure necessary to withstand most criticisms by the opposing attorney or forensic neuropsychological expert. The battery of tests should include: the Bender Visual-Motor Gestalt Test — Recall Version; the Wechsler Adult Intelligence Scale-III; the Wechsler Memory Scale-III; Symbol Digit Modalities Test; the Comprehensive Halstead-Reitan Neuropsychological Evaluation; the Sentence Completion Test; The Minnesota Multiphasic Personality Inventory-II; The Beck Depression Inventory-Revised; and the Structured Interview of Reported Symptoms.

With the exception of the Sentence Completion Test, clinical utilization of the tests just mentioned is supported by a plethora of studies. They affirm the appropriateness of the tests in the context of the objectives of the neuropsychological examination. In order to comply with the specific guidelines of the American Psychological Association for test administration, the manuals, instructions, and/or any other restrictions indicated in the test manuals should be adhered to with utmost compliance. Accordingly, it is the responsibility of the clinical neuropsychologist to provide direct, consistent, and clear evidence that the impact of any confounding variables does not interfere with the appropriate administration of the various tests.

3.1.4 BENDER VISUAL-MOTOR GESTALT TEST — RECALL VERSION

The inclusion of this version of the test in the first phase of the neuropsychological examination facilitates the examinee's motivation and decreases anticipatory anxiety. The Bender-Gestalt Test has been studied and researched extensively, partially due to its relative parsimony, including brief, rapid administration. However, it is very revealing when compared with other tests that require fine visual-motor dexterity, and immediate, short-term, and delayed recall. A comprehensive review of this test is available (Hutt, 1985), and the applicability of the test to the neuropsychological assessment is discussed. The main goal is the appraisal of the examinee's visual-constructional skills and memory. Hence, it provides an initial indication of the possibility of dyspraxia (and can be used as a projective technique). The forensic neuropsychologist must consider the fact that most individuals with direct evidence of brain dysfunction might not demonstrate any objective impairment when requested to perform drawing tasks alone (Lezak, 1995). Patients with compromised brain functioning will most likely have difficulty when the integration of fine visual-motor dexterity and retrieval is called for.

The content of the Bender test includes nine designs that assess the perceptual organization of parts into a configurational entity (i.e., Gestalt). The initial phase of this assessment instrument was utilized for examining developmental disabilities in children. However, its clinical application rapidly extended, and it is presently utilized with other populations. The discriminant validity of the Bender is found when the Wepman's version (Lezak, 1995) is chosen by the clinician. The addition of two recall phases is added after the initial copying. The immediate and the short-term recalls of the 9 figures are administered several seconds and 30 minutes, respectively, after the completion of the initial phase. Normal subjects usually recall five or more designs; thus, when the examinee recalls less than five designs, the possibility of brain dysfunction is raised (Pirozzolo, 1978).

Although the specific administration, scoring, and interpretations have not been standardized, Hutt (1985) proposed the following quantitative and qualitative criteria and scores. Hutt's model includes these organizational factors: sequence, position, use of space, collision, and shift of paper. The factors refer to difficulties with or due to: closure, crossing, curvature, angulation, perceptual rotation, retrogression, simplification, fragmentation, overlapping, elaboration, perseveration, and redrawing.

A comprehensive summary of the efficiency of neuropsychological instruments for discriminating between neurological and psychiatric patients provided supportive evidence for the present author's suggestion to include the Bender in the proposed battery. In their review, Heaton, Brade, and Johnson (1978) reported a median score for percent of correct classifications of 76% for the Bender test. This high accuracy was compared to four other reputable instruments: Benton Visual Retention Test; Memory for Designs; Trail-Making Test; and the Background Interference Procedure, i.e., BIP of the Bender (Canter, 1966). The accuracy of the Bender's discrimination was exceeded only by that of the BIP.

Validly impaired responses to the Bender's tasks and difficulties with fine visual-motor graphic abilities are associated with parietal lobe lesions, and predominantly due to lesions of the right parietal lobe (Diller, Ben-Yishai, Gersthan et al., 1974). Right hemisphere dysfunction is usually manifested by errors of rotation, fragmentation, and omission. While bilateral dysfunction results in omission, left hemisphere impairment manifests in additions. Noteworthy is the finding of poor performance on the Bender test due to pre-existing learning disabilities, left-hand dominance, and/or dyslexia.

3.1.5 THE WECHSLER ADULT INTELLIGENCE SCALE — THIRD EDITION

The Wechsler Adult Intelligence Scale — Third Edition (WAIS-III) is the most recent version of Wechsler's ecological approach; it adheres to the premise that intelligence is a multi-dimensional construct. The initial attempt by Wechsler to compile a set of skills and tasks as an appraisal of the individual's intelligence originated in 1939

(Wechsler, 1939). The outcome of Wechsler's conceptual framework resulted in the formation of the Wechsler-Bellevue Intelligence Scale. His dynamic definition of intelligence focused on the individual's capacity to behave purposefully, to think rationally, and to cope efficiently with his external world (Wechsler, 1944). Wechsler's construct of intelligence was global and included an aggregate of specific abilities. Wechsler opined that intelligence should be assessed via verbal and performance tasks which appraised ability in various ways, yet could be integrated to formulate a global construct. His cogent and insightful approach consistently evolved and resulted in an expansion of the concept of intelligence. He later proposed the inclusion of items that evaluate the individual's abilities to perceive and react to various moral, social, and aesthetic tasks (Wechsler, 1975). Wechsler proposed that several cognitive attributes explained the variance in factor analytic studies, including: motivation, attitudes, goal awareness, and persistence. Therefore, the clinical neuropsychologist should consider a compound of factors when quantitative parameters and the content of responses are interpreted. Interpretation of the WAIS-III (as well as all other test results) should entail the assessment of strengths, weaknesses, social-personal history, and background, including ethnic, cultural, and medical factors. Moreover, the clinician must assess the potential impact of depression, anxiety, apprehension, and any other relevant emotional factors.

The most recent edition, the WAIS-III, incorporates several revisions, including: updating the norms; extension of the age range through 89 years of age; modification of outdated items; updating artwork to minimize the interference of visual acuity problems and left-handedness; extension of floor effect and enhancement of clinical utility by including easier items; decreased reliance on timed performance; enhancement of fluid reasoning by adding the Matrix-Reasoning subtest; and the additional new subtests that appraise processing speed and working memory (the Symbol Search and Letter-Number Sequencing, respectively). The addition of the subtests mentioned above contributes to the strengthening of the theoretical bases. Moreover, statistical linkage to other measures of cognitive functioning and achievement was insured.

Of utmost importance are the extensive studies of reliability and validity. The averaged reliability coefficients for the WAIS-III IQ sub-scales and indexes (Verbal Completion, Perceptual Organization, Working Memory, and Processing Speed) range from .88 to .97 and are higher than those of the subtests that comprise the IQ scale or index. This distinction is due to the fact that specific subtests are only based on part of the individual's intellectual functioning, while the IQ and Index scores are based on the individual's performance on numerous tasks. However, a closer examination of the detailed table of reliability coefficients of the WAIS-III subtests, IQ Scales, and Indexes by Age Groups, in the Technical Manual raises a significant clinical issue. The variance of the reliability coefficients among 13 age groups when the 14 subtests are examined revealed a marked discrepancy, and a larger variance is apparent, ranging from .93 to .70 averaged coefficients of reliability. Moreover, when the various subtest scores of reliability are examined, the range is extended from .94 to .50. The association of this variance with age becomes more pronounced for very specific subtests when the age of the individual examined is above 70 years. The smallest degree of variance is shown with the Vocabulary and Digit Symbol subtests; the most widespread reliability coefficients are indicated in reference to the Picture Arrangement and Object Assembly subtests. Hence, it is the neuropsychologist's responsibility to consider those factors when appraising any unusual variance among the subtests of the WAIS-III.

A recent comprehensive publication by Kaufman and Lichtenberger (1999) includes a review of the administration, scoring, interpretation, strengths, and weaknesses, as well as the clinical applications of the WAIS-III. Kaufman et al. (1999) provide specific guidelines for formulating interpretive data based on the quantitative parameters of the WAIS-III. The interested forensic expert may benefit from utilizing the informative content of this text to arrive at a concise, accurate assessment of the patient's cognitive functioning.

3.1.6 THE WECHSLER MEMORY SCALE — THIRD EDITION

The most recent edition of the Wechsler Memory Scale (WMS) was published and became available to clinical neuropsychologists in 1997. The inclusion of this test in the comprehensive neuropsychological evaluation is essential for the assessment of memory and learning. A very concise and meaningful definition of the association between these functions was initially provided by Squire in his outstanding book, *Memory and Brain,*(1987). Squire's definition of learning addressed the process of acquiring new information; he described memory as learning that persists and can then be accessed at a later time. Contemporary studies and hypotheses (Squire, 1987; Squire and Butters, 1992) postulate the temporal differentiation of memory into two main phases. Short-term memory varies from several seconds to 1 to 2 minutes; long-term memory refers to the permanent storage of memory. Long-term memory was then further subdivided into declarative and procedural memory. The latter, i.e., procedural memory, refers to behavioral changes based on actual experiences that might be beyond the individual's conscious awareness. Declarative memory refers to the storage and retrieval of units of information or knowledge. It is then further divided into semantic and episodic memory. These constructs refer to: (1) memories for general facts or concepts; and (2) memory of information that is context specific. The Wechsler Memory Scale — Third Edition (WMS-III) is primarily an assessment of declarative episodic memory. Noteworthy is that the WMS-III utilizes the term "working memory" as a substitute for short-term memory.

Similar to the WAIS-III's development, the first edition of the WMS was constructed more than 50 years ago (Wechsler, 1945). It included the following seven subtests: Information; Orientation; Mental Control; Memory Passages; Digits Total; Visual Reproduction; and Associate Learning (of verbal-auditory input). The patient's age constituted the only demographic correction factor and ranged from 20 to 64 years.

The second phase in the development of the WMS was in the formation of the Wechsler Memory Scale — Revised (Wechsler, 1987). The WMS-R utilized 13 subtests, including questions often used as part of a general mental status examination (Information and Orientation Questions). The eight subtests that followed measured short-term learning and recall of both verbal and visual material. The remaining subtests assessed delayed-recall and retention of verbal and visual stimuli, including the measurement of the retention of meaningful and integrated material. The age-correction factor was extended to include groups from 16 to 74 years of age. Various combinations of the subtests yielded scores for: General Memory; Attention/Concentration; Verbal and Visual Memory; and Delayed-Recall Composite.

The most recent revision of the WMS is the WMS-III includes the following normative/psychometric updates: the standardization sample of individuals ranging in age from 16 to 89 years; and measures of recognition memory that are administered immediately after measures of delayed-recall. Although the WMS-III includes 17 main sections, the integration of the various scores results in 8 Primary Indexes: Auditory Immediate; Visual Immediate; Immediate Memory; Auditory Delayed; Visual Delayed; Auditory Recognition Delayed; General Memory; and Working Memory. Quantitative percentile scores are provided, in addition to the qualitative descriptions which range from Very Superior to Extremely Low. Moreover, eleven Primary Subtest scores and four Auditory Composite scores are provided.

It is highly recommended that the forensic expert consider the reliability of various components. The averaged reliability coefficients of the WMS-III Primary Subtest Scores and Primary Indexes range from .74 to .93 and are lower for the Primary Subtest Scores. This discrepancy becomes more pronounced when the averaged reliability coefficients for the Primary Subtest Scores are compared with those for Primary indexes across the 13 age groups. Indeed, when these parameters are thoroughly examined, they range from .64 to .96, for the Primary Subtest Scores, and from .64 to .95 for Primary Indexes. Noteworthy is that the majority of the lowest reliability coefficients occur in reference to the Auditory Recognition Delayed Index. This pattern of quantitative variance is not correlated with aging. The reliability coefficients for the Auditory Recognition Delayed Indexes were .69 and .64 for the 16 to 17 and 18 to 19 year age group, respectively. The highest correlation coefficients were for the following age groups: 20 to 24, 75 to 79, 80 to 84, and 85 to 89. These unique findings are quite relevant when the standard errors of measurement are examined. The parameters previously mentioned provide an estimate of the amount of error in an individual's observed test score. Since the standard error of measurement is inversely related to the reliability of a subtest, the greater the reliability, the smaller the standard error of measurement. Worth mentioning is that the examination of the standard errors of measurement of the WMS-III Primary Scores and Primary Indexes showed the smallest reliability for the Verbal Paired Associates I.

It is the responsibility of the neuropsychologist to consistently examine these parameters when interpreting the quantitative data obtained from the WMS-III in order to insure appropriate and valid analysis of the examinee's performance.

3.1.7 THE COMPREHENSIVE HALSTEAD-REITAN NEUROPSYCHOLOGICAL EVALUATION

The seminal contribution of Halstead (1947) to the foundation of the Halstead-Reitan Neuropsychological Battery (HRNB), included seven tests that were initially selected for the differential diagnosis among patients with frontal lobe lesions, patients with other lesions, and/or normal individuals. Throughout the years this battery has been modified by the deletion of the Critical Clicker Fusion and the Time Sense Test, and the addition of the Trail Making Tests (A and B) and the Reitan-Indiana Aphasia Screening Test (Reitan and Davison, 1974; Reitan and Wolfson, 1993). In spite of numerous controversies regarding the content and validity of the HRNB (Lezak, 1995; Reitan, 1955; Reitan and Wolfson, 1993; Reitan et al., 1995; Golden and Van Den Borek, 1998; Russell, 1998), it is considered the major neuropsychological battery in the United States (Golden, Zillmer, and Spiers, 1992a; Reitan, 1955). The two additional versions of the HRNB were proposed by Russell and his colleagues and a joint effort by Heaton and his co-contributors (Russell, Neuringer, and Goldstein, 1970; Heaton, Grant, and Matthews, 1986, 1991). The most significant modification in the interpretation of the quantitative scores obtained via the administration of the HRNB is the alternate scoring system proposed by Heaton, Grant, and Matthews in 1986. The utilization of demographic correction factors (age, education, and gender-corrected T-scores) for the HRNB, the WAIS, and the WAIS-R (Heaton, Grant, and Matthews, 1991, 1992) renders them highly comprehensive because they also include additional tests. The administration of the Expanded HRNB, including the WAIS, recommended by Heaton, Grant, and Matthews (1991), provides for the following tests: the Halstead Impairment Index; Average 40 Index; Category Test; Trail Making Tests A and B; Tactual Performance Test (TPT) - Time (minutes per block); TPT-Memory; TPT-Location; TPT-Dominant and Non Dominant hand (minutes per block); Seashore Rhythm; Speech Sounds Perception; Aphasia Screening; Spatial Relations; Sensory-Perceptual, Finger Tapping and Hand Dynamometer; Grooved Pegboard, Sensory Perceptual, and Tactile Forum Recognition - each one of these subtests appraises the functioning of both hands; Thurstone Word Fluency; Boston Naming; Boston Diagnostic Aphasia Examination (BDAE); Wisconsin Card Sorting Test, perseverative responses; Seashore Total Memory; Digit Vigilance, time and number of errors; Story Points/Trials and percent loss for the Story Memory Figure Learning; Peabody Individual Achievement Test, Reading Recognition, Reading Comprehension and Spelling. Heaton, Grant, and Matthews (1991) provided thorough explanations of the need for demographic corrections, the data collection, development and validation of the demographic correction system, and precise directions for the utilization of their findings. Therefore, the interested reader is encouraged to review that publication for any additional information. Noteworthy is that Heaton, Grant, and Matthews (1991) tentatively suggested T-scores parameters for the classification of the seven clinical categories, ranging from severe impairment (T-scores: 1 to 19) to above average (T-scores: 55+).

The impact of the clinical application of Heaton, Grant, and Matthews' (1991, 1992) scoring system was simultaneously: (a) challenged and questioned (Reitan and Wolfson, 1995); (b) considered important (Van Der Ploeg, Axelrod, Sherer, and Scott, 1997; Shutteworth-Jordan, 1997); and (c) appraised as "equally sensitive" when compared with the raw score system (i.e., Reitan and Wolfson's approach) (Golden and Van Den Broek, 1998). A thorough review of the discussions regarding the benefit of utilizing the demographic correction factors is quite revealing. For example, Golden et al., (1998) believed that the value of the scoring system was related to the population studied. He postulated that Heaton's system might be more accurate when applied to a population with general head injuries, while the Halstead-Reitan system might be more readily applicable to a stroke population. However, Golden and Van Den Broek's (1998) description of the participants in their retrospective examination of the data included in their study is very interesting: out of the 68 patients "chosen from archival files," 54 represented vascular disorders, 10 suffered from tumors, and only 4 patients in the study suffered from head trauma.

It is not necessary to include the coefficients of reliability and validity of every test in Heaton, Grant, and Matthews' (1991) expanded neuropsychological battery. However, this is contingent upon the inclusion of all the other tests recommended in this chapter. Therefore, it is the ethical and clinical responsibility of the clinician to be cautious and review the scientific literature regarding the various structured tests included in the battery and ascertain their relevance in each unique test situation.

3.1.8 THE SYMBOL DIGIT MODALITIES TEST

The Symbol Digit Modalities Test (SDMT) is a screening instrument for brain dysfunction in children and adults. It calls for the conversion of meaningless geometric forms into written and/or oral number responses. The two methods of administering the SDMT are: (1) a written version that may be given to individuals or groups; or (2) an oral version that is given individually. This test is relatively free of cultural bias and requires approximately five minutes to complete. Smith (1972) confirmed the sensitivity of the SDMT to the presence of brain dysfunction and spontaneous recovery from brain injury. The norms are provided for male and female children, ranging in age from 8 to 17 years, for the written and oral versions, and adults ranging from 18 to 78 years of age. The educational norms are available for adults only, with two groups: (1) 12 years or less of education; or 2) 13 years or more of education. The test-retest correlations for a sample of normal adults were .80 and .76, for the written and oral versions, respectively. The most relevant information is in Tables 13, 14, and 15 of the manual (Smith, 1972) and includes the following information: (1) mean written and oral SDMT scores for adults with chronic aphasia following stroke or brain trauma; (2) norms for normal adults and adults with chronic lesion, by age groups; and (3) percentages of correct classification of various cut-off scores on written SDMT for groups of normal and adults with chronic lesions. The correct classifications range from 81.3 to 93.7% for the 17 to 34 year age group and 82.6 to 100% for the 35 to 54 year age group, but decline markedly to range from 30.7 to 53.8% for the 55 to 75 year age group. However, when the correct classification on the oral SDMT for chronic lesions is examined, a more accurate trend is indicated. The positive classifications range between 70.3 to 87.5% for the 17 to 34 year age group, 82.6 to 100% for the 35 to 54 year age group, and 53.8 to 61.5% for the 55 to 75 year age group.

Although the SDMT is considered a very sensitive test in patients with confirmed brain dysfunction, SDMT scores could be lowered by other factors. Therefore, written or oral scores alone should not be considered diagnostically definitive.

3.1.9 THE SENTENCE COMPLETION TEST

The Incomplete Sentence Blank-Adult Form, originally proposed by Julian B. Rotter in 1950, is considered a testing instrument for the assessment of the individual's emotional status. It includes forty incomplete sentences. Each of those sentences starts with one to four words and the instructions request the expression of "real feelings," by making a complete sentence. Although the majority of the beginnings express emotional content: (1) I feel ... (2) I suffer ... (3) I hate ... etc., others are more neutral, such as: (1) People ... (2) Reading ... (3) Sometimes ... etc., or suggestive; (1) I can't ... (2) I want to learn ... (3) This place .... The clinical neuropsychologist can utilize this screening instrument for other purposes, as well. A rudimentary impression of the following functions can be formulated: handwriting; fine visual-motor coordination, grammatical ability, language skills, and emotional status.

The test does not have any quantitative parameters for scoring or analysis.

3.1.10 THE MINNESOTA MULTIPHASIC PERSONALITY INVENTORY-II

The initial version of the Minnesota Multiphasic Personality Inventory (MMPI) was constructed as a 566-item paper-and-pencil personality test during the 1930s in a medical facility in Minneapolis. The goal of the test was to facilitate the diagnostic impression of psychiatric inpatients. The most significant clinical questions arise when the construction of the original version is reviewed (Hathaway and McKinley, 1951; Dahlstrom, Welsh, and Dahlstrom, 1975). The patient's gender was the only demographic factor included in the norms, without consideration for age, education, or medical status. The interested reader should review the reference books by Hathaway and McKinley (1951) and Dahlstrom, Welsh, and Dahlstrom (1975). Since the revision of the original test is recommended, an examination of the most recent version, the MMPI-II, is provided in this section.

The MMPI-II includes 567 items, which are the result of several modifications indicated in the manual (Butcher et al., 1989). These modifications included the addition of one item and substitutions of several items due to their content (i.e., sexual preference, religion, or gastro-intestinal functions). The patient's age or education was not considered in the scoring and interpretations. The reliability and internal consistency of the basic scales in the profile range from .67 to .92 for men and .58 to .91 for women. Hence, the typical standard error of measurement of the basic clinical scales is two to three raw score points. This statistical data should be utilized especially when the patient is requested to retake the MMPI-II questionnaire after either a brief or an extended period of time, in order to evaluated any changes in the test results. Butcher et al. (1989) recommended indicating the actual number of the standard error of measurement above and below the actual raw scores.

The ten original scales of the MMPI are included in the MMPI-II, with the addition of three validity indicators: The Back F, Variable Response Inconsistency (VRIN), and True Response Inconsistency (TRIN). These indicators were designed for identifying: (a) when the patient stopped paying attention to the test items and shifted to a random pattern of responding; and (b) the tendency to respond to items in ways that are inconsistent (VRIN) or contradictory (TRIN).

A relatively recent contribution to the clinical utilization of the MMPI-II was provided by Butcher (1992) who formulated a computerized program for interpreting test results. The forensic practitioner can access this information in addition to the routine scorings. The clinical benefits of this scoring and interpretation program are several: minimizing the chance of human errors, increasing objectivity, and the inclusion of demographic correction factors, including education (four levels) and age (ten groups). The total number of approximately 100 scales and subscales is divided into four main categories that appraise the validity, clinical, supplementary, content, experimental, and critical items sets.

A more recent contribution to the scientific database regarding the MMPI-II in the forensic context investigated the MMPI-II validity indicators to detect response distortion or bias. The utilization of the traditional MMPI-II indicators was proposed on the basis of empirical data. The comparative analysis of MMPI-II responses of child custody and personal injury litigants provides a base rate of several validity indicators (Posthuma and Harper, 1998). Personal injury litigants are hypothetically motivated to make false allegations of suffering (i.e., malingering). Indeed, numerous studies were performed and provided data for the detection of over-reporting of problems and symptoms. However, Butcher (1995) opined that there were no particular personality test profile patterns that appeared in personal injury litigants. The study by Posthuma and Harper (1998) explained the efficacy of both (a) a number of MMPI-II scales designed to assess response bias, and (b) the standard validity scales: L, F, K, F-K (Dissimulation Index), and L+K and L+K-F (fake good indexes). The other scales were: Wiggins Social Desirability Scale (WsL), the Positive Malingering Scale (Mp), Obvious and Subtle Subscales (WHD), Critical items, the Lees-Haley Fake Bad Scale (FBS), the Variable Response Inconsistency Scale (VRIN), the Back Page Infrequency Scale, the Family Problem; the Psychopathic Deviate (PL) and Paranoia (Pa) subscales: Pd1 (Family Discord), PL4 (Social Alienation), Pa2 (Poignancy), and Pa3 (Naiveté).

Posthuma and Harper (1998) found that among the 13 validity measures utilized, 10 showed statistically different scores for the personal injury litigants, the majority of those statistically different scores being higher. The following indicators were not statistically significant: (1) L-scale; (2) L+K, for males; (3) Wsd for females; and (4) Mp, for females. Posthuma and Harper (1998) concluded that the supplemental scales provide a more accurate result than the standard scales of negative or positive response distortion. However, this exploratory study did not indicate that exaggeration of symptoms and/or problems is the norm for personal injury litigants. The interpretation of the MMPI-II profile validity scores, especially with cases of alleged brain dysfunction, should include consideration for various additional factors: the nature and extent of the alleged injury, the circumstances leading to litigation, clinical interviews, objective test results, and third party data must all be considered by the forensic expert.

3.1.11 THE BECK DEPRESSION INVENTORY — SECOND EDITION

The Beck Depression Inventory — Second Edition (BDI-II), is a relatively recent modification (Beck, Steer, and Brown, 1996) of the 21-item self-report instrument that was initially constructed more than 35 years ago (Beck, Ward, Mendelson, Mock, and Erbaugh, 1961). It is used for the assessment of the severity of depression in adolescents and adults aged 13 years and older. The recent revision of the BDI-II was developed in order to comply with the diagnostic criteria of depressive disorders according to the most recent edition of the American Psychiatric Association's *Diagnostic and Statistical Manual of Mental Disorders — Fourth Edition* (DSM-IV, 1994). In the revised edition, four items from the original instrument were deleted and replaced by four new items, in order to assess symptoms of severe depression or the need for hospitalization, and two items were changed.

The quantitative Total Score of the BDI-II ranges from 0 to 63, with the following four classifications: minimal degree of depression is indicated by a score of 0 to 13; mild depression by a score of 14 to 19; moderate depression by a score of 20 to 28; and severe depression by a score of 29 to 63. The reliability of the BDI-II is very high when internal consistency is appraised. The coefficients are .92 for outpatients and .93 for college students. However, closer examination of the internal consistency showed that the corrected total item correlations of the BDI-II range from .39 to .70 for the psychiatric outpatient and .27 to .74 for the college student sample.

The intercorrelations among the 21 BDI-II items were utilized for the factorial validity study and revealed two factors. The standardized regression coefficients and final community estimates for a sample of psychiatric outpatients included two main factors. The first factor represented a Somatic-Affective dimension and the second factor reflected a Cognitive dimension. Noteworthy is that among the 12 items included in the Somatic factor, 10 items could be possibly attributed to compromised brain functioning (e.g., crying, agitation, changes in sleeping pattern and appetite, irritability, tiredness, or fatigue). Hence, it is the purview of the forensic expert to cautiously hypothesize the etiology of the somatic items for the purpose of the differential diagnosis.

3.1.12 THE STRUCTURED INTERVIEW OF REPORTED SYMPTOMS

The Structured Interview of Reported Symptoms (SIRS) is a 172-item questionnaire that was primarily developed to assess the possibility and extent of feigning (Rogers, Bagly, and Dickens, 1992). Therefore, the objective of this instrument is to systematically evaluate deliberate distortion in the self-reporting of symptoms. Rogers, Bagly, and Dickens (1992) stated that the SIRS has not been validated to assess feigned neuropsychological impairment. However, they also stated that the SIRS could be utilized to investigate cases in which the clinician suspected psychopathology associated with organic deficits. Indeed, it is the responsibility of the forensic neuropsychologist to insure that a comprehensive assessment of the patient's emotional status and personality attributes are included in the battery of tests. Moreover, a comparative analysis of results of the SIRS with at least one more test (i.e., the MMPI-II) ought to be performed in order to insure an accurate appraisal. Furthermore, the SIRS is intended for use with adults 18 years or older, where questions arise with respect to the self-reporting of psychiatric symptoms. The SIRS should not be administered to grossly psychotic individuals.

The patient's responses to the items of the SIRS are utilized for the evaluation of malingering and other forms of dissimulation. It provides the forensic expert with relevant data regarding malingering and factitious disorders with psychological symptoms and honest responding. This information is based on the thirteen scales of the SIRS, eight primary and five supplementary scales. Since detailed descriptions are provided in the manual (Rogers, Bagly, and Dickens, 1992), the following list of the various scales is included in order to familiarize the forensic expert with the content of the test results. The eight primary scales are: Rare Symptoms; Symptoms Combination; Improbable and Absurd; Blatant; Subtle; Selectivity of -; Severity of -; and Reported vs. Observed Symptoms, respectively. The Supplemental scales are entitled: Direct Appraisal of Honesty; Defensive Symptoms; Overly Specified Symptoms; Symptoms Onset and Resolution; and Inconsistency of Symptoms. Noteworthy is that two simple cognitive tasks are included in the test, but not in the quantitative scales mentioned previously. Four items provide rudimentary information regarding the patient's ability when naming opposites and rhyming are required. The intention of Rogers, Bagly, and Dickens (192) was to appraise the individual's tendency for feigning gross cognitive impairment. However, the items (numbered 57, 58, 143, and 144) have not been validated for this purpose.

The SIRS manual provides specific guidelines for the interpretation of the obtained results for determining the possibility of: honest response pattern; indeterminate, probable, or definite feigning. The classification of feigners and honest responders vs. probable feigners based on single primary scale scores ranges from 58.0 to 98.9%, and 35.5 to 68.8%, respectively. The reliability of these classifications is very high. Indeed, the coefficient of correlation when internal consistency is considered, ranges from .66 to .92. The interrater reliabilities for the 13 scales of the SIRS are uniformly high; they range from .89 to 1.00, with the mean interrater reliability of .98.

The reliability of the individual scores is expressed in terms of the standard error of measurement. Honest responders are expected to have relatively low scores, while feigners would manifest greater variability. Accordingly, the standard errors of measurement ranged from: 1.06 to 2.31 with an average of 1.51 for clinical honest responders, and .64 to 1.8 with an average of 1.19 for non-clinical honest responders. However, the suspected malingering group demonstrated markedly higher standard errors of measurement: .64 to 4.66, with a mean of 2.64. The simulators manifested a range from 1.66 to 3.16, with an average of 2.38.

The criterion groups provide primary evidence for the validation of the SIRS based on their consistent discrimination. However, the forensic expert is encouraged to review the data provided in the manual in order to insure accurate interpretation of the scores obtained as a part of the neuropsychological examination.

3.2   ASSESSMENT OF MALINGERING: CLINICAL vs. FORENSIC EVALUATION IN THE NEUROPSYCHOLOGICAL REPORT

The assessment of malingering in the forensic context is probably the most challenging and complicated task of the neuropsychological evaluation. The assessment of various symptoms associated with traumatic brain injury (TBI) includes: peripheral injuries, i.e., pain, paresthesias, orthopedic fractures; emotional, i.e., depression, anxiety, apprehension, malaise; and cognitive/neuropsychological dysfunctions, i.e., impaired memory, agnosia, apraxia, dysphasia, and/or dysnomia. The symptoms mentioned above probably constitute only a small proportion of the multitude of complaints and allegations that the forensic expert must evaluate. In addition, the possibility of malingering, hypochondriasis or conversion disorder are diagnostic categories that the clinical neuropsychologist should consider while evaluating the valid complaints with which the patient presents. This section, however, will only examine the diagnostic classification of malingering. The interested reader is referred to the comprehensive issue of the DSM-IV for succinct definitions of conversion disorder or hypochondriasis. The most acceptable definition of malingering is also adapted from the DSM-IV, due to its utilization in various arenas throughout the United States and in certain international research.

The following definition of malingering has been adapted from the Quick Reference to the Diagnostic Criteria from DSM-IV (American Psychiatric Association, 1994b).

> The essential feature of malingering is the intentional production of false or grossly exaggerated physical or psychological symptoms motivated by external incentives such as avoiding military duty, avoiding work, obtaining financial compensation, evading criminal prosecution, or obtaining drugs. Under some circumstances, malingering may represent adaptive behavior - for example feigning illness while a captive of the enemy during wartime. (p. 296–297)

The following information is also included in the definition of malingering according to the DSM-IV:

> Malingering should be strongly suspected if any combination of the following is noted:
>
> 1. Medicolegal context of presentation (e.g., the person is referred by an attorney to the clinician for examination).
>
> 2. Marked discrepancy between the person's clinical stress or disability and the objective findings.
>
> 3. Lack of cooperation during the diagnostic evaluation and in complying with the prescribed treatment regiment.
>
> 4. The presence of Antisocial Personality Disorder. (p. 297)

The essence of malingering is quite explicit in the first sentence from the quote mentioned previously. It entails the intentional misrepresentation or "production of false or grossly exaggerated physical or psychological symptoms motivated by external incentives." Therefore, malingering implies the direct, planned, and conscious fabrication of various dysfunctions via deliberate embellishment, feigning, dissimulation, and confabulation of various symptoms of emotional, cognitive, and/or physical origin. Rogers (1988) considered malingering as one response style, among six distinct styles. The other five styles are: (1) defensiveness, which is the opposite of malingering by its virtue of being a conscious denial or gross minimization of physical and/or psychological symptoms; (2) irrelevant responding; (3) random responding; (4) honest responding; and (5) hybrid responding. The three gradations of malingering proposed by Rogers (1988, 1997) are:

1. Mild malingering: indicated by unequivocal evidence that the patient is attempting to malinger, primarily through exaggeration. The degree of distortion is minimal and plays only a minor role in differential diagnosis.
2. Moderate malingering: characterized by exaggeration and/or fabrication, limited to a few clinical symptoms.
3. Severe malingering: manifested by extreme fabrication of dysfunctions or symptoms, the degree of which is fantastic or preposterous.

3.2.1 THE CLINICAL MANIFESTATION OF MALINGERING

Due to patients' various and often concomitant complaints of emotional, cognitive, and/or neuropsychological allegations, this section is divided into the two main categories mentioned previously. However, it is pertinent to first provide definitions and examples of the constructs of clinical vs. forensic evaluation of malingering.

The clinical evaluation of malingering entails certain steps incumbent upon the forensic expert prior to and during the neuropsychological evaluation.

1. Reviewing the patient's medical history prior to and after the date of the alleged injury. This review should include any and all records with an emphasis on examining the patient's history for onset of any medical complications, e.g., hypertension, diabetes, attention deficit disorder, learning disability, cardiac or endocrinological dysfunctions, neurological diseases, psychiatric problems, and any form of hospitalization or extended medical care.
2. Reviewing the patient's educational history via formal records, i.e., school records, GPAs, PSAT, SAT, and college records of relevance. The clinician must search for any significant decline in functioning and/or the lack of any significant change.
3. Examining the patient's occupational background. This information should include, if possible, names of employers, duration of positions held, type of occupation, performance evaluations, dismissals from work, periods of unemployment, and/or employment of any form after the alleged injury.
4. Personal-developmental background, including: family history, stability of the patient's life as a child, adolescent, and adult, quality and duration of intimate relationships and/or losses, separations, or grief. Any form of abuse imposed on the patient or elected by the patient, i.e., substance abuse, must be examined.
5. Mental status examination: this part of the evaluation is more informal and allows the malingering patient to be cooperative and at ease. It is, therefore, potentially quite revealing. In the absence of formal instructions, read verbatim from a manual; the malingerer's responses constitute a

significant illustration of more routine daily functioning. Indeed, the patient's composure, alertness, physical endurance, eye-contact, tone of voice, emotional behavior (i.e., crying, laughing, or disinhibition), speech and language, and motor and sensory-perceptual functioning, are all subject to the expert's observation. Thus, it is strongly recommended that the examiner record (throughout the clinical interview and the structured tests administered) detailed notes, remarks, questions, and answers encompassing all of the patient's behavior. *The concept of the mental status examination is therefore extended for the entire duration of the interaction with the patient.* This aspect of the examination commences from the first moment of contact between the patient and clinician and spans the entire duration of the evaluation process. The clinical component of the neuropsychological report provided by the forensic expert for either plaintiff or defendant should be performed carefully. The absence of any aspect of the patient's history (medical, educational, occupational, social-developmental, and psychiatric complications) renders the clinical validity of the neuropsychological report open to doubt.

The cardinal indicators of malingering in both clinical and forensic components of the evaluation are: (a) incongruity between the patient's subjective presentation of symptoms and the forensic expert's objective observations of behaviors; (b) inconsistency in the clinical symptom presentation; (c) complaints about implausible symptoms; and (d) reporting incapacitating inadequacies in various aspects of daily life.

Of the indicators mentioned previously, the two most prevalent are the patient's complaints, responses, and actual behavior characterized by inconsistencies and incongruities. For example, a patient complains about extremely poor sleep, yet is able to remain alert and does not manifest significant fatigue throughout the intense 10 to 12 hours of the comprehensive evaluation; or, the subjective report of persistent and excruciating headache while answering a medical questionnaire, but lack of complaints during several hours with the examiner. Incongruities are also observable during the extended evaluation. If the patient reports any extreme functional shift, but denies the expected outcome of such a marked change, the validity of the complaint is probably very poor and should be further examined.

Complaints about implausible symptoms are also central to malingering and feigning. Among such allegations might be difficulties with various cognitive functions, predominantly memory, word-finding, and impaired concentration. Yet, the patient is able to provide a detailed description of the alleged accident, including time, places, names of physicians, medications, etc. Similar complaints can relate to emotional functioning. Moderate or severe depression, suicidal ideation and/or thought disorders (i.e., hallucinations, delusions, or other psychotic-like symptoms) are often reported by the malingering patient. These patients lack insight and awareness of the contradictions between their subjective complaints, objective observations, and the often unbearable degree of symptoms reported (Rogers, 1988, 1997). The syndrome constellation is often unclear to the malingering patient. Hence, the complaints are often preposterous in either the reported frequency or severity. Some patients present a facade of extreme effort during the evaluation. For example, when asked to demonstrate grip strength, they grimace, tightening all their facial and neck muscles, yet then fail to produce any muscular tension in their hands! Others indicate an alleged inability to solve simple problems. Their verbal responses are extended in latency and lack clarity. They are indirect, vague, and incomplete in content. Yet their responses to questions from the structured testing which require central processing are appropriate in content and don't require excessive response time. A patient might report inability to concentrate, yet solve mathematical problems quickly and accurately.

Overwhelming inadequacy in routine daily functions is often reported by the malingering patient. During the neuropsychological evaluation the malingering patient might ask for frequent rest periods, or refuse to continue with the assessment process. These patients tend to make their participation conditional, e.g., "If we don't take a break right now, I won't do any more." While the clinician must always prepare the patient for the fact that some tests cannot be interrupted because of timing factors, the malingerer's frustration tolerance is poor and impulse control is often very inconsistent.

3.2.2 The Forensic Evaluation of Malingering

The psychometric assessment of malingering and deception in individuals who allegedly suffered from TBI is probably the most complex aspect of the forensic neuropsychological evaluation. Malingering individuals might complain about various ailments or disorders which are physiological, emotional, cognitive/intellectual, or neuropsychological in nature. This tangle of presenting complaints can initially be quite challenging for the forensic expert to unravel. The present section addresses the various assessment techniques and specific tests recommended for inclusion in the forensic neuropsychological evaluation. It provides guidelines for making appropriate differential diagnoses.

3.2.2.1 The Structured Assessment of Malingering: Emotional Disorders

Objective assessment of feigned emotional disorders, specifically malingering, requires utilization of this basic triad: the Sentence Completion Test, the MMPI-II, and the Structured Interview of Reported Symptoms (SIRS). The forensic expert's goal is to appraise the most common denominators of malingering: (a) inconsistencies and incongruities; (b) complaining about implausible symptoms; and (c) subjective reporting of overwhelming inadequacies.

Meehl and Hathaway (1946) proposed that the malingering patient's tendency is to respond favorably when a favorable response would most likely be untrue. Therefore, the Lie(1) scale was constructed and specific items were included among the rest of the MMPI items. Another early suggestion by Gough (1947) proposed the Dissimulation Scale (Ds-R) for the detection of malingering. However, as research progressed and the MMPI-II was formulated, other indicators of malingering were identified. The scales that were considered valid indicators of malingering were the F and F-K scales (Green, 1980, 1991). The presentation of the MMPI-II (Butcher et al., 1989) resulted in the development of other specific indicators of faking bad, i.e., malingering. These indicators included: Fb (Back F Scale); F(p) (Infrequency Psychopathology Scale); and the FBS (Lees-Haley Fake Bad Scale)(Butcher et al., 1989; Arbisi and Ben-Porath, 1995; Lees-Haley, English, and Glenn, 1991, respectively). Additionally, the IR index (Inconsistent Response) was proposed (Bagby, Rogers, and Buis, 1994; Bagby et al., 1994).

Prior to the review of the various scales and/or indexes mentioned previously, it seems pertinent to examine the utility of the validity scales and indexes for detecting random responding. Most malingering patients' approach to the MMPI-II is characterized by exaggeration and deliberate simulation of an illness or disability. However, on occasion, random responding to MMPI-II items is shown by malingerers in addition to the paradoxical presentation of a combined mixture of fake good and fake bad self-reports (Lees-Haley, English, and Glenn, 1991). It is commonly accepted that the first step in assessing the validity of the MMPI-II profile is to evaluate the number of items omitted. However, the term "item omission" is a misrepresentation, since it includes: unendorsed items, items endorsed as both true and false, and items endorsed on the answer sheet other than in the allotted spaces. Hence, there might be some association between item omission and random responding. It should be noted that while omission of items is not a common issue when malingering is examined, some patients do omit a significant number of items due to the subjective complaints of multiple impairments which allegedly prevent the completion of the MMPI-II items (Green, 1997; Wetter, Baer, Berry, Smith and Larsen, 1992).

Several validity scales of the MMPI-II are considered sensitive to content non-responsivity. These indexes are the Infrequency (F), Infrequency Back (Fb) and VRIN scales, (Berry et al., 1991a, 1991b). The detection of random responding was recently refined by the inclusion of positive and negative predictive powers and hit rates. The study concluded with an alternative index, which includes the following components: VRIN Scale plus the Infrequent Scales (F) minus the Infrequency Back (Fb). This index provided the highest hit rate across all examined base rates.

The detection of personal injury malingering was also examined by the Fake Bad Scale (FBS). Although initially constructed for the appraisal of emotional distress injuries (Lees-Haley et al., 1991), more recent studies show that it is useful in the assessment of somatic malingering, e.g., cases alleging physical injuries or pain, and neuropsychological complaints (Larrabee, 1996, 1997, 1998). Larrabee's proposal (1997) was that when elevations on scales 1 and 3 exceed T-80 and are accompanied by elevation on the FBS, the possibility of somatic malingering is raised. Posthuma and Harper (1998) confirmed the efficacy of the FBS index, while simultaneously utilizing other validity measurements, as useful in the detection of personal injury claimants who were malingering,

Due to the complexity of the detection of exaggeration and fabrication of psychological symptoms, most studies utilize varied methodologies. The two main approaches involve: (1) individuals with no diagnosed psychological disorder who are simulating a disorder; or (2) various groups of clinical populations. Berry, Baer, and Harris (1991) provided a meta-analysis of the literature regarding detection of malingering on the MMPI and suggested that the two approaches might be conceptualized as complimentary. Utilizing this integrative approach, Berry, Baer, and Harris (1991) studied the over-reporting indexes by dividing patients into two groups based on their inferred motivation to exaggerate symptoms of their disorder, e.g., whether or not seeking compensation for injury (Berry et al., 1995). The four groups involved male and female subjects who comprised the following: (1) non-clinical participating subjects answering under standard instructions; (2) non-clinical participants instructed to fake closed-head injury (CHI) symptoms; (3) non-compensation-seeking CHI patients; and (4) compensation-seeking CHI patients. The four groups were demographically comparable (e.g., age, education, gender, and race). Moreover, data regarding: (a) time elapsing from injury to evaluation, and (b) injury severity, assessed by duration of loss of consciousness, were utilized to insure comparability of the two CHI groups. Berry et al.'s (1995) results included eight validity scales (L, F, K, Fb, F-K, Fp, DsZ, and VRIN) in addition to the ten clinical scales of the MMPI-II. The highest scores on over-reporting scales were obtained by non-clinical participants faking CHI, and significantly higher scores on these scales were obtained by compensation-seeking relative to non-compensation-seeking CHI patients. This finding occurred in regard to the following validity scale scores: K, F, Fb, F-K, Fp, and DsZ. The clinical scales that differentiated the groups were: 1, 2, 3, 6 (Paranoia), 7, 8, and 0 (Social Intervention). In general, the highest clinical scale scores were obtained by group 2 (non-clinical participants instructed on fake CHI). Group 4 (compensation seeking CHI patients) had the next highest clinical scale scores, although for several scales, group 4 was significantly lower than group 2. The major finding of Berry et al. (1995) was a general correspondence between MMPI-II over-reporting indexes and known or inferred motivation to over-report symptoms of CHI. In the analogue portion of the study, the normal group fabricating CHI symptoms showed elevated over-reporting validity scores (F, Fb, F-K, DsZ, and Fp) and a lowered score on under-reporting scale (K). Similarly, compensation-seeking CHI patients had higher scores on F, Fb, F-K, and DsZ and a lower score on K, when compared with non-compensation-seeking CHI patients. Although Berry et al.'s (1995) study suggests that MMPI-II over-reporting scales rise in the face of fabrication and possible exaggeration of symptoms of CHI, absence of elevations on these scales does not rule out the possibility of malingering of neuropsychological problems.

The relatively recent contribution of the SIRS provides another valid and reliable instrument for the assessment of malingering (Rogers et al., 1992). The SIRS is based on Rogers' (1984) proposal of four distinct basic response styles in psychiatric patients: (1) reliable; (2) irrelevant; (3) defensive; and (4) malingering. Rogers (1988) also recommended two additional terms for cases when motivation or response style are questionable: (1) dissimulation, referring to a response style in individuals who are deliberately distorting or misrepresenting their psychological or physical symptoms; and (2) unreliability, referring to self-reports which are inaccurate, although the reasons for the inaccuracy may not be known. The SIRS appears to be a unique instrument in its ability to distinguish malingering from genuine disorders. (Rogers, 1995). Since no formal studies utilized the SIRS specifically in order to assess malingering with patients who are alleging TBI, caution should be exercised by the forensic neuropsychologist. However, relatively high correlation coefficients with the MMPI fake-bad indicators were reported: 97.50% of the correlations were greater than .60, and 75.0% of them exceeded .70 (Rogers et al., 1991). Since most patients who complain about TBI report various emotional difficulties, the utility of the SIRS for the forensic expert is evident. However, it is essential that the SIRS be administered in addition to the MMPI-II and the other instruments recommended, since the diagnosis of malingering should be based on a comprehensive and interpretive approach. The SIRS constitutes an important source of collateral information for the composition of the diagnostic impression.

3.2.3 THE ASSESSMENT OF MALINGERING: COGNITIVE AND NEUROPSYCHOLOGICAL FUNCTIONS

The assessment of malingering of cognitive and neuropsychological dysfunctions is probably one of the most complicated and intriguing aspects of the forensic neuropsychological evaluation. It requires the expert's meticulous attention to numerous variables, parameters, and the detailed findings obtained via the administration of both complex and/or relatively effortless tasks. The clinical definition of malingering according to the DSM-IV implies that the malingering patient is deliberately responding in a deceptive and unusual fashion. Therefore, the outcome of the deceptive response is characterized clinically as not valid. Hence, the onus is on the forensic neuropsychologist to provide sufficient evidence to substantiate the individual's deliberate efforts to perform poorly, i.e., in a way that is not up to par with his/her ability. Malingering is often manifested by marked discrepancies between: (1) subjective complaints and objective test results; (2) differences between expected scores and norms and those obtained via the structured testing; and (3) incongruities among results obtained by various assessment instruments which appraise similar cognitive or behavioral skills (Franzen, Iverson, and McCracken, 1990). The three indicators of malingering previously mentioned aid the forensic expert in the detection of response distortion. It is important to note that detection of response distortion requires a diverse approach that includes the assessment of various skills. The reliability of obtained results is insured by: (a) repeated measures and the comparison of two or more administrations of the same tests, or (b) comparing different tests administered at the same time (Reitan and Wolfson, 1995, 1997). Moreover, a battery of tests can provide quantitative indicators that enable the forensic expert to compare the patient's performance across a range of tests (e.g., WMS-III and WAIS-III; the Bender and the Symbol Digit Modalities tests; or Sentence Completion vs. the MMPI-II and SIRS). This conceptual framework for the assessment of compromised brain-behavior was initially proposed by Halstead (1947). The challenge of assessing the relevant functions or dysfunctions was approached by subdividing the factors of brain dysfunctions into several independent variables. Consequently, the various neuropsychological instruments that later constituted the HRNB were constructed and formulated the well-known battery. A variation of Halstead's approach and Reitan's adaptation was proposed by Nies and Sweet (1994) who argued for the use of a number of measures rather than a single test in assessing the potential for malingering. Accordingly, Nies and Sweet (1994) concluded that no single test showed satisfactory hit rates for malingering. However, prior to and after Nies and Sweet's (1994) assertion, research efforts to identify malingering delineated patterns of such tests for the identification and assessment of malingering.

Most of the single tests that attempt to determine the presence of malingering follow a simple construct. The patient is usually informed or given the impression that the test is quite difficult, or that the next step is a difficult phase, when it is actually not true. Therefore, patients who perform worse under these circumstances are assumed to be malingering. The false hypothesis inherent in such an assumption is that the patient who performs well on any of these tests is not malingering. It is essential to substantiate the lack of malingering on the basis of objective parameters. These indicators should be obtained from various tests that appraise numerous functions, including cognitive/neuropsychological, emotional and personality attributes (the MMPI-II and the SIRS). The suggestions mentioned previously are substantiated by the DSM-IV inclusion of the presence of antisocial personality disorder as one of the four corollaries of malingering.

A succinct review of some of these instruments is pertinent at this time. The four tests that were designed specifically for the detection of biased responding in neuropsychological evaluations are: Digit Memory Test (Brown, Sherbenou, and Johnson, 1982; Lezak, 1995); Portland Digit Recognition (Binder, 1993); Rey's Dot Counting Test (Rey, 1946; Lezak, 1995); and Symptom Validity Testing (Pankatz, 1983; Pankatz, Fausti, and Peed, 1975). Detailed descriptions of these tests are available in the primary references mentioned above or in the compendium of neuropsychological assessment by Lezak (1995).

The Digit Memory Test is a forced-choice test that requires the patient to identify which of two 5-digit numbers presented on a card was the same as a number shown previously before a delay of 5-, 10-, or 15- seconds, respectively. As the time of the delay increases, the patient is told that the task is becoming more difficult. The task entails simple recognition of the first digit alone; therefore, recognition is not usually related to a very small temporal interval. The malingering patient is expected to perform gradually worse, in accord with the length of the delay. The Portland Digit Recognition Test (PDRT) is a modification of the Digit Memory Test. The identification/recognition of the five-digit number is the same. However, in the PDRT, the examiner first reads the number and the patient is asked to select the target number from a visual presentation. Longer delay intervals are employed when the task described becomes more difficult and interference is utilized.

The Rey's Dot Counting Test involves the presentation of 3x5 inch cards with groups of dots. The patient is asked to count the number of dots that are either randomly distributed or are grouped in an orderly fashion (making them easier to count). When the time taken to count the grouped dots meets or exceeds that for the random dots, biased responding is suspected. The three tests mentioned above utilize similar constructs: they are predominantly visual-spatial in nature and are an assessment of simple recognition memory. However, the Symptoms Validity Testing is an assessment of memory and sensory losses (Pankatz, 1983; Pankatz, Fausti, and Peed, 1975). In this paradigm, the patient is instructed to indicate whether an audible tone was heard in a series of multiple trials when randomly presented on 50% of the trials. Therefore, the scores of correct responses, by chance alone, should be correct approximately 50% of the time, even if the patient is unable to hear the stimulus. Thus, scores that are significantly above or below chance result from purposeful responding. Indeed, when the score is markedly below the 50% level, the possibility of malingering is raised. However, the vulnerability of this approach is apparent to the expert examiner. Although sensory-perceptual functions are strongly correlated with the age of the patient (or healthy subject) no age-correction norms are available for this test. Surprisingly, this issue was not studied in regard to forensic or routine clinical neuropsychological assessments.

The clinical utility of a test depends on its ability to classify patients into correct diagnostic categories. The goal of a neuropsychological test instrument is to correctly classify patients TBI vs. those without TBI (Parsons and Prigatano, 1978). A recent study replicated a previous finding that suspected malingerers often perform at a level worse than patients with unequivocal brain dysfunction on the Digit Memory Test (Prigatano et al., 1997). It was also shown that patients suffering from aphasia, as well as temporal and "frontal lobe" damage, perform at a higher level than suspected malingerers. However, Prigatano et al. (1997) found that performance of patients with true dementia was difficult to distinguish from suspected malingers. They concluded that if a patient is not demented and performs at a level less than 95% across three trials of the Digit Memory Test, the question of malingering must be considered.

The difficulty indicated by Prigatano et al. (1997) was studied when the base rates of deficient neuropsychological test performance were evaluated among neurologically healthy older normal adults using a variety of measures (Palmer et al., 1998). The neuropsychological battery included various tests (the Boston Naming, Ray-Osterrieth Complex Figure, and the Wisconsin Card Sorting tests) and subtests (the Digit Span from the WAIS, Logical Memory and Visual Reproduction from the WMS, and WMS-R). The subjects were divided into three age groups (50 to 59, 60 to 69, and 70 to 79 years). Palmer et al. (1998) asserted that even though the sample was composed of healthy individuals, the test results indicated that a proportion of subjects scored in the borderline and impaired range (1.3 and 2.0 standard deviations below the age-group mean, respectively). Palmer et al. (1998) also indicated that 73% of subjects scored in the borderline range on at least one measure, and 20% earned at least two scores in the impaired range on separate tests. However, the proportion of subjects consistently earning borderline or impaired scores across multiple measures within specific cognitive domains was generally lower. Palmer et al. (1998) concluded that any strong assertions regarding the incidence of neuropsychological impairment appear difficult to justify solely on the basis of a few unrelated and "abnormal" test scores. These findings provide supportive evidence to Heaton's et al. (1991, 1992) strong assertion regarding the utilization of demographic correction factors for the expanded HRNB. Indeed, Palmer et al. (1998) acknowledged that gender and education are not included in the subdivisions of sample groups, yet all subjects had at least high school education.

The significance of variation in test results was addressed when the raw data obtained by administering the WAIS-R to normal individuals was examined (Matarazzo, 1990). Although normally distributed around a mean difference of zero, differences between Performance and Verbal IQs showed an unusually large standard deviation (11 points) and a range from minus 42 to plus 43 points. Moreover, normal individuals showed substantial scatter in subtest scores and test-retest scores were markedly different. Hence, diagnosis of brain dysfunction could not be based on intra-individual variability that was similarly found in normal individuals. This conclusion lends further support for the unique and remarkable contribution of Heaton et al. (1992, 1993) and their persistent adherence to the utilization of demographic correction factors (Heaton, Grant, and Matthews, 1986). Indeed, in an earlier study, when no demographic corrections were utilized, the hit rate based on neuropsychological results varied from chance to only 20% above chance (Heaton et al., 1978).

The essential task of the forensic neuropsychologist is to provide a valid and reliable assessment of the presence and degree of malingering by providing objective, quantitative parameters, in addition to the conglomerate of clinical observations. The neuropsychological examination should be based on the comparative analysis of intra-individual and inter-individual scores. The various guidelines to achieving this complex goal are presented in Table 3.1. A rigorous adherence to the six techniques recommended for the detection of malingering provides the forensic neuropsychologist with the most comprehensive and valuable clinical data possible. These six guidelines combine theoretical, pragmatic, statistically derived and substantiated approaches for the assessment of malingering.

The first guideline suggested is based on comparisons of the subjective complaints obtained from the patient vs. the objective findings. This is accomplished via review of the medical records, the patient's complaints, the forensic neuropsychologist's clinical observations, and the specific quantitative indices derived from the test results.

The second guideline can be implemented by the inspection of incongruities and inconsistencies when the same functions are assessed via two or more tests and/or subtests. For example, various memory skills are assessed by the WMS-III and the WAIS-III (e.g., the Digits Forward and Backward, and the Letter-Number Sequencing). When precisely identical functions, assessed during the same day, and unaffected by other biasing factors (i.e., effects of medication, fatigue, neurobehavioral factors) show a variance which exceeds the acceptable margin of error of the variance, the possibility of malingering is clearly indicated. Additionally, subtest pattern clusters from various tests, although presently unavailable for the WAIS-III or WMS-III, may constitute a robust comparative index. This approach was utilized with the WAIS-R when pattern clusters in TBI patients and healthy subjects were studied (Crawford et al., 1997). Although there was a significant difference in the number of TBI and healthy participants in each cluster, there was a high degree of cluster membership. Crawford et al.'s (1997) study should be replicated with the newer tests (WAIS-III and WMS-III) and demographic correction factors.

The third guideline for the detection of malingering and invalid test results using the HRNB can be implemented with the utilization of the Response Consistency and Dissimulation Indices proposed by Reitan and Wolfson (1995, 1996, 1997). However, the forensic neuropsychologist is cautioned since Reitan and Wolfson do not advocate the utilization of demographic factors.

TABLE 3.1
Guidelines for the Detection of Malingering

1. Compare the patient's subjective complaints with the quantitative parameters obtained via the structured tests.
2. Evaluate similarities and discrepancies among obtained scores when certain specific functions are assessed via the various tests included in the neuropsychological battery.
3. Compare the patient's performance on prior neuropsychological batteries with the results obtained by the current examination process.
4. Utilize all available correction factors.
5. Evaluate the patient's performance and obtained scores by comparison with expected norms of the Epplicable populations.
6. Integrate the results from the tests assessing emotional functioning with the findings obtained from the psychological/neuropsychological components of the forensic examination.

The fourth guideline for the detection of malingering relies on the persistent utilization of all demographic correction factors, including: age, education, gender, ethnic background, handedness, the native language of the patient, and the medical condition reported.

The fifth guideline concerns the evaluation of the patient's performance and obtained scores via comparison with expected norms of applicable populations. For example, all scores obtained in the testing of a patient who reports or is diagnosed with Parkinson's, diabetic, or endocrinological conditions should ideally be compared with the averaged scores of the same population. A further illustration of this guideline can be seen in the following citation: the errors and impairments manifested by college students were significantly different when compared to those manifested by patients with TBI. This trend was apparent even when the college students were provided with specific instructions regarding the common mistakes associated with brain injury (Bruhn and Reed, 1975). Moreover, qualitative errors on the Bender-Gestalt were indicated when cross-validation of the results was utilized to detect faked insanity (Schretlen et al., 1992).

The sixth guideline is probably the most challenging, time-consuming, yet valuable part of the forensic neuropsychological evaluation. It entails the comparative analysis and integration of numerous cognitive, emotional, and neuropsychological indices. Functions such as memory, word-finding, concept formation, abstract reasoning, praxis, gnosis, visual-motor coordination, fine and gross motor, and sensory-perceptual could form a hologram of the patient's over-all status. For example, it is documented that the scores obtained on the Categories, Trails B, and TPT-Location of the HRNB are the most reliable indicators of TBI. Therefore, the patient's performance on these subtests from the HRNB could be compared with the results on the Block Designs, Symbol Digit and Similarities from the WAIS-III. Moreover, the complexity of the tasks when the same function is required could also be compared. Malingerers often fake deficits on subtests which assess simpler tasks while performing well on more difficult tasks. Malingerers showed severe deficits on simple measures of manual dexterity and tactile sensation (Heaton et al. 1978a; Binder and Willis, 1991). However, when memory tasks were appraised, malingerers often evidence better performance on delayed-recall tasks when compared with scores on recognition memory tasks (Lezak, 1995). Even more revealing is a malingering patient's complaint about impaired concentration and attention while retention and recall are allegedly intact. The epitome of malingering can be observed in the patient who complains about severe emotional distress, i.e., depression, but performs well on tasks which require sustained attention and information processing (i.e., the Arithmetic subtest of the WAIS-III). These functions are known to be significantly affected by emotional disorders, specifically depression. The most valuable utilization of the sixth guideline can be seen in the administration of the SIRS, especially when compared with the MMPI-II and the quantitative parameters regarding the cognitive tasks appraised. Inconsistencies and incongruities among task results, preposterous complaints which are contradicted by objective evidence, and poor insight constitute the main indicators of malingering.

The forensic expert is advised to follow the recommended guidelines and information in this section with prudent care. The ever present goal is to reduce or avoid the potential impact of biasing factors in the circumspect complaints presented by the litigating patient.

3.3 CORRELATION BETWEEN NEUROPSYCHOLOGICAL TESTING AND NEUROLOGICAL EXAMINATION/DIAGNOSTIC STUDIES

The introduction in 1973 of computerized topography (CT) and then in 1982 of Magnetic Resonance Imaging (MRI) modified the manner in which TBI strokes and brain tumors were diagnosed and followed. Prior to the advent of the CT and MRI, evaluation by diagnostic imaging (arteriography, pneumoencephalography) was limited by lack of soft tissue detail and the invasiveness of these procedures. Often the information provided was incomplete or inaccurate, since it was based on indirect evidence, distortion or displacement of vessels or cerebrospinal spaces rather than actual visualization of a lesion. Modern imaging has revealed lesions not suspected clinically or not detected by the more invasive techniques (Zimmerman and Bilaniuk, 1989). During the last 15 to 20 years, advanced techniques of electrophysiological, metabolic, and neurological assessment have enabled the detection of central nervous system (CNS) pathologies after TBI. The goal of this section is to explore the correlation between the neuropsychological evaluation and neurodiagnostic studies in order to confirm the association of functional with structural evidence.

Zimmerman and Bilanluk (1989) opined that most contusions that are diagnosed by imaging techniques are usually seen by CT, except when they are obscured by imaging techniques or are hemorrhagic. Large contusions are usually seen by CT, except when they are obscured by partial voluming, with adjacent bone or motion artifacts. However, since contusions are edematous, the high signal intensity of the edema outlines the contused gyri, provided the MRI technique is utilized. Moreover, an MRI can be performed in a sagittal or coronal plane that shows the surface cortex. A second major form of injury to the brain tissue that occurs as a result of trauma is diffuse axonal injury. In various contexts (i.e., falling from tall buildings or high speed motor vehicle accidents) the force that is imparted to the brain results in shearing and tearing of axons at sites of stress. If these torn axons are accompanied by rupture of local blood vessels, then the area becomes hemorrhagic. The areas of hemorrhage are quite small and may or may not be seen on CT. However, MRI is highly sensitive in showing both hemorrhage and/or edema (Zimmerman et al., 1986). These are the two major tissue components of diffuse axonal injury, which is a result of shearing and tearing (Reitan and Wolfson, 1988). The clinical efficacy of MRI is primarily more accurate than CT in the temporal lobes, posterior fossa, brain stem, and spinal cord.

While many studies have addressed the neuropsychological consequences of TBI, very few publications to date have correlated these with the psycho-physiological diagnosis of central information processing in humans with cortical and subcortical damage. Only a handful of studies indicates the amalgamation of psycho-physiological responses and the ability to orient to, process, organize, and recall information obtained via sensory perceptual modalities (Ohman, 1979). An exception is the Brouwer and Von Wolfelaar (1985) study of sustained attention and sustained effort utilizing vigilance and heart rate in a group of patients with TBI vs. one of normal controls. The groups were examined at two intervals, during a six-month, post-trauma time period. Brouwer and Von Wolfelaar (1985) reported no evidence of impairment in sustained efforts in the patients with TBI when performance on a low event vigilance task and recordings of heart rate variability were analyzed. However, differences in response latencies and in discrimination of small variations in loudness, especially during the early recovery period, were observed. Those results indicate that patients with TBI do not necessarily experience impaired sustained attention and effort in task performance.

3.3.1 The Electroencephalogram (EEG) and Evoked Potentials

A multi-modal comprehensive diagnostic evaluation was administered to 162 patients with TBI within 1 to 21 days post-injury (Thacter et al., 1991). Each evaluation consisted of: (1) power spectral analysis of electroencephalogram (EEG); (2) brainstem auditory evoked potentials; (3) CT scan; and (4) Glasgow Coma Score at time of admission (GCS-A) and at time of EEG test (GCS-T). Functional outcome at one year following injury was assessed using the Rappaport Disability Rating Scale (DRS) (Rappaport et al., 1977, 1981) which measures the level of disability in six diagnostic categories. These categories are: (1) eye opening; (2) best verbal response; (3) best motor response; (4) self-care ability for feeding, grooming, and toileting; (5) level of cognitive functioning; and (6) employability. The ability of the different diagnostic measures to predict outcome at one year following injury was assessed statistically. The best combination of predictor variables was EEG and GCS-T. The best single predictors of outcome in the two statistical approaches (discriminant and regression analyses) were EEG coherence and phase from frontal scalp leads. This is consistent with the features of high velocity accidents (Bigler, 1987).

A more recent review of the applicability of auditory brain stem evoked potential findings revealed that these findings were most frequently found in patients who suffered from severe TBI; only 10 to 20% of patients with mild TBI had abnormal evoked potentials (Goodman, 1994; Adams, Victor, and Ropper, 1997). Noteworthy is that positron emission tomography (PET) showed a generalized diffuse decrease in cerebral blood flow and cerebral glucose metabolism. A positive correlation between temporal proximity to the time of injury was found with these metabolic dysfunctions. They were most frequently present during the six months after the injury (Adams, Victor, and Ropper, 1997). Another usage of the PET is found in Silbersweig and Stern's (1997) publication, underscoring the efficacy of this instrument in localizing the systems-level brain dysfunction that underlies certain psychiatric symptoms.

The clinical efficiency of two different approaches to the evaluation of TBI was examined by comparing neuropsychological assessment and neurophysiological assessment. The neuropsychological dysfunctions (cognitive and emotional), and neurophysiological (reflexes, pupillary responses, eye movements, and motor functions, including balance and gait) were compared in patients with TBI. These studies revealed that the neuropsychological means of assessment were more actively efficient than the neurophysiological. Indeed, neurophysiological dysfunctions were more severe than neuropsychological impairments in only about 25% of a large number of patients with TBI (Jennet and Teasdale, 1981). This finding may be due to the fact that the main distinction between neuropsychological and neurological examinations is the former's reliance on statistically standardized, objective parameters, as opposed to the more impressionistic approach of the latter (Freedman, Stuss, and Gordon, 1991). The common neurological evaluation appraises various functions: speech and language; concentration and attention; memory and retrieval (e.g., retrograde and anterograde amnesia); higher order abstract reasoning; and evaluates the patient's emotional state (e.g., mood and affect), via observation and the mental status examination.

The forensic neuropsychologist's role in the assessment of potentially compromised brain-behavior functioning is to expand the appraisal of any behavioral changes following an alleged TBI. Hence, the purpose of the inclusion of various tests recommended in this chapter is to identify strengths and vulnerabilities manifested by the patient. The goal of the neuropsychological evaluation is to achieve a thorough understanding of the various converging operations of the brain. This goal is accomplished by adhering to the extended evaluation of the individual's CNS information processing of numerous sensory-perceptual and cognitive stimuli, as well as various motor tasks. Therefore, the forensic neuropsychologist must include the assessment of: (1) verbal and language abilities; (2) visual, spatial, simultaneous abilities; (3) concept-formation and concept utilization. Categories of these functions are controlled by the left-, right-, or both hemispheres, respectively. However, the concomitant inclusion of more primitive functions (e.g., alertness, endurance, etc.) is essential for the achievement of the comprehensive evaluation. It is essential to accept the concept of levels of the central nervous system (e.g., cortical, sub-cortical) as an integral component of the forensic neuropsychological evaluation.

3.3.2 Functional Magnetic Resonance Imaging

The Functional Magnetic Resonance Imaging (fMRI) is based on the sensitivity of the MRI to certain neurophysiological fluctuations within the brain. Magnetic effects are caused by variations in the oxygenation state of hemoglobin; this, in turn, is induced by local changes in blood flow during task activation. Most commonly, the signal of the MRI increases slightly during brain activation, because blood flow and oxygen supply increase. An excellent combination of spatial and temporal resolution of brain activation images is obtained via non-invasive measures. Visual, sensory-motor, or auditory stimuli, and cognitive processes (i.e., language, or mental imagery) are used to derive these results. The crucial significance of this technique is that it allows for the correlation of anatomy with function, in repeated studies of the same patient. This method is presently considered the optimal assessment of cognitive and emotional processes, and is being utilized to monitor recovery from TBI. Additionally, these cutting edge technologies afford clinicians the opportunity to observe changes in regional brain chemistry and activity for studying brain functions in illness and health. For example, positron emission tomography (PET) studies of depressive states due to limbic-cortical dysregulation were utilized for diagnosis of clinical depression. A functional MRI study of the cognitive generation of affect depicted activation of similar areas in the medial frontal gyrus and right anterior cingulate gyrus when positive and negative picture-caption pairs were presented to normal subjects. Activation of these sites by a range of evoked affects is in accord with areas of the medial prefrontal cortex, which mediates the processing of affect-related meanings. (Teasdale et al., 1999).

fMRI does not involve exposure to ionizing radiation, is repeatable and noninvasive and has a temporal resolution of several seconds for whole brain studies. Therefore, fMRI can be utilized for specific cognitive tasks to study differential responses to stimulus property or other item features. For example, component processes in language, memory, concentration, attention, problem solving, and higher order abstract reasoning could be assessed. Therefore, the forensic neuropsychologist can utilize the fMRI as a corollary approach for the verification of subjective complaints, presentation, and reports by patients. This combined method is likely to provide a more comprehensive appraisal of brain-behavior functioning. The forensic expert can utilize the findings of such examinations in order to validate or discredit the patient's symptom presentation.

3.4   CONCLUDING REMARKS

This chapter included the fundamental concepts and clinical principles which are essential for the understanding of the complexity of the neuropsychological evaluation. It described the various functions that must be assessed, the rationale for each component, and reliability and validity of the recommended instruments. The section on the assessment of malingering is crucial for understanding the valid appraisal of the subjective vs. the objective components of neuropsychological evaluation. The simultaneous significance of the neurological examination and the various neurodiagnostic studies, cannot be underestimated. Therefore, following is the introduction of a proposed model of the neuropsychological examination, based on the convergence of multifaceted sources of information (see Figure 3.1).

As elaborated in the various sections of this chapter, the assessment should include the comparative analyses of the patient's subjective complaints, the medical,

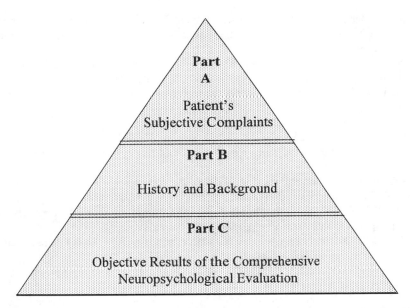

FIGURE 3.1 Neuropsychological examination model based on convergence of multifaceted sources of information.

personal-developmental (educational, occupational, etc. histories), and the compendium of all the tests administered. The convergent assessment thus proposed will most likely yield inclusive information regarding every constituent element of the patient's skills, abilities, and attributes.

REFERENCES

Adams, R.D., Victor, M., and Rooper, A.M., (1997). *Principles of Neurology.* McGraw-Hill, New York.

American Psychiatric Association, (1994a). *Diagnostic and Statistical Manual of Mental Disorders* (4th ed.). Washington, D.C.

American Psychiatric Association, (1994b). *Quick Reference to the Diagnostic Criteria from DSM-IV.* Washington, D.C.

American Psychological Association, (1985). Standards for educational and psychological testing. American Psychological Association, Washington, D.C.

Anderson-Parente, J.K., Dicesare, A., and Parente, R., (1990). Spouses who stayed. *Cognitive Rehabilitation,* 8, 22-25.

Arbisi, P.A. and Ben-Porath, Y.S., (1995). An MMPI-2 infrequent response scale for use with psychopathological populations: the Infrequency-Psychopathology Scale F. *Psychological Assessment,* 7, 424-431.

Armstrong, C., (1997). Selective versus sustained attention: a continuous performance test revisited. *The Clinical Neuropsychologist,* 11, 18 - 33.

Aylward, G.P., Gordon, M., and Verhulst, S.J., (1997). Relationships between continuous performance task scores and other cognitive measures: Causality or commonality. *Assessment,* 4, 325-336.

Bagby, R.M., Rogers, R., and Buis, T., (1994). Detecting malingering and defensive respond-ing on the MMPI-2 in a forensic inpatient sample. *Journal of Personality Assessment*, 62, 191-203.

Bagby, R.M., Rogers, R., Buis, T., and Kalemba, V., (1994). Malingered and defensive response style on the MMPI-2: an examination of validity scales. *Assessment*, 1, 31-38.

Banich, M.T. and Belger, A., (1990). Interhemispheric interactions. How do the hemispheres divide and conquer tasks? *Cortex*, 26, 77–94.

Basso, M.R., and Bornstein, R.A., (1998). Neuropsychological deficits in psychotic versus non-psychotic unipolar depression. *Neuropsychology*, 13, 69-75.

Beck, A.T., (1967). *Depression: Clinical Experimental and Theoretical Aspects.* Hoeber, New York.

Beck, A.T., Steer, R.A., and Brown, G.K., (1996). *Beck Depression Inventory — Second Edition.* The Psychological Corporation, San Antonio, TX.

Beck, A.T., Ward, C.H., Mendelson, M., Mock, J., and Erbaugh, J., (1961). An inventory for measuring depression. *Archives of General Psychiatry*, 4, 561-571.

Bender, L., (1938). A visual motor gestalt test and its clinical use. American Orthopsychiatric Association, *Research Monographs*, No. 3.

Bender, L., (1946). *Instructions for the Use of the Visual Motor Gestalt Test.* American Orthopsychiatric Association, New York.

Benton, A.L., (1989). Historical notes on the post-concussive syndrome, in *Mild Head Injury*, Levine, M.S., Eisenberg, H.M., and Benton, A.L., Eds., Oxford University Press, New York, p. 3-7.

Berenstein, J.G., (1988). *Handbook of Drug Therapy in Psychiatry* (2nd ed.). PSG Publishing, Littleton, MA..

Berry, D., Baer, R.A., and Harris, M., (1991). Detection of malingering on the MMPI: a meta-analysis. *Clinical Psychology Review*, 11, 585-598.

Berry, D.T.R., Wetter, M.W., Baer, R.A., Widiger, T.A., Sumpter, J.C., Reynold, S.K., and Hallan, R.A., (1991). Detection of random responding on the MMPI-2: utility of F, back F and VRIN scales. *Psychological Assessment*, 3, 418-423.

Berry, D.T.R., Wetter, M.W., Baer, R.A., Youngjohn, J.R., Gass, C.S., Lamb, D.G., Franzen, M.D., MacInnes, W.D., and Buchholz, D., (1995). Over-reporting of closed-head injury symptoms on the MMPI-2. *Psychological Assessment*, 7, 517-523.

Beetar, J.T. and Williams, J.M., (1995). Malingering response styles on the Memory Assess-ment Scales and symptom validity tests. *Archives of Clinical Neuropsychology*, 10, 57-72.

Bigler, G.D., (1987). Neuropathology of acquired cerebral trauma. *Journal of Learning Disability*, 20, 458-473.

Binder, L.M. and Willis, S.C., (1991). Assessment of motivation following financially com-pensatable minor head trauma. Psychological Assessment. *A Journal of Consulting and Clinical Psychology*, 3, 175-181.

Binder, L.M., (1990). Malingering following minor head trauma. *The Clinical Neuropsychol-ogist*, 4, 25-36.

Binder, L.M., (1992). Malingering detected by forced choice testing of memory and tactile sensation: a case report. *Archives of Clinical Neuropsychology*, 7, 155-163.

Binder, L.M., (1993). Assessment of malingering with the Portland Digit Recognition Test after mild head trauma. *Journal of Clinical and Experimental Neuropsychology*, 15, 170-182.

Binder, L.M., (1986). Persisting symptoms after mild head injury: a review of the post-concussive syndrome. *Journal of Clinical and Experimental Neuropsychology*, 8, 323-346.

Birber, R.B., (1998). Depression and aging too often do mix. Postgraduate Medicine, 104, 143-164.

Bishop, D.S. and Miller, I.W., (1988). Traumatic brain injury: empirical family assessment techniques. *Journal of Head Trauma Rehabilitation*, 3, 16-30.

Boles, D.B., (1992). Factor analysis and the cerebral hemispheres: temporal, occipital and frontal functions. *Neuropsychological*, 30, 963-988.

Boll, T. and Bryant, B.K., Eds.., (1988). *Clinical Neuropsychology and Brain Function: Research, Measurement and Practice.* American Psychological Association, Washington, D.C.

Boone, K.B., Ponton, M.D., Gorsuch, R.L., Gonzalez, J.J., Miller, B.L., (1998). Factor analysis of four measures of prefrontal lobe functioning. *Archives of Clinical Neuropsychology,* 13, 585-595.

Brandt, J., (1988). Malingered amnesia,. in *Clinical assessment of malingering and deception,* Rogers, R., Ed., The Guilford Press, New York, p. 65-83.

Brandt, J., Rubinsky, E., and Larson, G., (1985). Uncovering malingered amnesia. *Annals of the New York Academy of Science,* 44, 502-503.

Bremner, J.D., Randall, P., Scott, C.M., Bronen, R.A., Seibyl, J.P., Southwick, S.M., Delaney, R.C., McCarthy, G., Charney, D.S., and Innis, R.B., (1995). MRI-based measurement of hippocampal volume in combat-related post traumatic stress disorder. *American Journal of Psychiatry,* 152, 973-981.

Brooks, N., Campsie, L., Symington, C., Beattie, A., and McKinlay, W., (1987). The effects of severe head injury on patient and relative within seven years of injury. *Journal of Head Trauma Rehabilitation,* 2, 1-13.

Brouwer, W.H. and Van Wolffelar, P.C., (1985). Sustained attention and sustained efforts after closed-head injury: detection and 0.10 H_z heart rate variability in a low event rate vigilance task. *Cortex,* 21, 111-119.

Brown, L., Sherbenou, R.J., and Johnson, S.K., (1982). *Test of Nonverbal Intelligence: A Language-free Measure of Cognitive Ability.* Pro-Ed., Austin, TX

Bruhn, A.R. and Reed, M.R., (1975). Simulation of brain-damage on the Bender-Gestalt test by college students. *Journal of Personality Assessment,* 39, 244-255.

Bryant, R.A. and Harvey, A., (1998). Relationship between acute stress disorder and post traumatic stress disorder following mild traumatic brain injury. *American Journal of Psychiatry,* 155, 625-629.

Burgess, P.W., Alderman, N., Wilson, B.A., Evans, J.J., and Emslie, H., (1996). The dysexecutive questionnaire, in *Behavioral Assessment of the Dysexecutive Syndrom,* Wilson, B.A., Alderman, N., Burgess, P.W., Emslie, H., and Evans, J.J., Eds., Thames Valley Test Company, Bury St. Edmunds, U.K.

Butcher, J.N., Dahlstrom, W.G., Graham, J.R., Tellegen, A., and Kaemmer, B., (1989). *Manual for administration and scoring the Minnesota Multiphasic Personality Inventory — II.* University of Minnesota Press, Minneapolis, MN.

Butcher, J.R., (1995). Personality patterns of personal injury litigants: the role of computer-based MMPI-2 evaluations, in *Forensic Applications of the MMPI-2,* Ben-Porath, Y.S., Graham, J., Hall, G., Hirschman, R., and Zaragsa, M., Eds., Sage, Thousand Oaks, CA, Sage, p.179—201.

Cavallo, M.M., Kay, T., and Ezracki, O., (1992). Problems and changes after traumatic brain injury: differing perceptions, within and between families. *Brain Injury,* 6, 327-335.

Canter, A., (1966). A background interference procedure to increase sensitivity of the Bender Gestalt test to organic brain disorder. *Journal of Consulting Psychology,* 30, 91-97.

Cercy, S.P., Schretlen, D.J., and Brand, J., (1997). Simulated amnesia and pseudo-memory phenomena, in *Clinical Assessment of Malingering and Deception* (2nd ed.), Rogers, R., Ed., The Guilford Press, New York, p. 85-107.

Classen, C., Koopman, C., Hales, R., and Spiegel, D., (1998). Acute stress disorder as a predictor of post traumatic stress disorder. *American Journal of Psychiatry*, 155, 620-624.

Conoley, J.C. and Impara, J.C., (1995). *Supplement to the 11th Mental Measurements Yearbook*, University of Nebraska Press, Lincoln, NE.

Crawford, J.R., Garth waite, P.M., Johnson, D.A., Mychalkin, B., and Moore, J.W., (1997). WAIS-R Subtest pattern clusters in closed-head injured and healthy samples. *The Clinical Neuropsychologist*, 11, 249-257.

Dahlstrom, W.G., Welsh, G.S., and Dahlstrom, L.E., (1975). *An MMPI Handbook. Volume I: Clinical interpretation*. University of Minnesota Press, Minneapolis, MN.

Del Orto, A. and Power, P.W., (1994). *Head injury and the Family: A Life and Living Perspective*. PMD Publishers Group, Winter Park, FL.

Deptula, D., Singh, R., and Pomara, N (1993). Aging, continuous state, and memory. *American Journal of Psychiatry*, 150, 429-434.

Derogatis, L.R., (1983). *SCL-90-R Administration, Scoring and Procedures Manual — II for the Revised Version and Other Instruments of the Psychopathology Rating Scale Series*. Clinical Psychometric Research, Towson, MD.

Derogatis, L.R., (1975). *Brief Symptom Inventory*, Clinical Psychometric Research, Baltimore, MD.

Diller, L., Ben-Yishai, Y.,Gersthan, L.J. et al., (1974). *Studies in cognition and rehabilitation in hemiplegia.,* (Rehabilitation Monograph, No. 50). New York University Medical Center Institute of Rehabilitation Medicine, New York.

Geschwind, N., (1970). The organization of language and the brain. *Science*, 170, 940 - 944.

Geschwind, N., (1985). Brain disease and the mechanisms of mind, in *Functions of the Brain*, Cohen, C.W., Eds., Clarendon Press, Oxford.

Eamses, P., (1989). Behavior disorders after severe head injury: their nature and causes and strategies for management. *Journal of Head Trauma Rehabilitation*, 3, 1-6.

Emery, O., (1988). *Pseudodementia: A theoretical and Empirical Discussion: Interdisciplinary Monograph Series*. Western Reserve Geriatric Education Center, Cleveland, OH.

Epstein, J.N., Conners, C.K., Sitareniss, G., and Erhardt, D., (1988). Continuous performance test results of adults with attention deficit hyperactivity disorder. *The Clinical Neuropsychologist*, 12, 155-168.

Epstein, N.B., Baldwin, L.M., and Bishop, D.S., (1983). The MacMaster Family Assessment Device. *Journal of Marital and Family Therapy*, 9, 171-180.

Eviatar, Z., Hellige, J.B., and Zaidel, E., (1997). Individual differences in lateralization: effects of gender and handedness. *Neuropsychology*, 11, 562-572.

Fowler, K.S., Saling, M.M., Conway, E.L., Semple, J.S., and Louis, W.J., (1997). Computerized neuropsychological tests in the early detection of dementia: prospective findings. *Journal of the International Neuropsychological Society*, 3, 139-146.

Folstein, M., McHugh, P., (1978). Dementia syndrome of depression, in Alzheimer's Disease. Senile Dementia and Related Disorders in *Aging*. Katzman, R., Terry, R.D., and Bick, K.L., Raven Press, New York.

Fox, D.D., Lees-Haley, P.R., Earnest, K., and Dolexal-Wood, S., (1995). Base-rates of post-concussive symptoms in health maintenance organization patients and control. *Neuropsychology*, 9, 606-611.

Frankowski, R.F., (1986). Descriptive epidemiological studies of head injury in the United States: 1974-1984, in *Psychiatric Aspects of Trauma*, Peterson, L.G. and O'Shanick, G.J., Eds., Karger, New York.

Franzen, M.D., Iverson, G.L., and McCracken, L.M., (1990) The detection of malingering in neuropsychological assessment. *Neuropsychology Review*, 1, 247-279.

Freedman, M., Stuss, D.T., and Gordon, M., (1991). Assessment of competency: the role of neurobehavioral deficits. *Annals of Internal Medicine,* 115, 203-208.

Fristoe, N.M., Salthouse, T.A., and Woodard, J., (1997). Examination on age-related deficits on the Wisconsin Card Sorting Test. *Neuropsychology,* 11, 428-436.

Gallen, R.T. and Berry, D.T.R., (1996). Detection of random responding in MMPI-2 protocols. *Assessment,* 3, 171-178.

Galski, T., Palasz, J., Bruno, R.L., and Walker, J.E., (1994). Predicting physical and verbal aggression on a brain trauma unit. *Archives of Physical Medicine and Rehabilitation,* 75, 380-383.

Gasquoine, P.G., (1998). Historical perspective on post-concussion symptoms. *The Clinical Neuropsychologist,* 12, 315-324.

Gasquoine, P.G., (1997). Post-concussion symptoms. *Neuropsychology Review,* 7, 77-85.

Gasquoine, P.G. and Gibbons, T.A., (1994). Lack of awareness of impairment in institution-alized severely and chronically disabled survivors of traumatic brain injury: a preliminary investigation. *Journal of Head Trauma Rehabilitation,* 9, 16-24.

Gass, C. and Russell, E., (1991). MMPI profiles of closed-head trauma patients: impact of neurological complaints. *Journal of Clinical Psychology,* 47, 253-260.

Gass, C., (1991). MMPI-2 interpretation and closed-head injury: a correction factor. *Psychological Assessment,* 3, 27-31.

Gelenberg, A.J., Bassuck, E.L., and Schooner, S.C., Eds., (1991). *The Practitioner's Guide to Psychoactive Drugs* (3rd ed.). Plenum Publishing Corp., New York.

Geschwind, N., (1965). Disconnection syndromes in animals and men. *Brain,* 88, 237-294.

Geschwind, N. and Galaburda, A.M., (1987). *Cerebral Lateralization. Biological Mechanisms, Associations and Pathology.* MIT Press, Cambridge, MA.

Gewirtz, G., Squires-Wheeler, E., Sharif, Z., and Honer, W.G., (1994). Results of computerized tomography during first admission for psychosis. *British Journal of Psychiatry,* 164, 789-795.

Gierz, M., Sewell, D.D., Kramer, R., Gillin, J.C., and Jeste, D.V., (1995). Psychotic versus non-psychotic depression in older patients. *American Journal of Geriatric Psychiatry,* 164, 789-795.

Goebel, R.A., (1983). Detection of faking on the Halstead-Reitan Neuropsychological Test Battery. *Journal of Clinical Psychology,* 39, 731-742.

Goodman, J.C., (1994). Pathologic changes in mild head injury. *Seminars in Neurology,* 14, 19-24.

Golden, C.J. and Van Den Broek, A., (1998). Potential impact of age- and education-corrected scores on HRNB score patterns in participants with focal brain injury. *Archives of Clinical Neuropsychology,* 13, 683-694.

Golden, C.J., Zillmer, E., and Spiers, M., (1992). *Neuropsychological Assessment and Rehabilitation.* Charles G. Thorne, Springfield, IL.

Goldstein, G. and McCue, M., (1995). Differences between patient and informant functional outcome ratings in head-injured individuals. *International Journal of Rehabilitation and Health,* 1, 25-35.

Goran, D.A., Fabiano, R.J., and Crewe, N., (1997). Employment following severe traumatic brain injury: the utility of the Individual Ability Profile System. *Archives of Clinical Neuropsychology,* 12, 691-698.

Gough, H.G., (1947). Simulated patterns on the MMPI. *Journal of Abnormal and Social Psychology,* 42, 215-225.

Graham, J.R., (1990). *MMPI-2 Assessing Personality and Psychopathology.* Oxford University Press, New York.

Green, R., (1980). *The MMPI: An Interpretive Manual.* Grune and Stratton, New York.

Green, R., (1991). *The MMPI-2/MMPI: An Interpretive Manual.* Allyn and Bacon, Boston.

Green, R.L., (1997). Assessment of malingering and defensiveness by multi-scale personality inventories, in *Clinical Assessment of Malingering and Deception* (2nd ed.), Rogers, R., Ed., The Guilford Press, New York, p. 169-207.

Greene, R.L., (1988). Assessment of malingering and defensiveness by objective personality inventories. In Rogers, R., (Ed.) *Clinical Assessment of Malingering and Deception,* The Guilford Press, New York, p.169-207.

Greiffenstein, M., Baker, W., and Gola, T., (1994). Validation of malingered amnesia. Measures with a large clinical sample. *Psychological Assessment,* 6, 218-224.

Greiffenstein, M., Gola, T., and Baker, W., (1995). MMPI-2 validity scales versus domain specific measures in the detection of factitious traumatic brain injury. *The Clinical Neuropsychologist,* 9, 230-290.

Groom, K.N., Shaw, T.G., O'Conner, M.E., Howard, N.I., and Pickens, A., (1998). Neurobehavioral symptoms and family functioning in traumatically brain-injured adults. *Archives of Clinical Neuropsychology,* 13, 695-711.

Guidelines for the Evaluation of Dementia and Age-Related Cognitive Decline, (1998). *American Psychologist,* 53, 1298-1303.

Hall, S., Pinkston, S.L., Szalda-Petree, A.C., and Coronis, A.R., (1996). The performance of healthy older adults on the Continuous Visual Memory Test and the Visual-Motor Integration Test: preliminary findings. *Journal of Clinical Psychology,* 52, 449-454.

Hall, K.M., Karzmark, P., Stephens, M., Englander, J., O'Hare, P., and Wright, J., (1994). Family stressors in traumatic brain injury: a two year follow-up. *Archives of Physical Medicine and Rehabilitation,* 75, 876-883.

Halstead, W.C., (1947). *Brain and Intelligence.* University of Chicago Press, Chicago, IL.

Hammarberg, M., (1992). Penn Inventory for post traumatic stress disorder: psychometric properties. *Psychological Assessment,* 4, 67-76.

Hathaway, S.R. and McKinley, J.C., (1951). *The Minnesota Multiphasic Personality Inventory manual* (rev.). The Psychological Corporation, New York.

Heaton, R., Smith, H., Lehman, R., and Vogt, A., (1978a). Prospects for faking believable deficits on neuropsychological testing. *Journal of Consulting and Clinical Psychology,* 46, 892-900.

Heaton, R.K., Brade, L.F., and Johnson, K.L., (1978b). Neuropsychological test results associated with psychiatric disorders in adults. *Psychological Bulletin,* 85, 141-162.

Heaton, R.K., Grant, I., and Matthews, C.G., (1991). *Comprehensive Norms for an Expanded Halstead-Reitan Battery,* Psychological Assessment Resources, Odessa, FL.

Heaton, R.K., Grant, I., and Matthews, C.G., (1986). Differences in test performance associated with age, education and sex, in *Neuropsychological Assessment in Neuropsychiatric Disorders: Clinical Methods and Empirical Findings,* Grant, I. and Adams, K., Eds., Oxford University Press, New York.

Heaton, R.K., Matthews, C.G., Grant, I., and Avitable, N., (1996). Demographic corrections with comprehensive norms: An overzealous attempt or a good start. *Journal of Clinical and Experimental Neuropsychology,* 181, 121-141.

Hellige, J.B., (1995). Coordinating the different processing biases of the left and right cerebral hemispheres, in *Hemispheric Communication: Mechanisms and Models,* Erlaum, Hillsdale, NJ, p. 347-362.

Hellige, J.B., (1993). *Hemispheric Asymmetry: What's Right and What's Left.* Harvard University Press, Cambridge, MA.

Hellige, J.B., Block, M.I., Cowin, E.L., Eng, T.L., Eviatar, Z., and Sergent, V., (1994). Individual variation in hemispheric asymmetry: multitask study of effects related to handedness and sex. *Journal of Experimental Psychology: General,* 123, 235 - 256.

Higgins, K. and Sherman, M., (1978). The effect of motivation on loose thinking in schizo-phrenics as measured by the Bermister-Fransella Grid Test. *Journal of Clinical Psychology*, 34, 624-628.

Hiscock, M. and Hiscock, C.K., (1989). Refining the forced choice method for the detection of malingering. *Journal of Clinical and Experimental Neuropsychology*, 11, 964-967.

Hodges, J.R., Gerrard, P., Perry, R., Patterson, K, Ward, R., Bak, T., and Gregory, C., (1999). The differentiation of semantic dementia and frontal lobe dementia (temporal and frontal variants of frontotemporal dementia) from early Alzheimer's Disease: a comparative neuropsychological study. *Neuropsychology*, 13, 31-40.

Hom, J., (1992). General and specific cognitive dysfunctions in patients with Alzheimer's disease. *Archives of Clinical Neuropsychology*, 7, 121-133.

Horton, M., (1993). Post-traumatic stress disorder and mild head trauma: follow-up of a case study. *Perceptual and Motor Skills*, 76, 243-246.

Hutt, M.L., (1985). *The Hutt Adaptation of the Bender-Gestalt Test: Rapid Screening and Intensive Diagnosis* (4th ed.). Grune and Straton, Orlando, FL.

Impara, J.C. and Plake, B.S., (1998). *Mental Measurement Yearbook*. Buros Institute of Mental Measurements, University of Nebraska–Lincoln, NE.

Ivnik, R.J., Smith, G.E., Lucas, J.A., Peterson, R.C., Boeve, B.F., Kokmen, E., and Tangalos, E.G., (1999). Testing normal older people three or four times at 1-2 year intervals: defining normal variance. *Neuropsychology*, 13, 121-127.

Jarvis, P.E. and Barth, J.T., (1994). *The Halstead-Reitan Neuropsychological Battery: A Guide to Interpretation and Clinical Application*. Psychological Assessment Resources, Odessa, FL.

Jennet, B. and Teasdale, G., (1981). *Management of Head Injuries*. F.A. Davis, Philadelphia.

Jordan, B.D., (1997). Emerging concepts in sports neurology. *Annals of the New York Academy of Sciences*.

Julien, R.M., (1995). *A Primer of Drug Action: Concise, Non-Technical Guide to the Actions Woes, and Side Effects of Psychoactive Drugs* (7th ed.). W.H. Freeman and Company, New York.

Katzung, B.G., Ed., (1995). *Basic and clinical pharmacology* (6th ed.). Appleton and Lange, Norwalk, CT.

King, D.A., Cox, C., Lyness, J.M., Conwell, Y., and Caine, E.D., (1998). Quantitative and qualitative differences on the verbal learning performance of elderly depressives and healthy controls. *Journal of the International Neuropsychological Society*, 4, 115-116.

Kotrla, K.J., Chacko, R.C., Harper, R.G., and Doody, R., (1995). Clinical variables associated with psychosis in Alzheimer's disease. *American Journal of Psychiatry*, 152, 1377-1379.

Kraus, M.F., (1995). Neuropsychiatric sequelae of stroke and traumatic brain injury: the role of psycho-stimulants. *Interactive Journal of Psychiatry in Medicine*, 25, 39-51.

Kreutzer, J.S., Gervasion, A.M., and Camplair, P.S., (1994). Primary caregiver's psycho-logical status and family functioning after traumatic brain injury. *Brain Injury*, 8, 197-210.

Kreutzer, J.S., Marwitz, J.H., and Kepler, K., (1992). Traumatic brain injury: family response and outcome. *Archives of Physical Medicine and Rehabilitation*, 73, 771-778.

Kwasnica, C.M., and Heinemann, A., (1994). Coping with traumatic brain injury: represen-tative case studies. *Archives of Physical Medicine and Rehabilitation*, 75, 384-389.

Lanson-Kerr, K., Smith, P., and Beck, D., (1991). Behavioral neuropsychology. Past, present, and future direction with organically based affect/mood disorders. *Neuropsychology Review*, 12, 65-107.

Larrabee, G.J. and Curtiss, G., (1995). Construct validity of various verbal and visual memory tests. *Journal of Clinical and Experimental Neuropsychology*, 17, 536-547.

Larrabee, G.J., (1996). *Somatic malingering on the MMP/MMPI-2 in litigating subjects.* Presented to the National Academy of Neuropsychology annual conference, New Orleans, LA.

Larrabee, G.J., (1997). Neuropsychological outcome, post concussion symptoms, and forensic considerations in mild closed-head trauma. *Seminars in Clinical Neuropsychology, 2,* 196-206.

Larrabee, G.J., (1998). Somatic malingering on the MMPI and MMPI-2 in personal injury litigants. *The Clinical Neuropsychologist,* 12, 129-188.

Lees-Haley, P.R., (1997). MMPI-2 base rates for 492 personal injury plaintiffs: implications and challenges for forensic assessment. *Journal of Clinical Psychology,* 53, 745-755.

Lees-Haley, P.R., English, L.T., and Glenn, W.J., (1991). The fake bade scale on the MMPI-2 for personal injury claimants. *Psychological Reports,* 68, 203-210.

Lester, D.S., Felder, C., and Lewis, E.N., Eds., (1997). Imaging brain structure and function. *Annals of the New York Academy of Sciences,* Vol. 820, New York.

Levin, M.J. and Guermy, M., (1991). Applications of psychophysiology in clinical neuropsychology, in *Windows on the Brain. Annals of the New York Academy of Science,* Zappula, R.A., LeFever, F.F., Jagger, J., and Bilder, R., Vol. 620, p. 208-216, New York.

Levin, H.S., Williams, D.H., Eisenberg, H.M., High, W.M., and Guinto, F.C., (1992). Serial MRI and neurobehavioral findings after mild to moderate closed head injury. *Journal of Neurology, Neurosurgery, and Psychiatry,* 55, 255-262.

Levin, H.S., High, W.M., Goethe, K.E., Sisson, R.A., Overall, J.E., Rhoades, H.M., Eisenberg, H.M., Kalisky, Z., and Gary, H.E., (1987). The Neurobehavioral Rating Scale: assessment of the behavioral sequelae of head injury by the clinician. *Journal of Neurology, Neurosurgery, and Psychiatry,* 50, 183-193.

Levine, S.C., (1995). Individual differences in characteristic arousal asymmetry: implications for cognitive functioning, in *Hemispheric communication: Mechanisms and models,* Kitterle, F., Ed., Erlbaum, Hillsdale, NJ, p. 255-270.

Levine, S.C., Banich, M.T., and Koch-Weser, M., (1984). Variations in patterns of lateral asymmetry among dextrals. *Brain and Cognition,* 3, 317-344.

Lezak, M.D., (1995). *Neuropsychological Assessment* (3rd ed.). Oxford University Press, New York.

Lezak, M.D., (1986). Psychological implications of traumatic brain damage for the patient's family. *Rehabilitation Psychology,* 31, 241-250.

Lezak, M., (1978). Living with the characterologically altered brain injured patient. *Journal of Clinical Psychiatry,* 39, 592-598.

Linn, R.T., Allen, K., and Willer, B.S., (1994). Affective symptoms in the chronic stage of traumatic brain injury: a study of married couples. *Brain Injury,* 8, 135-147.

Livingston, M.G., Brooks, D.N., and Bond, M.R., (1985). Three months after severe head injury: psychiatric and social impact on relatives. *Journal of Neurology, Neurosurgery and Psychiatry,* 48, 870-875.

Machuloa, M.M., Berquist, Ito, V., and Chew, S., (1998). Relationship between stress, coping, and post-concussion symptoms in a healthy adult population. *Archives of Clinical Neuropsychology,* 13, 415-424.

Matarazzo, J.D., (1990). Psychological assessment versus psychological testing. *American Psychologist,* 45, 999-1017.

McGlynn, S.M. and Schacter, D.L., (1989). Unawareness of deficits in neuropsychological syndromes. *Journal of Clinical and Experimental Neuropsychology,* 11, 143-205.

McKinzey, R.K., Podd, M.R., Kreihbiel, M.A., Mensch, A.J., and Trombka, C.C., (1997). Detection of malingering on the Luria-Nebraska neuropsychological battery: an initial and cross-validation. *Archives of Clinical Neuropsychology,* 12, 505-512.

McNeill, D.E., Schuler, B.A., and Ezrachi, O., (1997). Assessing family involvement in traumatic brain injury rehabilitation. The development of a new instrument. *Archives of Clinical Neuropsychology,* 12, 645-660.

Meehl, P.E. and Hathway, S.R., (1946). The K factor as a suppresser variable in the MMPI. *Journal of Applied Psychology,* 30, 525-564.

Melamed, S. Rahamani, L., Greenstein, Y., Groswasser, Z., and Najenson, T., (1985). Divided attention in brain injured patients. *Scandinavian Journal of Rehabilitation Medicine,* 12, 16-20.

Mesulam, M.M., (1985). *Principles of Behavioral Neurology,* F.A. Davis Company, Philadelphia.

Meyers, J.E. and Volbrecht, M., (1998). Validation of Reliable Digits for detection of malingering. *Assessment,* 5, 303-307.

Millis, S.P., (1992). The Recognition Memory Test in the detection of malingered and exaggerated memory deficits. *Clinical Neuropsychologist,* 6, 405-413.

Mishkin, M. and Appenzeller, T., (1989). The anatomy of memory. *Scientific American,* 256, 80-89.

Mitchell, J., (Ed.) *The Ninth Mental Measurement Yearbook.* 1985. University of Nebraska Press, Lincoln, NE.

Nelson, L.D., Drebing, C., Satz, P, and Uchimaya, C., (1998). Personality change in head trauma: a validity study of the Neuropsychology Behavior and Affect Profile. *Archives of Clinical Neuropsychology,* 13, 549-560.

Newell, A., (1973). Productions system: models of control structures, in *Visual Information Processing,* Chase, W.G., Ed., Academic Press, New York.

Niemann, H. Ruff, R.M., and Kramer, J.H., (1996). An attempt towards differentiating attentional deficits in traumatic brain injury. *Neuropsychology Review,* 6, 11-46.

Nies, K.J. and Sweet, J.J., (1994). Neuropsychological assessment and malingering: a critical review of past and present strategies. *Archives of Clinical Neuropsychology,* 9, 501-552.

O'Boyle, M., Amadeo, M., and Self, D., (1990). Cognitive complaints in elderly depressed and pseudo-demented patients. *Psychology and Aging,* 5, 467-468.

Ohman, A., (1979). The orienting response, attention and learning: on information processing perspective, in *The Orienting Reflex in Human,* Kimmel, M.D., Van Olst, G.M., and Orlegeke, J.F., Eds., Lawrence Erlbaum Associates, Hillsdale, N.J, 443-471.

Oldfield, R.C., (1971). The assessment and analysis of handedness. The Edenburg Inventory. *Neuropsychologia,* 9, 97-113.

Palmer, B.W., Boone, K.B., Lesser, I.M., and Wohl, M.A., (1998) Base rates of "impaired" neuropsychological test performance among healthy older adults. *Archives of Clinical Neuropsychology,* 13, 503-511.

Pankatz, L., Fausti, A., and Peed, S., (1975). A forced choice technique to evaluate deafness in the hysterical or malingering patient. *Journal of Consulting and Clinical Psychology,* 43, 421-422.

Pankatz, L., (1983). A new technique for the assessment and modification of feigned memory deficit. *Perceptual and Motor Skills,* 57, 367-372.

Pankatz, L., (1988). Malingering on intellectual and neuropsychological measures, in *Clinical Assessment of Malingering and Deception,* Rogers, R., Ed., The Guilford Press, New York, p. 169-194.

Pankatz, L. and Binder, L., (1997). Malingering on intellectual and neuropsychological measures, in *Clinical Assessment of Malingering and Deception* (2nd ed.), Rogers, R., Ed., The Guilford Press, New York, p. 223-238.

Panting, A. and Merry, P.M., (1972). Long term rehabilitation of severe head injuries with particular reference to the need for social and medical support for the patient's family. *Rehabilitation,* 38, 33-37.

Paolo, A.M., Troster, A.I., and Ryan, J.J., (1998). Continuous Visual Memory test performance in healthy persons 60–94 years of age. *Archives of Clinical Neuropsychology,* 333-337.

Parasuraman, R., Mutter, S.A., and Malloy, R., (1991). Sustained attention following mild closed-head injury. *Journal of Clinical and Experimental Neuropsychology,* 13, 789-711.

Parkin, A.J., (1998). The central executive does not exist. *Journal of the International Neuropsychological Society,* 4, 518-522.

Parsons, O.A. and Prigatano, G.P., (1978). Methodological considerations in clinical neuropsychological research. *Journal of Consulting and Clinical Psychology,* 46, 608-619.

Penry, J.K., (Ed.) (1991). *Epilepsy and Life Performance.* Raven Press, New York.

Perlesz, A., Kinsella, G., and Crowe, S., (1999). Impact of traumatic brain injury on the family: a critical review. *Rehabilitation Psychology,* 44, 6-35.

Peters, L.C., Stambrook, M., Moore, A.D., and Esse, L., (1990). Psychosocial sequelae of closed head injury: effects on the marital relationship. *Brain Injury,* 4, 39-47.

Pirozzolo, F.J., (1978). Disorders of perceptual processing, in *Handbook of Perception* (Vol. 9), Carterette, E.C. and Friedman, M.P., Eds., Academic Press, New York.

Podd, M.H., Krehbiel, M.A., Mensch, A.J., and Trombka, C.C., (1997). Detection of malingering on the Luria-Nebraska neuropsychological battery: an initial and cross-validation. *Archives of Clinical Neuropsychology,* 12, 505-512.

Pope, H.S., Butcher, J.N., and Seelen, J., (1993) *The MMPI, MMPI-2 and MMPI-A in court. A practical Guide for Expert Witnesses and Attorneys.* American Psychological Association, Washington, D.C.

Posthuma, A.B. and Harper, J.F., (1998). Comparison of MMPI-2 response of child custody and personality injury litigants. *Professional Psychology: Research and Practice, 29,* 437-443.

Posner, M.I. and Rafal, R.D., (1987). Cognitive theories of attention and the rehabilitation of attentional deficits, in *Neuropsychological Rehabilitation,* Meier, M., Benton, A., and Diller, L., Eds., The Guilford Press, New York, p. 182-201.

Potter, S.M. and Graves, R.E., (1988). Is inter-hemispheric transfer related to handedness and gender? *Neuropsychologia,* 26, 319-325.

Pribram, K.M. and McGuinness, D., (1975). Arousal, activation and effort in the control of attention. *Psychological Review,* 82, 176-179.

Prigatano, G.P. and Amin, K., (1993). Digit Memory Test: unequivocal cerebral dysfunction and suspected malingering. *Journal of Clinical and Experimental Neuropsychology,* 15, 537-546.

Prigatano, G.P., Parsons, O.A., and Bortz, J.J., (1995). Methodological considerations in clinical neuropsychological research: 17 years later. *Psychological Assessment, 7,* 396-402.

Prigatano, G.P., Smason, I., Lamb, D.G., and Bortz, J., (1997). Suspected malingering and the Digit Memory Test: a replication and extension. *Archives of Clinical Neuropsychology, 12,* 609-619.

Prigatano, G.P., Altman, I.M., and O'Brien, K.P., (1990). Behavioral limitations that traumatic-brain-injured patients tend to underestimate. *The Clinical Neuropsychologist,* 4, 163-176.

Prigatano, G.P. and Altman, I.M., (1990). Impaired awareness of behavioral limitations after traumatic brain injury. *Archives of Physical Medicine and Rehabilitation,* 71, 1058-1069.

Rappaport, M.C., Hall C.K., Hopkins, H.K., and Belleza, T., (1977). Evoked brain potentials and disability in brain damaged patients. *Archives of Physical Medicine and Rehabilitation,* 58, 333-338.

Rappaport, M.C., Hall C.K., Hopkins, H.K., and Belleza, T., (1981). Evoked potentials and head injury: I rating of evoked potential abnormality. *Clinical Electroencephalography,* 12, 154-156.

Rawling, P. and Brooks, N., (1990). Simulation index: a method for detecting factitious errors on the WAIS-R and WMS. *Neuropsychology,* 4, 234-238.

Ray, E.C., Engum, E.S., Lambert, E.W., Bane, G.F., Nash, M.R., and Bracy, O.L., (1997). Ability of cognitive behavioral Driver's Inventory to distinguish malingerers from brain-damaged subjects. *Archives of Clinical Neuropsychology,* 12, 491-503.

Reitan, R.M. and Wolfson, D., (1997). *Detection of Malingering and Invalid Test Scores.* Neuropsychology Press, Tucson, AZ.

Reitan, R.M., (1955). An investigation of the validity of Halstead's measures of biological intelligence. *Archives of Neurology and Psychiatry,* 73, 28-35.

Reitan, R.M. and Davison, L.A., (1974). *Clinical Neuropsychology: Current Status and Applications.* Winston/Wiley, New York.

Reitan, R.M. and Wolfson, D., (1993). *The Halstead-Reitan Neuropsychological Test Battery.* Neuropsychology Press, Tucson, AZ.

Reitan, R.M. and Wolfson, D., (1995a). Influence of age and education on neuropsychological test results. *Clinical Neuropsychologist,* 9, 151-158.

Reitan, R.M. and Wolfson, D., (1995b). Consistency of response on re-testing among head-injured subjects in litigation versus head-injured subjects not in litigation. *Applied Neuropsychology,* 2, 67-71.

Reitan, R.M. and Wolfson, D., (1996). The question of validity of neuropsychological test scores among head-injured litigants: Development of a Dissimulation Index. *Archives of Clinical Neuropsychology,* 11, 573-580.

Reitan, R.M. and Wolfson, D., (1997a). Consistency of neuropsychological test scores of head-injured subjects involved in litigation compared with head-injured subjects not involved in litigation: development of the Latest Consistency Index. *The Clinical Neuropsychologist,* 11, 69-76.

Reitan, R.M. and Wolfson, D., (1997b). *Detection of Malingering and Invalid Test Scores.* Neuropsychology Press, Tucson, AZ.

Reitan, R.M. and Wolfson, D., (1988). *Traumatic Brain Injury. Vol. II. Recovery and Rehabilitation.* Neuropsychology Press, Tucson, AZ.

Reitan, R.M. and Wolfson, D., (1999). The two faces of mild head injury. *Archives of Clinical Neuropsychology,* 12, 191-202.

Reitan, R.M. and Wolfson, D., (1998). *Mild Head Injury: Intellectual, Cognitive and Emotional Consequences.* Neuropsychology Press, Tucson, AZ.

Resnick, P.J., (1988). Malingering of post-traumatic disorders, in *Clinical Assessment of Malingering and Deception,* Rogers, R., Ed., The Guilford Press, New York, p. 84-103.

Resnick, P.J., (1997). Malingering of post-traumatic disorders, in *Clinical Assessment of Malingering and Deception* (2nd ed.)., Rogers, R., Ed., The Guilford Press, New York, p. 130-152.

Rey, A., (1946). L'Examen psychotechnique dans le cas d'ence'phalopathie traumatique. *Archive de Psychologie,* 28, 286-340.

Reynolds, C.F., Dew, M.A., Frank, E., Begley, A.E., Miller, M.D., Cornes, C., Mazumdar, S., Perel, J.A., and Kupfer, D.J., (1998). Effects of age at onset of first lifetime episode of recurrent major depression on treatment response and illness course in elderly patients. *American Journal of Psychiatry,* 6, 795-799.

Richardson, E.D. and Marottoli, R.A., (1996). Education — specific normative data on common neuropsychological indices for individuals older than 75 years. *The Clinical Neuropsychologist,* 10, 375-381.

Ridenour, T.A., McCoy, K.D., and Dean, R.S., (1998). Discriminant function analysis malingerer's and neurological headache patients' self-reports of neuropsychological symptoms. *Archives of Clinical Neuropsychology,* 13, 561-567.

Rivara, J.B., Jaffa, K.M., Polissar, N.L., Fay, G.C., Martin, K.M., Shurtleff, H.A., and Liao, S., (1994). Family functioning and children's academic performance and behavior problems in the year following traumatic brain injury. *Archives of Physical Medicine and Rehabilitation,* 75, 369-379.

Robinson, R.G. and Szetta, B., (1981). Mood change following left hemisphere brain injury. *Annals of Neurology,* 9, 447-453.

Rogers, R., (1984). Towards an empirical model of malingering. *Behavioral Sciences and the Law,* 2, 93-112.

Rogers, R., (1988). *Clinical Assessment of Malingering and Deception.* The Guilford Press, New York.

Rogers, R., (1995). *Diagnostic and Structured Interviewing: A Handbook for Psychologists.* Psychological Assessment Resources, Odessa, FL.

Rogers, R., (Ed.) (1997). *Clinical Assessment of Malingering and Deception* (2nd ed.). The Guilford Press, New York

Rogers, R., Bagby, R.M., and Dickens, S.E., (1992). *Structured Interview of Reported Symptoms.* Professional Manual. Psychological Assessment Resources, Odessa, FL.

Rogers, R., Gillis, J.R., Dickens, S.E., and Bagby, R.M., (1991). Standardized assessment of malingering: validation of the Structured Interview of Reported Symptoms. *Psychological Assessment,* 4, 89-96.

Romano, M.D., (1974). Family responses to traumatic brain injury. *Scandinavian Journal of Rehabilitation Medicine,* 6, 1-4.

Rose. F.E., Hall, S., and Szalda-Petree, A.D., (1998). A Comparison of four tests of malingering and the effects of coaching. *Archives of Clinical Neuropsychology,* 13, 349-363.

Rotter, J., (1950, 1977). *Incomplete Sentence Blank — Adult Form.* The Psychological Corporation, San Antonio, TX.

Russell, E.W., (1998). In defense of the Halstead-Reitan Battery: a critique of Lezak's review. *Archives of Clinical Neuropsychology,* 13, 365-381.

Russell, E.W., Neuringer, C., and Goldstein, E., (1970). *Assessment of Brain Damage: A Neuropsychological Key Approach.* John Wiley & Sons, New York.

Sakow, D., (1963). Psychological deficit in schizophrenia. *Behavioral Science,* 8, 275-305.

Sanders, C.M., Mauger, P.A., and Strong, P.N., (1985). *A Manual for the Grief Experience Inventory.* Consulting Psychologists Press, Palo Alto, CA.

Saykin, A.J., (1998). Advances in Brain Mapping with fMRI: implications for clinical neuropsychology. *The Bulletin of the National Academy of Neuropsychology,* 14, 3-7.

Sbordone, R.J., (1991). *The side effects of neuro-pharmacological medications on neuropsychological test performance in the traumatically brain injured patient.* Abstract. Annual Meeting of the American Psychological Association, San Francisco.

Schlegel, S., Maier, W., Philipp, M., Aldenhoff, J.B., Heuser, I., Kretzschmar, K., and Benkert, O., (1989). Computed tomography in depression: Association between ventricular size and psychopathology. *Psychiatry Research,* 29, 221-230.

Schretlen, D., Wilkins, S.S., Van Gorp, W.G., and Bobholzf, J.H., (1992). Cross-validation of a psychological test battery to detect faked insanity. *Psychological Assessment,* 4, 77-83.

Shalev, A.Y., Freedman, S., Peri, T., Brandes, D., Sahar, T., Orr, S.P., and Pitman, R.K., (1998). Perspective study of post traumatic stress disorder and depression following trauma. *American Journal of Psychiatry,* 155, 630-637.

Shallice, T. and Burgess, P., (1991). Deficits in strategy application following frontal lobe damage in man. *Brain,* 114, 727-741.

Shallice, T., and Burgess, P., (1993). Supervisory control of action and thought selection, in *Attention: Selection, Awareness and Control: A Tribute to Donald Broadbent,* Baddeley, A. and Weistrantz, L., Eds., Clarendon Press, Oxford, U.K., p. 171-187.

Sherman, A.G., Shaw, T.G., and Glidden, H., (1994). Emotional behavior as an agenda in neuropsychological evaluation. *Neuropsychological Review,* 4, 45-69.

Shuttleworth-Jordan, A.B., (1997). Age and education effects on brain damaged subjects: "negative" findings revisited. *Clinical Neuropsychologist,* 11, 205-209.

Silbersweig, D.A., and Stern, E., (1997). Symptom Localization in Neuropsychiatry: a functional neuroimaging approach, in *Frontiers of Neurology: A Symposium in Honor of Fred Plum.,* Reis, D.J. and Posner, J.B., *Annals of the New York Academy of Sciences,* 835, 410-420.

Small, G.W., La Rue, A., Komo, S., Kaplan, A., and Mandelkern, M.A., (1995). Predictors of cognitive change in middle-aged and older adults with memory loss. *American Journal of Psychiatry,* 152, 1757-1764.

Smith, A., (1972). *Symbol Digit Modalities Test — Revised.* Western Psychological Services, Los Angeles, CA.

Snyder, P.J. and Nussbaum, P.D., Eds., (1998). *Clinical Neuropsychology: A Pocket Handbook for Assessment.* American Psychological Association, Washington D.C.

Specialty guidelines for forensic psychologists, (1990). American Psychology-Law Society News, II, 8–11.

Speedie, L. Rabins, P., Pearlson, G., and McBerg, P., (1995) Confrontation naming deficit in dementia of depression. *Journal of Neuropsychiatry and Clinical Neurosciences,* 2, 59-63.

Spreen, O. and Strauss, E., (1991). *A Compendium for Neuropsychological Tests,* Oxford University Press, New York.

Squire, L., (1987). *Memory and Brain.* Oxford University Press, New York.

Squire, L.R. and Butters, N., Eds., (1992) *Neuropsychology of Memory* (2nd ed.). Guilford Press, New York.

Squire, L.R., (1992). Declarative and non-declarative memory: multiple brain systems supporting learning and memory. *Journal of Cognitive Neuroscience,* 4, 232-243.

Standards for Educational and Psychological Testing, (1985). The American Psychological Association, Washington, D.C.

Stein, R.A. and Strickland, T.L., (1998). A review of the neuropsychological effects of commonly used prescription medications. *Archives of Clinical Neuropsychology,* 13, 259-284.

Storandt, M. and Van Den Bos, G.R., Eds., (1994). *Neuropsychological Assessment of Dementia and Depression.* American Psychological Associations, Washington D.C.

Stuss, D.T. and Benson, D.F., (1986). *The frontal lobes.* Raven Press, New York.

Suchy, Y., Blint, A., and Osmon, D.C., (1997). Behavioral dyscontrol scale: criterion and predictive validity in on inpatient rehabilitation unit population. *The Clinical Neurologist,* 11, 258-265.

Sweet, J., (1983). Confounding effects of depression on neuropsychologist testing. Five illustrative cases. *Clinical Neuropsychology,* 5, 103-109.

Symonds, C.P., (1937). Mental disorder following had injury. *Proceedings of the Royal Society of Medicine,* 30, 1081-1094.

Teasdale, J.D., Howard, R.J., Cox, S.G., Ha, Y., Brammer, M.J., Williams, S. C. R., and Checkley, S.A., (1999). Functional MRI Study of the Cognitive Generation of Affect. *American Journal of Psychiatry,* 2, 209-215.

The Psychological Corporation, (1997). *Scoring Assistant for the Wechsler Scales for Adults.* San Antonio, TX.

Thacter, R.W., Cantor, D.S., McAlister, R., Geisler, F., and Krause, P., (1991). Comprehensive predictions of outcome in closed-head injured patients, in *Windows on the Brain,* Zappula, R.A., LeFever, F.F., Jaeger, J., and Bilder, R., Eds., *Annals of the New York Academy of Sciences,* New York., Vol. 620, p.82-101.

Tromp, E. and Mulder, T., (1991). Slowness of information processing after traumatic head injury. *Journal of Clinical and Experimental Neuropsychology,* 13, 821-830.

Truebold, W. and Schmidt, M., (1993). Malingering and other validity considerations in the neuropsychological evaluation of mild head injury. *Journal of Clinical and Experimental Neuropsychology,* 15, 578-590.

Tucker, D.M., (1981). Lateral brain functions, emotion and conceptualization. *Psychological Bulletin,* 89, 19-46.

Van Der Kolk, B.A., Burbride, J.A., and Suzuki, J., (1997). The psychobiology of traumatic memory: clinical implications of neuroimaging studies, in *Psychobiology and Post-traumatic Stress Disorder,* Yehuda, R. and McFarlane, A.C., *Annals of the New York Academy of Sciences,* New York, Vol. 82, 99-113.

Van Der Ploeg, R.D., Axelrod, B.N., Sherer, M., and Scott, J., (1997). Importance of demographic adjustment on neuropsychological test performance: a response to Reitan and Wolfson (1995). *Clinical Neuropsychologists,* 11, 210-217.

Van Zomeren, A.M., Brouwer, U.H., and Deelman, B.G., (1987) Attentional deficits: the riddles of selectivity, speed and alertness, in *Closed Head Injury: Psychological, Social and Family Consequences,* Brooks, N., Ed., Oxford University Press, New York, p. 74-107.

Watson, C.G., Davis, W., and Gaser, B., (1978). The separation of organics from depressives with ability and personality-based tests. *Journal of Clinical Psychology,* 34, 393-897.

Watts, F.N., (1995). Depression and anxiety, in *Handbook of Memory Disorders,* Baddeley, A.D., Wilson, B.A., and Watts, F.N., Eds., John Wiley and Sons, Chichester, U.K., p. 293-317.

Wechsler Adult Intelligence Scale — 3rd Edition, (1997).. The Psychological Corporation, San Antonio, TX

Wechsler, D., (1939). *Wechsler-Bellevue Intelligence Scale.* The Psychological Corporation, New York.

Wechsler, D., (1944). *The Measurement of Adult Intelligence* (3rd ed.). Williams and Wilkins, Baltimore, MD.

Wechsler, D., (1945). A standardized memory scale for clinical use. *The Journal of Psychology,* 19, 89-95.

Wechsler, D., (1955). *Wechsler Adult Intelligence Scale.* The Psychological Corporation, New York.

Wechsler, D., (1975). Intelligence defined and undefined: a relativistic appraisal. *American Psychologist,* 30, 135-139.

Wechsler, D., (1981). *Wechsler Adult Intelligence Scale-Revised.* The Psychological Corporation, San Antonio, TX.

Wechsler, D., (1987). *Wechsler Memory Scale-Revised.* The Psychological Corporation, San Antonio, TX.

Weinstein, G.A., and Kahn, R.L., (1955). *Denial of illness.* Charles Thomas, Springfield, IL.

Wetter, M.W., Baer, R.A., Berry, D.T.R., Smith, G.T., and Larson, L.H., (1992). Sensitivity of MMPI-2 validity scales to random responding and malingering. *Psychological Assessment,* 4, 369-374.

Yehuda, R. and McFarlane, A.C., (1995). Conflict between current knowledge about post-traumatic stress disorder and its original conceptual basis. *American Journal of Psychiatry,* 152, 1705.

Zaidel, E., Aboitiz, F., Clarke, J., Kaiser, D., and Matteson, R., (1995). Sex differences in inter-hemispheric language relations. in *Hemispheric Communication: Mechanisms and Models,* Kitterle, F., Ed., Erlbaum, Hillsdale, NJ, p. 85-175.

Zappalá, G. and Trexler, L.C., (1992). Quantitative and qualitative aspects of memory performance after minor head injury. *Archives of Clinical Neuropsychology,* 7, 145-154.

Zimmerman, R.A. and Bilaniuk, L.T., (1989). CT and MR: diagnosis and evaluation of head injury, stroke and brain tumors. *Neuropsychology,* 3, 191-230.

Zimmerman, R.A., Bilaniuk, L.T., Johnson, M.H., Hershey, B., Joffe, S., Gonori, J.M., Goldberg, H.I., and Grossman, R.I., (1986). Magnetic resonance imaging: early clinical results at 1.5 tesla. *American Journal of Neuroradiology,* 4, 587-594.

Zinner, E.S., Ball, J.D., Stutts, M.L., and Philput, C., (1997). Grief reactions of mothers and adolescents and young adults with traumatic brain injury. *Archives of Clinical Neuropsychology,* 12, 435-449.

4 The Forensic Psychological Evaluation of Traumatic Brain Injury

Joseph Yedid

CONTENTS

The forensic psychological and/or neuropsychological evaluation is an intricate, complex, and arduous clinical process. It is often subject to multidimensional biases which could overwhelm even the expert neuropsychologist, or result in a disputation during deposition or testimony. Therefore, an essential axiom in clinical neuropsychology is the expert's reliance on findings which are not spurious or subject to Type I error. The absolute necessity of abiding within strict clinical criteria is reflected in Heaton et al.'s (1991) finding that 53% of non-neurologically impaired normal subjects performed in the dysfunctional range on 10% of the WAIS-R and HRNB subtests scores. Moreover, 25% of the normal subjects performed in the dysfunctional range on 20% of the test scores. It is clear that without the accountability provided by a base rate of dysfunction, the scores of the normal subjects on cognitive or emotional tests could potentially distort the expert's opinion. The forensic expert ought to consider overt and covert biasing factors in the selection of assessment instruments and normative data utilized (Van Gorp and McMullen, 1997). In situations where normative data is not available, it is the responsibility of the forensic neuropsychologist to obtain access to this data and determine the most pertinent normative parameters. However, it is incumbent upon the forensic expert to clearly specify these facts as an integral component of the report, whether written or verbal.

The field of forensic clinical neuropsychology is fraught with various controversies, ambiguities, and unanswered dilemmas (Puente, 1991; Fuast, 1991; Wedding, 1991). Some of the problems and limitations we will consider are: contrasts between the clinical and forensic context; the base-rate problem; lack of standardized practices; problems assessing credibility or malingering; difficulties determining prior functioning; controversies regarding the integration of complex data; and inconsistent application of rigorous credentialing standards regarding clinical qualifications. Accordingly the compendium of diagnostic categories such as personality disorders, post traumatic stress disorder (PTSD), organic brain syndrome (due to traumatic brain injury (TBI) or Alzheimer's dementia), and numerous emotional conditions might confound the accuracy of the diagnostic impression (Newman, 1992).

The present chapter endeavors to provide sufficient information, clinical armamentarium, and investigation into what might confound valid and reliable forensic diagnostic conclusions. We will accomplish this goal by addressing the following in the five sections of the chapter: (1) appropriate selection of tests in cases of TBI and PTSD; (2) the differential diagnosis of organic vs. emotional disorders; (3) the conglomerate of behavioral and personality changes associated with TBI; (4) issues related to loss and grief, consequent to the various difficulties manifested by patients with TBI; and (5) the various impacts on relationships, incurred as a result of TBI.

4.1. PSYCHOLOGICAL ASSESSMENTS/TESTS IN TBI AND PTSD

The application and utilization of objective, quantifiable psychological, and/or neuropsychological instruments for the assessment of TBI and the possible corollary onset of PTSD have contributed considerably to the appraisal of compromised brain functioning. These various tests or batteries (i.e., the HRNB or Luria-Nebraska) have been useful in deriving inferences regarding the presence and degree of brain dysfunction in patients who do not simultaneously manifest psychiatric disorders. However, there is controversy in the scientific literature over whether or not those fixed batteries are flexible enough to provide the forensic expert with the ability to distinctly assess a variety of functions and dysfunctional structures (Keefe, 1995; Luria et al., 1970; Luria, 1973, 1980). Therefore, the hypothesis that stipulates specific regional brain impairments when indicated by abnormal neuropsychological findings is frequently rejected. This problem often occurs when patients with TBI have otherwise uncomplicated emotional status and a normal history. The hypothesis is even less likely to be true in the assessment of patients with chronic psychiatric disorders. Further compounding the problems in integrated neuro-assessment is the following: while neuropsychological tests often facilitate the neuropathological understanding of psychiatric disorders by enabling a comparison between the functioning of psychiatric patients and TBI patients, neuroimaging techniques frequently do not correlate with patients' subjective reporting or objective neuropsychological assessment (Keefe and Harvey, 1994). Impaired neuropsychological test performance can be found in numerous psychiatric disorders without the presence of well-substantiated, localized brain dysfunction (Hoffman, 1986). Therefore, it is deemed appropriate and indispensable to utilize valid and reliable neuropsychological assessment instruments for the comprehensive appraisal of various psychological and/or neuropsychological functions. Chapter 3, "The Neuropsychological Evaluation" (Yedid, 2000) of this volume, includes detailed information regarding the content of the evaluation process. The selection of specific tests or subtests indicated is elaborated in the following section. However, it is important to note that the particular tests or subtests recommended are not the only assessment instruments which are appropriate and relevant. Selection criteria for inclusion in the list of recommended instruments are the following: reliability, validity, easy accessibility, relative freedom from biasing factors, and small margin of the error of variance. Specific functions and recommended tests are included in Table 4.1.

The forensic expert must be familiar with other references that provide information regarding the multitude of neuropsychological instruments available for the qualified professional. These references include the names of tests and relevant data for the assessment of: achievement; attention and memory; language; visual, visuomotor, and auditory modalities; tactile, tactile-visual, and tactile-motor tasks; motor ability; and adaptive behavior and personality tests. The forensic neuropsychologist must also be able to communicate with colleagues, conduct literature searches, obtain articles, and locate the most recent clinical and research findings regarding TBI via the Internet (Kerns, Mateer, and Brosseau, 1998).

4.2 DIFFERENTIAL DIAGNOSIS OF ORGANIC vs. EMOTIONAL DISORDERS

The focus of this section is an examination of the numerous manifestations of mild to moderate TBI in relation to various other diagnostic criteria. Many articles, manuscripts, presentations (e.g., Lezak, 1995; Hartlage, 1990; Russell, Neuringer, and Goldstein, 1970), and other references indicated in this chapter address the variety of cognitive, emotional, or behavioral dysfunctions associated with TBI and specific loci of the brain. Most of these studies examine specific categories of function. However, an integrated examination of the conglomerate of potential dysfunctions that can be associated with TBI has not been implemented in a thorough and comprehensive fashion. The term proposed by the present author for this examination is the *convergent neuropsychological assessment*. It should be noted that relatively few objective and scientific studies

TABLE 4.1
Assessed Functions and Recommended Tests/Subtests

Function	Recommended Tests/Subtests	
MOTOR	Hand Dynamometer	
Gross (Dominant vs. No-dominant hand)	HRNB:	Finger Tapping
Fine		Grooved Pegboard
SENSORY-PERCEPTUAL	HRNB:	Sensory Perceptual Examination
Visual, Auditory, Tactile	HRNB:	Tactile Form Recognition
ORIENTATION	WMS III:	Information and Ofientation
ATTENDING/SPEED OF	HRNB:	Seshore Rhythm Test
INFORMATION PROCESSING	HRNB:	Speech Sound Perception
	WAIS-III:	Digit Span (Forward and Backward; Arithmetic; Symbol Search)
	WMS III:	Spatial Span (Forward and Backward)
	Digit Vigilance	
	Test:	Time; Errors
VERBAL SKILLS	Reitan-Indiana Aphasia Screening Test	
	WAIS-III:	Information; Comprehension; Similarities; Vocabulary; Boston Naming; Thurston Word Fluency Sentence Completion Test
ABSTRACTION/FLEXIBIITY OF	WAIS-III:	Matrix Reasoning; Letter-Naming Sequencing
THINKING	HRNB:	Category Test; Trails B
LEARNING AND INCIDENTAL		
MEMORY		
Immediate Verbal-Auditory	WMS-III:	Digit Span
	WMS-III:	Logical Memory I
	WMS-III:	Verbal Paired Associates I
Immediate Visual-Spatial	WMS-III:	Family Pictures; Bender Visual Motor Gestalt
Auditory-Delayed	WMS-III:	Logical Memory II
	WMS-III:	Auditory Composite Scores; Verbal Paired Associates II
Visual-Delayed	WMS-III:	Family Pictures II Spatial Span Visual Reproduction II Bender Gestalt Visual Motor Recall
Tactile-Delayed	TPT:	Memory; Location
Recognition Memory Auditory Visual	WMS-III:	Verbal Paired Associates
	WMS-III:	Family Pictures Recognition Faces II Recognition
PSYCHOMOTOR SKILLS	WAIS-III:	PictureCompletion; Block Design; Digit Symbol
	HRNB:	TPT-Time Symbol Digit Modalities Test Dominant vs. Non-dominant; Both, total Trail A

TABLE 4.1
Assessed Functions and Recommended Tests/Subtests (continued)

Function	Recommended Tests/Subtests
EMOTIONAL STATUS Overall	MMPI-II: All Scores Beck Depression Inventory-II Sentence Completion Test
Malingering	Structured Interview of Reported Symptoms
PTSD	Trauma Symptoms Inventory
SUMMARY SCORES	WAIS-III: Verbal, Performance, Full-Scale IQ WMS-III: scores General Memory, Working Memory Halstead Impairment Index Average Impairment Rating

of cognitive dysfunctions associated with TBI simultaneously assess patients' affective states. Moreover, the assessment of affective symptomatology in the majority of studies relies primarily on non-objective measurements, e.g., rating scales, questionnaires, or relatives' reports. Currently, most studies employ either structured psychological or neuropsychological examinations and well-established diagnostic indicators, or rely solely on the subjective complaints of patients or collateral sources. To summarize, the principle components of the neuropsychological evaluation's differential diagnosis are: (1) the necessity of utilizing demographic correction factors; (2) integrating the results of tests that assess emotional status with cognitive and other findings; (3) including the impact of pre-existing and co-existing medical complications; and (4) utilizing more than one instrument for the assessment of specific functions to ensure the reliability, validity, and consistency of the diagnostic impression.

It seems pertinent to also list some of the potentially confounding variables that might, if not taken into consideration, have a direct, biasing impact on the forensic expert's diagnostic classification: (1) peripheral nervous system dysfunctions vs. central nervous system dysfunctions; (2) patient's native language, if other than English; (3) cross-cultural considerations; (4) fatigue or inconsistent physical endurance; and (5) PTSD or pre-existing personality disorders. The significance of some these factors has evoked arguments in the scientific literature (Youngjohn, Spector, and Mapon, 1998; Binder, 1997; Klein, 1996, 1998; Novak, Daniel, and Long, 1984; Youngjohn, Burrows, and Eroal, 1995). Particularly when the conglomeration of data compiled reveals a pattern of discrepancies, prudent utilization of the differential diagnosis process is essential. This comprehensive process ought to include the objective appraisal of various other functional/emotional diagnoses: (1) hypochondriasis or malingering; (2) conversion hysteria, somatoform, or dissociative disorder; and (3) factitious disorder. The forensic expert should always consider the possibility that any one of the functional/emotional disorders is a co-existing condition, superimposed on the presence of TBI (Cullum, Heaton and Grant, 1991; Putnam and Mills, 1994). Appropriate utilization of the convergent neuropsychological assessment (CVNA) provides critical data for the formulation of the differential diagnosis. This assessment approach consists of numerous ethical and clinical guidelines for the forensic expert. It also includes variables discussed in the following sections.

4.2.1 ESTIMATION OF THE PATIENT'S PRE-MORBID IQ AND COGNITIVE ABILITY

Conceptual and empirical data with a solid face validity for establishing putative, pre-morbid cognitive status is difficult to obtain. However, several measures have been deemed acceptable and include: (1) post injury residual skill levels; (2) predictions based on the residuum of various skills; (3) estimates predicated on residual functional abilities which are presumably resistant to TBI; and (4) cognitive capacities which are highly correlated with pre-morbid occupational background, avocational pursuits, and academic performance (Hartlage, 1997; Reynolds, 1997; Blair and Spreen, 1989; Black, 1974; Barona, Reynolds, and Chastain, 1984; Goldstein, Gary, and Levin, 1986; Wilson et al., 1978; Yates, 1956; Crawford, 1989; Franzen, Burgess, and Smith-Seemiller, 1997; Kaufman, Reynolds, and McLean, 1989).

More specific guidelines for accomplishing this complex task are based on the following indicators: percentile ranks on achievement tests at several grade levels, when available as part of the school records; performance on old, acquired academic skill measures, when conspicuously higher than present measurement of IQ level; and utilization of word knowledge, such as the Vocabulary Subtest of the WAIS-III, or the Shipley Institute of Living Scale and WRAT-R. While the Vocabulary subtest of any version of the WAIS (e.g., WAIS, WAIS-R, WAIS-III) is usually the best indicator of pre-morbid cognitive ability, patients with TBI might exhibit impaired word-finding due to neuropsychological dysfunctions. Additional complicating factors in this assessment can be: the presentation of exaggerated difficulty by patients seeking compensation; certain medications which interfere with word-finding; and the impact of any therapeutic intervention, e.g., speech therapy. Therefore, devising the most valid and reliable estimate of pre-morbid ability entails the following: (1) quantitative results of well standardized IQ tests or PSAT, SAT, and ACT scores administered prior to the TBI; (2) an IQ result obtained from an intelligence test administered to a monozygotic twin; and (3) estimates based on demographic variables, such as educational level, ethnicity, urban-rural habitation, and socioeconomic status. Reynolds (1997) opined that combination of current demographic data with pre-morbid obtained Wechsler subtest scores with high g-loadings (Vocabulary and Block Design), Verbal IQ (VIQ) or Performance IQ (PIQ), is the most superior approach. Indeed, a relatively recent study (Crawford and Allan, 1997) found that in a sample of 200 healthy adults representative of the United Kingdom population in terms of age, gender, and occupational classification, occupation was the best predictor of IQ for all three WAIS-R scales (VIQ, PIQ, and FSIQ). Age and years of education significantly increased the variance predicted. Together, these three variables accounted for 53%, 53%, and 32% of the variance of FSIQ, VIQ, and PIQ, respectively. The ability to predict PIQ was quite inferior to that achieved for FSIQ and VIQ (Crawford and Allan, 1997). This difficulty becomes more pronounced when estimating pre-morbid intelligence in the elderly, since they are more vulnerable to various neurological processes and/or dementias (Evans et al., 1989). Methods for estimating pre-morbid cognitive functioning have utilized deterioration indices, vocabulary and/or reading test scores, and demographic-based regression equations. Unfortunately, knowledge about the applicability of these formulas to very old patients (i.e., 75 years and older) is relatively limited. This problem is exacerbated by the fact that there is a high prevalence of dementia among individuals who are 75 years or older. There is a high correlation between the patient's cognitive status and the certain measurements of intelligence. The utility of two methods for estimating pre-morbid WAIS-R IQ (Barona, Reynolds, and Chastain, 1984; Barona and Chastain, 1986) were compared in a sample of normal elderly and a sample of neurologically impaired patients. For the normal subjects, the percent of obtained IQs that was in the range of one standard error of estimate of the formula-estimated IQs, demonstrated sufficient agreement of both methods for the FSIQ. However, a markedly lower accuracy was found for the PIQ. The VIQ was adequately predicted by the utilization of the 1984 method proposed by Barona et al. Yet, both estimation procedures overestimated the obtained IQs of patients with TBI. Therefore, three cautionary guidelines are noted by the studies mentioned above (Paolo and Ryan, 1992; Barona, Reynolds, and Chastain, 1984; Barona and Chastain, 1986): (1) the equations proposed are most useful for the prediction of WAIS-R FSIQ, but were not studied for the WAIS-III; (2) use of regression procedures for estimating pre-morbid intellectual functioning in the elderly should not be used in isolation; and (3) these procedures ought to be utilized in conjunction with other background information (education and occupation) and in combination with predicting memory functions.

4.2.2 THE APPROPRIATE UTILIZATION OF DEMOGRAPHIC VARIABLES IN ORDER TO INCREASE DIAGNOSTIC ACCURACY

Various demographic variables (e.g., age, sex, education, race, and litigation status) have been proved valid and significant in the context of the differential diagnosis of TBI (Heaton et al., 1991; Bowman, 1996; Karzmark, 1992; Uchiyama, Mitrushina, Satz and Schall, 1996). However, there is some controversy in the literature regarding this issue; some examples of opposing opinions can be found in the works of Reitan and Wolfson (1995), Russell, Neuringer, and Goldstein (1970), and Moses, Pritchard, and Adams (1999).

There is a significant association between educational level and performance on psychological and neuropsychological tests. The acquisition of formal education impacts a critical variable which significantly correlates with the scores obtained on standardized tests of intellectual function. An early study found that the correlation coefficients varied from 0.57 to 0.75 (Matarazzo, 1979). Noteworthy is that correlation with verbal intellectual subtests are customarily higher than correlation with performance intelligence subtests (0.66 to 0.75 vs. 0.57 to 0.61, respectively). Thus, the assessment of quantifiable cognitive/intellectual functions is significantly prejudiced by the educational background. Accordingly, the level of educational attainment (defined by number of years of formal schooling) was proven to have significant association with performance on neuropsychological tests (Ardilla, Rosselli, and Ostroski, 1992; Bornstein and Suga, 1988; Heaton et al., 1986; Rosselli, Ardilla, and Rosas, 1990). This spectrum of functions and abilities includes: motor skills, constructional and calculation abilities, language, memory, and problem solving. Without inclusion of educational variables, the expert might reach erroneous conclusions regarding impaired brain functioning. This was demonstrated when neuropsychological test performance in illiterate subjects was investigated by analyzing the effects of education across different age ranges. The impact of school attendance on neuropsychological test performance was appraised by comparing a group of 64 illiterate normal subjects with two marginally schooled control groups (1–2 and 3–4 years of schooling). The participating subjects' ages ranged from 16–85 years. In the second analysis the illiterate subjects were further matched by age and sex with individuals with 1-4, 5–9, and 10–19 years of formal education. The effect of educational background was significant on most of the tests. Interestingly, the most prominent educational effect was apparent when constructional abilities (i.e., copying a figure), language (comprehension), phonological verbal fluency, and concept formation (sequencing, calculation, and abstraction abilities) were assessed. The effect of aging was noted in visuoperceptual and memory functions. The researchers (Ostrosky-Solis et al., 1998) deduced that despite such limited educational range (from 0–4 years of formal education), and such a wide age range (from 16–85 years), schooling represented a stronger variable than age. The forensic expert must note that the study by Ostroski-Solis et al. (1998), was performed outside of the U.S. Therefore, a similar study should be performed with English speaking, American subjects prior to accepting this construct for a non-Mexican population. The effects of demographic, medical, and psychological variables on neuropsychological performance in normal geriatric subjects was studied by Uchiyama et al. (1996). The researchers postulated that these effects could be subclassified as direct and indirect in their study of 156 geriatric subjects. Uchiyama et al., concluded that the influence of demographic variables on neuropsychological functioning for geriatric subjects is complex and some variables should not be interpreted independently of each other, due to their significant interaction effects.

The impact of demographic variables becomes more pronounced when variance in clinical classification of raw test scores across normative data sets is examined. The forensic neuropsychologist's selection of normative data clusters for the interpretation of raw test data must be the most population-specific. Adherence to this suggestion will improve the interpretive validity of tests administered to an individual or group. (Axelrod and Goldman, 1996; FrommAusch and Yeudall, 1983; Butler, Retzlaff, and Van Der Ploeg, 1991; Selnes et al., 1991). The degree to which categorization of specific scores may be swayed by differences across various data sets was studied by applying published normative data to a group of fictitious patients (Kalechstein, van Gorp, and Rapport, 1998). Nine different tests (Trail Making Test A and B; Stroop, Color, Wood and Interference; Controlled Oral Word Association; Boston Naming; and Finger Tapping) were selected. The sample included 12 fictitious patients in 3 age groups (young adult, middle-aged, and older adults), who were counterbalanced across gender. Kalechstein et al. (1998) classified the percentile rankings into seven categories (Very Superior, Superior, High Average, Average, Low Average, Borderline-Impaired, or Impaired) on the basis of percentile ratings. The results revealed significant variability in score classification as a function of the specific normative data set utilized to interpret the raw test data. The demographic characteristics associated with the greatest variability across normative data sets were age and gender. Kalechstein et al. (1998) reported that interpretation of a single raw score spanned up to four clinical classifications, depending on which normative data set was used. Important to note is that the variance in the classification of test scores appeared greater for men than for women and greater for younger vs. older patients. Therefore, as indicated by Kalechstein et al. (1998) regardless of whether criterion norms would be based on a local, national, or statistical level, corrections for population-specific moderating variables should be cautiously implemented for each test. Thus, criterion normative data sets would preferably utilize weighted regression to adjust for the impact of a moderator variable rather than stratifying samples.

However, a recent study raised doubts regarding the adequacy of the demographic correction factors proposed by Heaton et al. (1991). Moses, Pritchard, and Adams (1999) reported that only 10% of the variance in standard score profiles were predictable by considering the patients' age and education. They also found that the overall level of the profile decreased with age, while education increased the relative scores on the aphasia test. Their main finding, however, was that when the standard scores were converted to age and education corrected T-scores, less than 1% of the variance could be predicted by age and education. Noteworthy is the fact that Heaton et al. (1991) also included gender as one of the significant demographic correction factors. Yet Moses et al. (1999) did not specify the inclusion of gender in their comparative research.

4.2.3 Verification of Pre-Existing and Co-Existing Medical Conditions

An essential, integral component of the differential diagnosis in the forensic neuropsychological evaluation is the review of pre-existing and co-existing medical conditions. It is equally important to consider the various categories of medications that are often prescribed by physicians with different arenas of expertise (neurology, physiatry, internal medicine, endocrinology, nephrology, or chronic pain) as a component of the comprehensive intervention regime. Due to the complexity of acute and/or chronic medical complications, only a sample of the various ailments are included in the present section. It is the responsibility of the forensic neuropsychologist to obtain a comprehensive set of medical records on each patient, to thoroughly review this information, and to consider the opinions of the medical experts involved in the evaluation (Hartman, 1995; Adams and Victor, 1989; Bernstein, 1988; Julien, 1995; Gelenberg, Bassuck, and Schoonover, 1991; Deptula, Singh, and Ponara, 1993; Penry, 1991; Kraus, 1995). Tables 4.2 and 4.3 represent partial lists of symptoms and behaviors that might be associated with TBI, and examples of the associations between medical conditions and these various symptoms and behaviors. The information in Table 4.2 is divided into four categories: physiological, emotional, cognitive, and active behavioral. Although a total of 36 indicators are included in Table 4.2, the possibility of other correlations must be considered.

The information contained in Table 4.3 includes numerous medical complications and the functions that are associated with these complications. A review of this information reveals a significant pattern. The medical conditions associated with the largest number of cognitive, emotional, and/or behavioral impairments or

TABLE 4.2
Classification of Dysfunctions and Impairments by Category

Physiological	Emotional	Behavioral/Active	Cognitive
Appetite	Apprehension	Agitation	Abstraction
Cardiac Palpitations	Anhedonia	Altered Personality	Confusion
Dizziness	Anxiety (Generalized)	Disinhibition Of Affect	Concentration/Attention
Fatigue	Depression		Deja-vue
Libido	Dysphoria	Poor Impulse Control	Delusion
Muscular	Fear	Violence	Hallucinations
Perspiration	Flat Affect		Incoherence
Respiration	Irritability		Deja-vue/Jamais-vue
Pain (Non Specific)	Poor Self Esteem		Learning
Startle Response	Poor Interpersonal Interaction		Memory: Immediate
Sexual	Suicidal Ideation		Memory: Short-term
Sleep	Psychomotor Retardation		Memory: Long-term
	Feelings Of Worthlessness		Perseveration
			Dysnomia
			Sensory-perceptual
			Dysarthria
12	13	5	16

dysfunctions are endocrinological or cardiovascular. Since these medical conditions may be either pre-existing or co-existing, the information detailed in Table 4.3 provides substantial support for the necessity to carefully verify the possibility of any non-injury-related conditions.

Additionally, consideration given to the medical dysfunctions and/or impairments mentioned previously could be misleading if the forensic expert does not factor medications used by a patient into the differential diagnosis process. For example, the majority of patients with TBI are prophylactically treated with anticonvalescent medications (Sbordone, 1991). Moreover, some of these patients are simultaneously treated with psychotropic medications for the alleviation of physiological symptoms (e.g., impaired sleep), as well as apprehension, dysphoria, irritability, or agitation. Furthermore, a smaller number of these patients are temporarily or permanently receiving other medications that are not psychotropic agents. Hence, the forensic expert is encouraged to review a recent publication regarding the neuropsychological effects of anti-depressants, anxiolytics, stimulants, seizure-controls, antihistamines, and hypertension medications (Stein and Strickland, 1998). The following are examples of the effects reviewed by Stein et al. (1998): (1) anticholinergic effects induced by anti-depressants resulting in impaired memory; (2) adverse dose-response effects on motor speed and motor pursuit while improving attention, secondary to intake of Imipramine; (3) impaired acquisition of new information during exposure to benzodiazepine, in addition to psychomotor and memory dysfunctions; (4) beneficial effects on memory and vigilance due to various stimulants; (5) significant psychomotor slowing, decreased attention /concentration, and general cognitive functioning accompanying anti-seizure agents; and (6) potent retarding effects on psychomotor, attentional, and to a lesser degree, memory performance, due to antihistamine intake. The various effects reported by Stein and Strickland (1998) involve the cardinal issues of anticholinergic and sedative impacts on neuropsychological functions. It is of utmost importance to note that impaired

TABLE 4.3
Examples of the Association Between Impairments, Dysfunctions, and Various Medical Conditions

Symptoms and Behaviors	Medical Conditions
Abstraction	Hyperadrenalism
Agitation	Hyperadrenalism (Cushing's Syndrome)
Altered Personality	Porphyria; Pernicious Anemia; Hyperthyroidism
Anhedonia	Hyperthyroidism; Adrenal Cortical Insufficiency
Anxiety	Hypoglycemia; Porphyria; Menopause
Appetite	Hypothyroidism; Pancreatic Carcinoma, Rheumatoid Arthritis
Cardiac Palpitations	Hypertension
Concentration/attention	Systemic Lupus Erythematosis
Confusion	Hypothyroidism; Systemic Lupus Erythematosis
Delusions	Hypothyroidism; System Lupus Erythematosis
Depression	Temporal Lobe Epilepsy; Hepatitis; Pernicious Anemia; Hyperadrenalism; Diabetes
Disinhibition Of Affect	XYY Syndrome
Dizziness	Menier's Syndrome
Dysarthria	Hypothyroidism
Fatigue	Hypoglycemia; Menopause; Hyperadrenalism; Asthma
Fear	Postpartum Complications; Male Hypoandrogen Secretion
Feelings Of Worthlessness	Cardiovascular Disease; Hyperadrenalism; Postpartum Complications
Flat Affect	Hyperthyroidism; Hypoglycemia; Cardiac Disease
Hallucination	Hypothyroidism; Metabolic Failure
Incoherence	Metabolic Failure; Vascular Disease
Irritability	Adrenam Cortical Dysfunction; Rheumatoid Arthritis
Learning	Seizure Disorder, Intractable; Cardiovascular
Libido	Hyperthyroidism
Memory	Cardiovascular; Hypothyroidism; Pernicious Anemia
Muscular Trembling	Pernicious Anemia; Hypoglycemia; Menopause
Pain Non-specific	Hypothyroidism; Pernicious Anemia
Perseveration	Adrenal Cortical Insufficiency
Perspiration	Hypoglycemia; Menopause; Hyperadrenalism; Asthma
Poor Impulse Control	Systemic Lupus Erythematosis
Poor Inter Personal	XYY Syndrome
Psychomotor Retardation	Adrenal Cortical Insufficiency
Respiration	Chronic Obstructive Pulmonary Disease And Other Bronchial Dysfunctions
Sensory/perceptual	Menier's Syndrome; Glaucoma; Peripheral Neuropathy
Sexual (Physical) Problems	Male Hypoandrogen Secretion; Systemic Lupus
Startle B	Systemic Lupus Erythematosis
Suicidal Ideation	Hyperadrenalism
Violence	XYY Syndrome; Severe Drug Intoxication

memory effects persist after the cessation of anti-cholinergic intake. However, visuospatial skills, language, and to a lesser extent, executive functioning, are more resilient to the effects of most drugs, primarily when psychomotor and timed assessments of these functions are of minimal importance. Thus, the forensic expert must be continuously cognizant of the various potentially confounding vectors in the process of the differential diagnosis.

4.2.4 INDIVIDUAL DIFFERENCES IN LATERALIZATION OF FUNCTIONS

A great compendium of research projects, journal articles, and monographs has addressed structural and functional differentiation of the right and left hemispheres of the healthy human brain. Moreover, the study of lateralized dysfunctions secondary to compromised brain structures has given impetus to numerous projects regarding the unique functional attributes of either unilateral or bilateral impairments. Focal lesions of right or left hemispheres have contributed to better understanding the functions uniquely attributed to either prefrontal, frontal, temporal, parietal, or occipital lobes of either hemisphere. Some of the more esoteric studies have investigated specific associations between or among cortical and sub-cortical structures, or have hypothesized additional connections between or among any of the divisions of the human brain (Geschwind and Galaburda, 1987; Boll and Bryant, 1988; Hellige, 1995; Boles, 1992; Hellige et al., 1994). The consequences of disconnection between the two hemispheres was also studied extensively (Geschwind, 1965, 1970, 1985; Hellige 1993; Potter and Graves, 1988). However, in the context of lateralization of function, the significance of handedness has generated relatively little research regarding correlation with cognitive and/or emotional functions (Zaidel et al., 1995; Oldfield, 1971). The issue of individual differences in lateralization of function becomes more complex when the effects of gender and handedness are operating simultaneously (Eviatar, Hellige, and Zaidel, 1997). Indeed, when male and female left and right handers participated in experiments designed to investigate cognitive performance in lateralized tasks, an intriguing variation was found. Eviatar, Hellige, and Zaidel (1997) provided data regarding quantitative differences in hemispheric abilities; furthermore, qualitative discrepancies in hemispheric strategies indicated that left-handers have a smaller performance asymmetry than right handers and that both groups have the same proportion of increased accuracy when stimuli were presented bilaterally. Handedness affected the qualitative measures of male functioning, but not of female functioning. However, when the nominal and physical letter-matching tasks with bilateral presentation measured the flexibility of callosal function, the results indicated that left handers have less flexible interhemispheric communication when compared to right handers, without any significant gender effect. Left-handers tended to have a higher level of arousal of the right hemisphere, albeit the distribution of right handers' arousal was centered around 0 (zero) arousal bias. Eviatar, Hellige, and Zaidal's (1997) results demonstrated that handedness affected the three precincts (hemispheric abilities, callosal flexibility, and arousal asymmetry), while gender was significant only in the context of handedness. These recent findings should be integrated with prior theoretical and research findings regarding the hemispheric specialization of the human brain in normal subjects or patients with TBI. The forensic neuropsychologist should integrate the findings indicated above into the differential diagnosis of neuropsychological status.

4.2.5 INCLUSION OF ATTENTIONAL FACTORS FOR INSURING ACCURATE ASSESSMENT OF TBI

The most common cognitive dysfunctions associated with TBI are marked declines in attention and memory. The vast majority of studies regarding impaired memory functions as an outcome of TBI focused on the presence of either short-term and delayed-recall dysfunction or post-traumatic amnesia (PTA). However, it is equally crucial to fully consider attentional processes. Due to the consistent manifestation of both impaired memory capacity and dysfunctional attention, the forensic neuropsychologist is obligated to assess these cognitive operations as an integral component of the differential diagnosis essential for the accurate appraisal of mild, moderate, or severe TBI (Pribram and McGuinness, 1975; Parasuramen, Mutter, and Malley, 1991; Van Zomeren, Brouwer, and Deelman, 1984; Melamed et al., 1985; Posner and Rafal, 1987). However, the various constructs of attention (i.e., arousal/alertness, selective attention, and alternating attention) merit specific consideration. The interested expert is advised to review the publication edited by Boll and Bryant (1988) for more detailed information, in addition to the literature review by Nieman, Ruff and Kramer (1996). These publications propose that the construct of attention includes four sub-categories: focusing, sustaining, shifting, and encoding. These subcategories refer to: selecting target information from a stimulus field; maintaining attentional focus over time; flexibility and change of attentional direction; and utilization of mnemonic techniques in immediate retention. Since emotional factors, such as depression or anxiety, often contribute to any variation in attention or memory, sufficient attention to and integration of emotional variables ought to be an essential part of the forensic evaluation.

The structural/anatomical components of the brain associated with specific attentional constructs were proposed by Mesulam (1985). The associations among the reticular formation, thalamus, limbic system, hypothalamus, and cerebral cortices were postulated as responsible for: arousal, focusing, sustaining, and shifting, respectively. Since temporal and frontal, cortical and sub-cortical structures are predominantly affected by TBI (Levin et al., 1992), it can be difficult to differentiate which structure is responsible for the impaired function. Fatigue, distractibility, and decreased vigilance also result in impaired alertness, sustained and/or selective attention by most patients with TBI; however, focused attention is seldom impaired.

Another confounding effect of TBI is slowed information processing, usually compounded by dysphoric mood associated with related depression. The cognitive functions of analysis, storage, retrieval, and manipulation of information are utilized simultaneously or sequentially for the goal of problem solving. All of those components of central information processing become vulnerable when TBI is incurred. Slowed information processing is indicated by longer reaction times and decline of performance in time-limited tasks (Brouwer and Van Wolffelaar, 1985; Tromp and Mulder, 1991). It was proposed that a substantial causative factor in slowed information processing involves a dysfunction in the activation of information stored in memory. Tromp and Mulder (1991) attributed this problem to a reduced redundancy of the memory representations. Indeed, the results of the study indicated that novelty, not complexity, was a discriminating task variable in mental slowness after TBI. This finding suggests that the fundamental memory dysfunction involves the general operation of memory activation, rather than a specific stage of processing, like motor preparation or perception. Tromp and Mulder (1991) concluded that a critical problem for TBI patients is the delayed retrieval of information stored in memory due to abated redundancy of memory representations. The behavioral measurement of reaction time included in Tromp and Mulder's (1991) study presumably reflects either information processing speed or attentional capacity. To elucidate this discrepancy, the behavioral reaction time (RT) and the within-subject variability of RT were examined as they pertain to electro-physiological measures of information processing and attention. Segalowitz, Dywan, and Unsal (1997) included the P300 latency component of the evoked potential as a reflection of stimulus evaluation time, P300 amplitude as an assessment of attentional allocation, and the pre-response component of the contingent negative variation (CNV), which represents the sustained attention. The variability and latency in behavioral RT of patients with TBI were not correlated with the latency or variability of the P300, indicating that stimulus evaluation time is not a major contributor to RT and its variability in the paradigm utilized by Segalowitz, Dywan, and Unsal (1997). However, among normal controls, RT was related to P300 amplitude, and thereupon to attentional allocation (which is a reflection of selective attention, associated with event or stimulus meaningfulness). For the TBI patients, the variability, not the rapidity of RT was related to P300 amplitude and the pre-response component of the CNV. These findings provide a helpful technique in the differential diagnosis between the patients with sincere TBI and those who are malingerers, feigning, or presenting with conversation reaction. Moreover, since depression is often associated with slowed thinking, the utilization of Segalowitz, Dywan, and Unsal's (1997) paradigm provides a further resource for the process of the differential diagnosis.

A more refined approach for the differentiation among the diagnoses of dementia, mild TBI, multiple sclerosis, and learning disability was found when the Auditory Selective Attention Test (ASAT) was utilized. The continuous performance test paradigm was implemented with the selective-set construct as the conceptual basis (Armstrong, 1997). A significant age-effect was found in subjects over the age of 60. Impairment in discrimination (omission errors), but not response bias, indicated that the ASAT requires cognitive search as defined by selective-set theory. Indeed, individuals older than 60 years of age had lower discrimination rates than the younger subjects, and omission was the most common error type. Worth mentioning is the fact that discrimination and omission rates differentiated the three neurological groups. The primary error of the neurological patients was their failure to identify targets following probability foils. Normal subjects between the ages of 10 and 60 did not make errors in responding to the foils for stimulus features. The false alarm rate was found in 38% of older individuals, but was not significantly higher than that of the other groups. Among the neurological groups, only the patients with dementia had an elevated rate of commission errors. However, TBI patients manifested a selective but not sustained attention impairment. Armstrong (1997) deduced that the total error and probability error were most effective in classifying neurological and control subjects.

A recent study attempted to assess the continuous performance test (CPT) functioning of 60 adults with attention-deficit-hyperactivity disorder (ADHD) when compared with normal subjects. Adults with current ADHD symptoms (according to DSM-IV criteria) were found to make more errors of omission and commission than did normal adults. Patients with ADHD were less sensitive to stimulus features than were normal patients. A marginally significant result suggested decreased RTs in adults with ADHD was in accord with the impulsivity characteristic of ADHD. Therefore, adults with ADHD are quick to respond to stimuli without sufficient consideration provided to the validity of the stimuli presented. In contrast to patients with dementia, ADHD patients respond impulsively due to their decreased ability to make sustained accurate stimulus discrimination secondary to poor attentional styles. This finding is in accord with Armstrong's (1997) conclusion that TBI patients showed impaired selective attention, but not impaired sustained attention. This distinction is probably due to the fact that TBI is most often characterized with cortical or sub-cortical frontal and temporal dysfunction, while ADHD is more likely due to brain stem impairment.

The study of attentional factors in the context of the differential diagnosis of TBI requires at least one additional piece of information. The significance of neuropsychological tests in discriminating between ADHD and depression is quite relevant when the potential presence of TBI is raised. Indeed, a comparison between adults with depression and with ADHD on several cognitive tests of attention and memory yielded interesting results. Both the ADHD and depression groups were subdivided with regard to co-morbid depression in the ADHD group and developmental learning disorder in both groups (Katz et al., 1998). The differential diagnosis process was even more challenging because of a multiplicity of inter-related diagnostic elements. Individuals with depression frequently manifest symptoms which are analogous to those presented as a result of ADHD or TBI. Those symptoms include: low level of arousal, decreased physical endurance, mood swings, inability to concentrate, impaired sustained attention, short-term memory dysfunctions, and psychomotor agitation. However, neuropsychological assessments of depression have discerned that memory problems are not the prominent manifestation of ADHD and poor performance on attention and memory tasks when sustained attention is called for (Watts, 1995). The test battery included the California Verbal Learning Test (CVLT); Paced Auditory Serial Addition (PASAT); Stroop; Speech Perception, Seashore Rhythm, Finger Tip Number Writing, Trail Making and TPT from the HRNB; WAIS-R; WMS-R; and the Conners Continuous Performance Tests, respectively. However, the only variables passing the default tolerance test included the PASAT, short and long delayed free recall from the CVLT, and the Color Naming and Interference from the Stroop Test. Most of the patients with ADHD were correctly classified when the discriminant function analysis was performed. However, 60% of the depressed patients were mis-classified into the ADHD group. Of the 30 cases with both ADHD and depression, 80% were classified as ADHD and 20% were classified as depressed. Hence, when depression and ADHD co-exist, the tests included in the discriminant function analysis most efficiently classified patients into the ADHD group. The variables entered did discriminate between pure ADHD and depressed patients with 82% accuracy, primarily accounted for by correct classification of the ADHD patients. The group with ADHD and depression was mainly classified into the ADHD group, consistent with the pattern found for the pure ADHD and depression cases. Katz et al. (1998) concluded that depression does not seem to mask ADHD based on neuropsychological determinants, and patients diagnosed with both ADHD and depression were not different from patients diagnosed with the ADHD alone. Although Katz et al. (1998) provided significant data in their study, they did not utilize any of the quantitative testing instruments for the appraisal of the severity of the depression, such as the BDI or the MMPI-II.

When attentional dysfunctions are manifested by TBI patients, Nieman et al.'s (1991) classification seems pertinent. They proposed the following: (1) patients with an overall decreased level of arousal due to brain stem lesions; and (2) patients with attentional deficits that result in impaired planning, divided into two sub-groups: (a) those with impaired initiative due to dorso-lateral frontal lesions and associated sub-cortical structures, who are slow but accurate, and (b) patients with impaired inhibition, due to orbitofrontal and associated sub-cortical structures, who are impulsive and over-inclusive in their functioning. In summary, attentional dysfunctions manifested by TBI patients are secondary to impairments in strategic organizational planning, self-monitoring and utilization of self-monitoring, and feedback.

4.2.6 DEPRESSION IN PATIENTS WITH ACUTE TBI

The neuropsychological correlates of depression constitute a potentially perplexing facet of the differential diagnosis when TBI is assessed. There are several confounding aspects of depression which are either related to the conceptual framework of brain-behavior correlation or to co-existing factors. The presence of cognitive deficits associated with depression was indicated in the previous sections of this chapter. However, the etiological factors can become obstacles when cause–effect distinctions factor into the forensic neuropsychological assessment. Indeed, early studies of TBI propounded controversial opinions. They either concluded that depression could: (1) result in decreased efficiency of the patient's performance on neuropsychological tests (Sweet, 1983); (2) be misperceived as TBI (Watson, Davis, and Gaser, 1978); or (3) suggest compromised brain functioning (Tucker, 1981).

The presence of cognitive dysfunctions in patients who suffer from depressive disorder was explained by two theoretical constructs. The first hypothesis relied on neuropsychological dysfunction due to neurological impairment of the right hemisphere. The second hypothetical proposition relied on the explanation that cognitive impairments manifested by depressed patients are due to abated motivation, which is usually a manifestation of depressive states (Beck, 1967). Consequently, neuropsychological dysfunctions are explained as an outcome of functional impairment, i.e., lowered motivation, rather than solely a right-hemisphere dysfunction.

The motivational effects on neuropsychological functioning were studied by comparing depressed vs. non-depressed individuals (Richards and Ruff, 1989). The extent of the effect of motivation on neuropsychological test performance of depressed patients and the degree to which their performance can be attributed to right-hemisphere impairment were studied. Richards and Ruff (1989) assessed the neuropsychological functioning of depressed patients and normal volunteers who were examined by the Beck Depression Inventory (BDI) and were determined to be relatively free of depressive symptoms (all had a score of 9 or less on the BDI). The functions appraised were those of memory, learning, and attention in the visuospatial and verbal-auditory modalities in addition to a brief assessment of motivational status. The main finding reported by Richards and Ruff (1989) was that the patients in the depressed group showed impairments of visuospatial short-term memory and learning in addition to verbal-auditory learning. Yet, the effects of motivation on neuropsychological tests' performance were minuscule. Hence, the results of the study by Richards and Ruff did not provide supportive evidence to the hypothesis that the motivational deficit of depressed patients detrimentally affected performance on cognitive tests. Indeed, while depressed patients evidenced decreased motivation, they did not manifest significantly different performance on neuropsychological tests when compared with the non-motivated group. Therefore, depression is a potentially confounding variable in neuropsychological assessment. Accordingly, the forensic neuropsychologist must exercise prudent consideration when depression is a possibility, if visuospatial impairments are observed, as proposed by early hypotheses (Flor-Henry, 1979, 1983; Taylor and Abrams, 1983). It would be sensible to include a quantifiable assessment of depression as an integral component of the forensic neuropsychological examination.

The presence of depression in patients with acute TBI was not studied to the same extent as the presence of cognitive dysfunctions. However, a comparative study regarding the severity of depression in patients who suffered from strokes and patients with TBI had a significant bearing on the issue of differential diagnosis. Although patients with stroke were more severely depressed than patients with TBI, the discrepancy in severity of depressive symptoms was initially explained primarily by differences in CAT-scanned visualized lesions in the left hemisphere. Moreover, in both stroke and TBI patients there was a significant correlation between proximity of the largest lesion to the left frontal pole and severity of depression (Robinson and Szetta, 1981). A more refined study re-investigated the presence of depressive disorder in patients with TBI by means of quantifiable interviews. These interviews were: a semi-structured psychiatric interview (i.e., Present State Examination); Hamilton Rating Scale for Depression; Mini-Mental State; Johns Hopkins' Functioning Inventory; Social Functioning Exam; and Social Ties Checklist. Out of the 64 patients interviewed, 17 met the DSM-III criteria for major depression and 47 had no diagnosis of mood disorder. There was significantly greater frequency of a previous history of psychiatric disorder in the group with major depression; however, this was then controlled by the exclusion of patients with a history of alcohol or other substance abuse. Nevertheless, two other patients with TBI were diagnosed with dysthymic disorder. The presence of left dorsolateral frontal lesions and/or left basal ganglia lesions, following TBI, and to a lesser extent, parietal-occipital and right hemisphere lesions, was associated with an increased probability of developing major depression (Fedoroff et al., 1992).

The studies reviewed above promulgate a dichotomous approach that views cognitive impairment as either organic or non-organic. However, the forensic neuropsychologist must also consider the significance of degenerative dementia of the Alzheimer's type (DAT). This clinical variable is a cardinal factor in the assessment of TBI, since depressive dementia tends to be dichotomized on the basis of irreversibility vs. reversibility, structural vs. functional, or organic vs. non-organic etiology. This perception was expanded by a relatively recent proposal to view depression, cognitive impairment, and degenerative dementia as interrelated continua. Emery and Oxman (1992) suggested five prototypical groups along those continua: (1) major depression without depressive dementia; (2) depressive dementia; (3) degenerative dementia without depression; (4) depression of degenerative dementia; and (5) independent co-occurrence of degenerative dementia and depression.

A relatively large number of studies regarding the neuropsychology of depression exists, but less data is available about the neuropsychology of depressive dementia. This problem is probably related to insufficient assessment of the severity of dementia. Nevertheless, studies of cognitive function that compare depressive dementia with both primary degenerative dementia and major depression revealed more significant differences between major depression and depressive dementia than between depressive dementia and primary degenerative disease (Speedie et al., 1978). The following cognitive functions illustrate the trend mentioned previously: free recall, delayed recall, and verbal delayed memory. However, the following functions were not affected: tests of delayed visual memory; language measures of repetition; confrontation naming; auditory word recognition; sequential commands; complex syntax; or reading comments. Noteworthy is that when abstract reasoning was assessed, patients with depressive dementia scored significantly lower than depressed patients without depressive dementia. Therefore, cognitive impairments observed in depressive disorder during late life is real, not pseudo or simulated. Depression and dementia may include a common patho-physiology but do not have a causative relationship.

4.2.7 THE INTERACTION OF NORMAL AGING, DEPRESSION, DEMENTIA, AND TBI

Prevailing knowledge regards the decline in cognitive and emotional functions as a part of normal aging, not pathological process. This decline corresponds with decreases in various physiological operations. Therefore, the guideline for obtaining the differential diagnosis among normal aging, dementia, depression, and TBI should include a general evaluation of common age-related changes. (American Psychological Association, 1994).

The most significant means for achieving this complex differentiation within the context of the forensic evaluation are the considerations for demographic correction-factors, as well as pre-morbid medical, emotional, and intra-personal conditions. Interestingly, the normative data recommended for most neuropsychological tests do not exceed the ages of 85 to 88 years. Moreover, the recommended criterion scores for inclusion in the impaired range often misclassify a significant proportion of healthy, cognitively normal elderly subjects (Hall et al., 1996; Paolo, Troster, and Ryan, 1998; Larrabee and Curtiss, 1995).

Neuropsychological assessment with the elderly population when the possibility of TBI is raised should include more than a single administration of the tests utilized. Since the degree of variance from the standardized norms is the criterion for determination of impaired functioning, follow-up evaluations are essential with elderly patients. This clinical approach is normally not utilized to the degree that it should be, when temporal factors are considered. A recent study reported both group-level and individual-level cognitive test data derived from a respectably sized sample and relating to multiple (three or more) serial assessments of cognitively normal subjects. However, it is important to remember that serial testing results in what is more commonly referred to as the practice effect. The most unexpected finding was that for subjects tested after 1 to 2 year intervals, practice effects were found only between the first and second assessments. Practice effects predominantly affected the results that were obtained at the first re-testing (Ivnik et al., 1999). Normative data were presented that delineated the upper and lower standards for determining whether various cognitive functions show reliable change when the Mayo Cognitive Factor

Scores were obtained. Five cognitive functions were assessed: established verbal knowledge, non-verbal reasoning, attention and concentration, new learning, and memory. Invik et al.'s (1999) findings indicated that: (1) greater changes in scores were needed for test-retest discrepancies to be considered reliable; (2) different cognitive abilities require change scores of different proportions at identical confidence levels even though the normative groups' psychometric properties for each variable were highly analogous; and (3) different cognitive proficiencies possess various degrees of temporal stability and it may be incorrect to attribute all observed instability to either measurement error or dysfunction. Ivnik et al. (1999) concluded that for each cognitive ability, a certain amount of test-retest change is normal. This proposition is extremely significant since the cognitive functions included in Ivnik et al.'s (1999) study are affected by either normal aging (new learning), depression (concentration and attention), dementia (delayed-memory), or TBI (new learning and delay-memory). Hence, the conceptual framework proposed by Ivnik et al. (1999) should be the cornerstone of every forensic neuropsychological examination when differential diagnosis is at stake. This suggestion is supported by the findings of another study that utilized the Continuous Visual Memory Test performance in healthy older persons. Hall et al. (1996) found that 7 to 63% of cognitively normal subjects scored below the suggested cut-offs. Consequently, these subjects were mis-classified as impaired.

The confounding effect of normal aging during late adulthood (e.g., older than 80 years) might potentially be explained by the examination of age related deficits. This phenomenon was studied via the administration of the Wisconsin Card Sorting Test (WCST) and the comparison of performance before and after statistical control of age-related differences (Fristoe, Salthouse, and Woodward, 1997). The magnitude of age-related variance was significantly decreased when measures of feedback usage, working memory, and perceptual-comparison speed were controlled in relation to a summary measure of the WCST. Moreover, the age-related variance associated with the feedback-usage measure declined subsequent to controlling for working memory and perceptual-comparison speed measures. Fristoe, Salthouse, and Woodward (1997) opined that age-related differences on the WCST are partly caused by adult age differences in feedback utilization which are affected by variations in working memory and decline in processing speed.

A substantial impact on neuropsychological performance was noted when education-specific normative data was implemented with individuals older than 75 years of age. The population studied was divided into 2 groups (76–80 and 81–91 years) with educational levels ranging from a 4th grade education to a college education. The tests administered were the: Logical Memory and Visual Reproduction subtests of the WMS-R; Trail Making Test, Part B; Hooper Visual Organization Test; and the Symbol Digit Modalities Test. The averaged performances of participants with 12 or more years of education were comparable to common norms (Heaton et al., 1991). Nonetheless, the averaged performances of those with less than 12 years of education were significantly inferior in comparison to the group with more than 12 years of education. These data corroborate the findings mentioned above regarding the association between education and cognitive efficiency (Richardson and Marottoli, 1996).

Limited educational experience and level of occupation were found to have an influence on the risk of DAT. When these two aspects of life experience were considered simultaneously, the risk of dementia was highest for individuals with both low education and low-level occupation. A large number (593) of individuals aged 60–99 years were evaluated with both neurological and neuropsychological measures. A follow-up evaluation was performed between 1–4 years after the initial evaluation. Of the 593 subjects, 106 were diagnosed with dementia, and of those, 101 met the criteria for DAT. The risk for developing dementia was higher in subjects with either low education or low life-time occupational attainment and greatest for subjects with both low education and low occupational attainment (Stern et al., 1994).

The forensic neuropsychologist must consider information regarding general and specific cognitive dysfunctions manifested by patients with DAT. However, a comparison ought to be performed with the functioning of a same age group of normal aging subjects. Even in the earlier stages, DAT affects an extensive range of cognitive functions. This array of dysfunctions includes: overall intelligence (FSIQ); attention and concentration; incidental memory; abstraction and problem-solving; and overall brain function (as assessed by the Halstead Impairment Index). These functions usually present regardless of a specific location or laterality of impairment. Significant group differences were found for all the specific brain functions, including: specific intelligence (VIQ and PIQ); academic and verbal learning (Reading, Spelling, and Arithmetic tests of the WRAT or WRAT-R); and semantic and figural memory. The exceptions indicated were motor output, and responses to bilateral, simultaneous tactile and auditory stimulation. Patients with DAT demonstrated more frequent language and visual-spatial construct deficits than controls, with a high incidence of dysnomia, dyscalculia, and auditory-verbal dysgnosia (Hom, 1992). The study of cognitive change in middle-aged and older adults with memory loss yielded similar results. It indicated that parietal asymmetry, sex of the patient, and baseline visual-spatial memory were significant predicators of change in visual-spatial memory; moreover, level of education and baseline verbal memory predicted change in verbal memory. However, neo-cortical asymmetry, age, family history of DAT, cerebral atrophy, and self-ratings of use of mnemonics were not significant predictors of cognitive change (Small et al., 1995). Furthermore, psychotic patients with DAT did not differ in cognitive functioning from non-psychotic patients with DAT, when rudimentary assessment was utilized, e.g., Mini-Mental State (Kortla et al., 1995).

Patients with clinically questionable dementia constitute a uniquely relevant population since they report memory deterioration (one of the cardinal symptoms of TBI), but are not impaired on standard neuropsychological tasks. Hence, a comparative assessment of normal controls, patients in the early stages of DAT, and individuals with questionable dementia (QD) is most relevant. At 6–12 months after initial presentation, almost half of the QD patients exhibited lower scores on the computerized subtests of Cambridge Neuropsychological Test Automated Battery (CANTAB). However, scores on standard testing (WAIS-R; WMS-R; Mini-Mental State Examination; and Controlled Oral Word Association Test) were maintained. Over the same period, control subjects maintained their performance levels, while

DAT patients deteriorated. QD patients, as a group, were indistinguishable from normal controls at initial assessment with paired associate learning and delayed matching to sample subtests. Over the 12-month re-assessment period, 43% of the QD group demonstrated a significant decline in scores on the CANTAB subtests. Over the same interval, their scores on all standard tests were stable. The hypothesis provided was that the deteriorating QD patients had or might develop DAT (Fowler et al., 1997). Worth mentioning is that DAT patients exhibited continued decline on all standardized tests across the course of the study. This was particularly pronounced on measures of recent memory and language.

At this juncture of the differential diagnosis process, the emphasis on emotional correlates of aging and dementia is imperative. Depression in the aged is construed as different than the common model of depression in a younger population. The clinical construct that elderly patients are not inclined to experience the common symptom of loss of self-esteem was proposed by Bieliauskas (1993). He postulated that the elderly present with feelings of distress and unhappiness that have no significant effect on cognitive functions. Accordingly, the hypothesis was proposed that the impact of depressive-like symptoms on cognitive capacities in the elderly is non-existent or null; similarly, when elderly patients manifest cognitive dysfunctions, they are likely to be the outcome of a disease process, rather than an emotional factor, e.g., depression. This is supported by an earlier study than compared cognitive dysfunctions of patients with depressive pseudo-dementia and patients with depression alone with average age of 68 years. The definition of pseudo-dementia involved the manifestation of reversible cognitive dysfunctions assessed by the Mini-Mental State Examination (MMSE), while patients with depression alone showed no such dysfunction. The predominant cognitive dysfunctions reported by the patients with pseudo-dementia were difficulties with concentration and recent memory, yet no significant difference was found in regard to impaired long term memory (O'Boyle, Amadeo, and Salf, 1990).

The studies indicated prviously (O'Boyle, Amadeo, and Salf, 1990; Bielauskas, 1993), are only a minute sample of both the contradictions and similarities discovered in the multitude of studies and numerous cautionary guidelines provided in this chapter. Additionally, a recently reported study compared qualitative and quantitative factors in the verbal learning performance of elderly depressed patients and healthy controls. When the verbal learning and memory of inpatients with unipolar major depression was compared with the performance of healthy, non-depressed controls, very different findings were obtained (King et al., 1998). While controlling for gender, education, and estimated level of intelligence, the effects of age were assessed. King et al.'s (1998) results indicated that with the exception of verbal retention, the depressed patients exhibited deficits in cued and uncued recall and delayed recognition memory. Moreover, the depressed patients' performance declined more expeditiously with age than did the performance of the controls. King et al. (1998) opined that depressed inpatients have significant deficits in a range of explicit verbal learning functions.

The forensic expert must cautiously weigh the discrepancies previously indicated, since the degree of mood disorders varies in severity, etiology, and symptom presentation, particularly in the elderly. Indeed, elderly dysthymic patients differ from young adult dysthymic patients, who are mostly female with an early onset of dysthymia and who frequently have comorbid emotional complications and/or personality disorders. Noteworthy, is that usually elderly dysthymic patients do not have a history of dysthymia (Devanand et al., 1994). As indicated previously, depression late in life differs from depression earlier in life, and is viewed as a spectrum rather than a categorical disease entity. This construct has significant bearing when the prevalence and correlates of dysthymic and major depressive disorders among patients with DAT are examined. Accordingly, when patients with DAT were assessed for psychiatric conditions, presence of cognitive dysfunctions, deficits in activities of daily living, social functioning, and anosagnosia, noteworthy findings were obtained. Of the patients asessed, 51% had depression (28% dysthymia and 23% major depression). Women had a significantly higher prevalence of both diagnostic entities than men. Prevalence of family history and personal history of depression, and personality disorder were equal for males and females. Moreover, there were no significant differences in cognitive deficits (based on subjective reports) and impairments in activities of daily living. Surprisingly, dysthymia was reported as starting after the onset of dementia and was significantly more prevalent in the early stages of dementia. Patients with dysthymia had a markedly better awareness of intellectual dysfunction than patients with no depression or major depressive disorder. Worth noting, is that patients with major depression had an earlier onset of depression (half of them before the onset of dementia). The authors concluded that a high prevalence of dysthymia and major depression is demonstrated among patients with DAT. Yet, the conclusion was that dysthymia is an emotional reaction to the progressive cognitive deterioration, while major depression may have a biological etiology (Migliorelli et al., 1995; Reynolds et al., 1998).

Before addressing the challenge of differentiation among TBI, aging, and DAT, a summary of information is provided in Table 4.4, derived from several sources (Storandt and Van Den Bos, 1994; Birrer, 1998).

Considering differences and similarities among diagnostic categories regarding cognitive and emotional functioning is essential for the differential diagnostic process. For example, patients with psychotic depression manifest distinctly different dysfunctions on neuropsychological tests when compared to non-psychotic patients. Moreover, patients with psychotic depression may suffer from structural brain abnormalities, such as cortical atrophy (Gewirtz et al., 1994) or enlarged third ventricles (Schlegel et al., 1989). Another complicating factor is that psychotic peculiarities are prevalent in elderly depressed individuals (Gierz et al., 1995). Therefore, the findings of a recent study on the comparative analysis of neuropsychological dysfunctions in psychotic vs. non-psychotic patients with unipolar depression are germane. Indeed, depressed patients with psychotic features manifested more severely impaired neuropsychological functioning than depressed patients without psychotic features. This pattern of performance was quite general and became apparent when non-verbal reasoning, visuospatial perception, verbal and non-verbal learning, dexterity, verbal fluency, and attention span were assessed (Basso and Bornstein, 1999).

Another potentially complicating variable relates to the differentiation of etiological factors associated with the localization of structural impairments and early DAT. This was studied via assessment of age-matched groups of patients with: (a)

TABLE 4.4
The Differentiation Between Features of Depression and Dementia

Feature	Depression	Dementia
Onset	Relatively hasty; Mood swings	Subtle; Indeterminate
Duration of symptoms	Brief and acute	Ordinarily chronic and extended
Frequency	Diurnal alternation of dysphoria and apprehension	Variable, inconsistent
Cognitive dysfunction	Fluctuating, limited	Consonant, fixed or deteriorating
Neuropsychological dysfunctions (Agnosia, Apraxia, Aphasia)	Lacking	Frequently manifested
Subjective complaints	Often Reported by Patient	Denied by patient
Depressive symptoms	Manifested	Manifested
Memory dysfunction	Depression precedes impaired: concentration, recent and remote recall	Depression is subsequent to loss of memory of recent events; frequently with no awareness
Premorbid history	Frequent prior depression	Absent
Motivation	Inconsistent; distress is manifested	Persistent attempts without emotional distress
Suicidal thoughts	Present or intermittent	Extremely rare
Sleep and appetite problems	Often manifested	Inconsistent

the frontal and temporal lobe variants of frontal temporal dementia; (b) early DAT; and (c) normal controls (Hodges et al., 1999). Patients with DAT manifested severe deficits in episodic memory, but less severe dysfunctions in semantic memory and visuospatial skills. Patients with semantic dementia manifested profoundly impaired semantic memory, but similar performance to DAT patients on a test of story recall. Patients with dementia due to frontal lobe dysfunction were the least impaired and presented with only mild deficits in episodic memory, verbal fluency, and intact semantic memory (Hodges et al., 1999).

The forensic neuropsychologist must consider evidence from focal lesions, TBI, and normal aging in comparison with diffuse brain damage while strategy application is appraised. Impairments in activities of daily living associated with compromised brain-behavior functioning have been associated with deficient executive control (Shalice and Burgess, 1993). Those impairments may not be observed on routine neuropsychological tests. Therefore, Shalice and Burgess (1991) proposed an unstructured array of numerous sub-goal tasks to appraise supervisory skills. More recently, a new test of strategy application was constructed for the assessment of supervisory capability (Levin et al., 1998). The validity of the test was assessed in three samples of individuals with varying levels of supervisory dysfunctions and frontal system impairment: focal frontal lesions, TBI, and normal aging. Levin et al. (1998) demonstrated that strategically impaired patients from a consecutive series can include patients with or without deficits shown by neuropsychological test performance. The prevalence of non-strategic performance regardless of the various sub-groups was in accord with Levin et al.'s (1998) prediction that performance would vary according to the severity of frontal lobe systems dysfunction. A moderate, yet significant degree of dysfunction was manifested by older adults with high intellectual ability, but without health problems that could bias cognition. The patients with TBI were impaired; however, the focal frontal sub-group showed the highest proportion of non-strategic participants, almost twice that of the focal posterior sub-group. Moreover, when neuropsychological impairment was present, it was more severe on executive functioning assignments. Among subjects with non-strategic performance, there was indication of a dissociation of knowledge from action. Differential effects of lesion locations on these processes showed that inferior medial frontal and right hemisphere lesions resulted in compromised efficiency scores. (Levin et al., 1998).

Worth mentioning is that when neuropsychological effects of TBI in older adults were compared with the correlates of DAT, a differential pattern was identified (Goldstein et al., 1996). When compared to patients with TBI, individuals with DAT demonstrated severe memory dysfunctions and did not exhibit normal performance on a category retrieval task. However, the patient groups showed similar degrees of categorical clustering and naming accuracy. Goldstein et al. (1996) concluded that memory and semantic processing could be useful in the differential diagnosis of cognitive dysfunctions associated with DAT when compared to TBI in older adults.

4.2.8 BEHAVIORAL AND PERSONALITY CHANGES ASSOCIATED WITH TBI

The most significant facet of the behavioral and personality changes associated with TBI is the presence of emotional distress with concomitant neuropsychological symptoms. The behavioral and personality changes are manifested along the continuum of severity of the TBI, ranging from concussion to severe injury. The patient's subjective perception of the corollary aspects of TBI can therefore be of even greater significance than the objective severity of the brain injury (Gasquoine, 1997, 1998). The predominant symptoms associated with mild TBI are the following: poor concentration and memory; depression; anxiety; fatigue, secondary to disrupted sleep; apprehension and anxiety; irritability; and dizziness (Binder, 1986; Benton, 1989; Fox et al., 1995). The forensic expert is advised that the diagnostic term of mild or minor head injury is often interchanged with that of post-concussion syndrome or TBI. Indeed, the gradation of the severity of TBI, in the context of the forensic neuropsychological evaluation, is a controversial issue. For example, the majority of patients with severe TBI tend to disclaim symptoms, primarily during the first year post-injury (Prigatano, Altman, and O'Brien, 1990; Prigatano, 1999; Golstein and McCue, 1995). This phenomenon is usually explained by the defense mechanism of denial or as a consequence of executive dysfunction (McGlynn and Schacter, 1989). Prigatano (1999) further refines the symptom of impaired self-awareness by proposing four syndromes of self-awareness correlated with different regions of the brain and their lateralized locations, as well as the severity of the injury. Prigatano opines that bilateral brain dysfunction results in "complete" syndromes of impaired awareness, while unilateral dysfunction results in "partial" impaired awareness.

The cornerstone of appraising the severity of any form of behavioral and/or personality changes attributed to TBI should be concern for demographic correction factors. Moreover, major emphasis should be placed on the developmental history and background of the patient. This step must be pursued regardless of whether or not the patient is engaged in any form of litigation. The patient's history should include any deviation from the normal course of development. In addition to age and gender, a thorough history should include all of the following: learning disability, conduct disorder, juvenile delinquency, criminal behavior, probation, imprisonment, genetic abnormality, psychiatric syndrome, substance abuse, or chronic pain. Gasquoine (1998) proposed four categories of behavioral and personality attributes consequent to TBI: organic, emotional, motivational, and personality syndromes. These categories primarily refer to: anatomical/structural; anxiety and depression; malingering; and pre-existing personality attributes. Although these categories are relevant when behavioral changes and personality alterations are considered, Gasquoine's (1998) proposal is not an exhaustive representation. This contention is supported by the information included in this chapter regarding PTSD and the array of other symptoms associated with TBI (see Table 4.2). It seems appropriate to assume that the post-injury behavioral repertoire and personality attributes are both the consequences of TBI, as well as an exaggerated representation of the pre-TBI personality constellation (Symonds, 1987; Eames, 1988; Lawson-Kerr, Smith, and Beck, 1991).

A significant controversy involving the lateralization of functions is inherent in the assessment of either behavioral or personality changes associated with TBI. The voluminous research and publications devoted to this topic should enable the forensic neuropsychologist to be aware of this controversy when either normal or abnormal functioning of the two hemispheres is addressed. However, it might be helpful to include a concise summary of the localizationist approach to brain-behavior relationship. It attributes qualitatively equal and opposite dysfunctions to lateralized TBI (Sherman, Shaw, and Glidden, 1994). An example of this approach is indicated in Table 4.5.

A more relevant and well-substantiated behavioral change is impaired awareness after TBI (Gasquoine and Gibbons, 1994; Weinstein and Kahn, 1955; Prigatano and Altman, 1990; Sherer et al., 1998). This complicated phenomenon is indicated by a patient's impaired or completely nonexistent awareness of his/her various dysfunctions. However, most TBI patients are more keenly aware of their physical dysfunctions than their emotional or cognitive dysfunctions. More severe injuries are usually associated with a decreased level of awareness. Consequently, independent functioning is highly correlated with behavioral determinants, such as poor cognitive flexibility, impaired mental programming, and minimal awareness of one's deficits (Suchy, Blint, and Osmon, 1997). The behavioral and personality changes associated with TBI are analogous to the effects of frontal lobe lesions. (Stuss and Benson, 1986; Prigatano, 1999). This hypothesis is substantiated by a recent empirical study that assessed psychosocial recovery after TBI. The principle components of the patients' social functioning were: inactivity, impulsiveness, and withdrawal. The ecological validity of tests of executive dysfunctions which are manifested by most patients with TBI was studied by utilizing the Dysexecutive Questionnaire (Burgess et al., 1996). This instrument revealed the following changes secondary to TBI: inability to inhibit a pre-potent response; inability to formulate appropriate goal-oriented plans and follow complex behavioral sequences; confabulation, perseveration, and temporal

TABLE 4.5
Post-TBI Lateralized Dysfunctions by Hemisphere

Right Hemisphere Dysfunction	Left Hemisphere Dysfunction
Euphoria	Depression
Decreased Sleep	Increased or Inconsistent Sleep
Impulsivity; Increased Libido; Hyperverbal Communications and Inappropriate Laughter	Psychomotor Retardation and Crying Spells

sequencing; variable motivation, aggression, euphoria, shallow effect, or apathy. These behavioral difficulties result in an enhanced susceptibility to lapses and mistakes in the performance of activities of daily living, a problem explained on the basis of limited capacity resources. Thus, the patient with dysexecutive dysfunction is easily distracted, poor at decision-making, and unable to perform tasks that require significant organization or planning. These findings support the contention that there is no single controlling resource, and different executive tasks involve non-overlapping control processes (Parkin, 1998; Boone et al., 1998; Bowman, 1996). It must be noted that other studies dispute the construct proposed by Parkin (1998) regarding the executive function of the frontal lobe. Thus, neither of the results of the studies mentioned previously provides substantial evidence to abandon the concept of executive functioning mediated by the frontal lobes.

The personality changes following TBI are often manifested by motivational difficulties, presumably due to damage to the frontal cerebral structures. Denial, anger, apathy, excessive enthusiasm, mistrust of health care professionals, and medical information seeking behavior are the main components of the motivational changes assessed. (Chervinsky et al., 1998; Levin et al., 1992). Denial of difficulties, irritability, apathy, problems with awareness of deficits, and dissatisfaction with treatment are manifested by patients with TBI (Chervinsky et al., 1998). Decreased motivation is often associated with impaired responsiveness to reward and impairment in the ability to generate effortful goal-directed responses. A functional separation between executive functions concerned with: (a) response initiation and, (b) strategic problem solving and response monitoring was utilized as the explanation for the impaired motivation. It is important not to infer a subjective state of depression from passive behavior in TBI patients. Indeed, the absence of any relationship between mood (i.e., depression) and motivation was found via the utilization of rigorous, quantitative test results (Al-Adawi, Powell, and Greenwood, 1998). Pre-injury history, including the quality of intra-familial relationships, is correlated with the patient's mode of adaptive problem-solving and positive re-appraisal of various situations (Kwasmica and Heinemann, 1994). Accordingly, when quantitative assessment was utilized by family members of TBI patients, a similar trend was apparent. Inappropriate or bizarre behavior, indifference, depressive symptomology, and prognosis (e.g., impaired social or pragmatic communication style) were manifested (Nelson et al., 1998).

Therefore, the forensic neuropsychologist is advised to insure the inclusion of various sources of information and data on pre-injury status in order to obtain an objective appraisal of any behavioral/personality changes.

4.2.9 GRIEF AND LOSS ISSUES

One of the most complex issues associated with the forensic psychological/neurop-sychological evaluation is that of grief and loss. Clinical literature supports the contention that a myriad of cognitive and emotional correlates are the sequelae to any psychological or physiological trauma. Patients with emotional trauma only, e.g., PTSD, will experience the loss of any function with resultant grief. However, patients with TBI simultaneously experience the emotional response to their physical dysfunctions as well as the emotional symptoms that accompany compromised brain functioning.

One of the primary manifestations of grief is depression, which can be a response to either psychological or physiological trauma; concentration, attention and there-fore memory, are also affected by depression. Therefore, the retrospective data obtained in a forensic evaluation can be compromised by the fact that the patient's recall and retrieval are impaired. Moreover, it is difficult to determine the relative contributions of the traumatic experience and any pre-existing psychopathology. This is an inherent problem when patients with different degrees of TBI are examined via a neuropsychological evaluation and manifest emotional symptomatology (see Table 4.5). The possibility of a pre-existing personality disorder can further confound the differential diagnostic process.

An additional complication is introduced by the controversy in the field of neu-ropsychology as to whether post traumatic stress disorder (PTSD) and TBI could simultaneously co-exist (Sbordone, 1991; Mishkin and Appenzeller, 1987; Horton, 1993). The severity of TBI is primarily defined by the duration of retrograde amnesia. If the hypothesis that the patient's memory is impaired by the TBI is accepted, and therefore the memory of the actual event that resulted in the TBI is potentially affected, how then could the patient be diagnosed with PTSD? This diagnosis presumes a memory of the distressing event, and the significant emotional distress seen in PTSD is explained by the extraordinary nature of the distressing event. Thus, the opposing expert might present this issue as a way of defeating the opinion of the claimant (Nemiah, 1995). Hence, it is the onus of the forensic expert to become familiar with the nature of stress induced syndromes, dissociative symptoms, and PTSD. Indeed, the use of a structured clinical interview for the assessment of dissociative symptoms in PTSD can yield significant findings. Amnesia, depersonalization, derealization, identity confusion, and identity alteration are examples of severe dissociative symp-toms manifested by patients with PTSD (Bremner et al., 1993). This constellation of symptoms is either partially or totally a common phenomenon associated with TBI. The presence of amnesia, disorientation to person, time, or place, confabulation, and confusion are some of the well-documented dysfunctions secondary to TBI. There-fore, it is imperative that the forensic neuropsychologist's clinical evaluation be based on a keen awareness of the various conceptual approaches to understanding PTSD, loss, and grief. The study of the conflict between current knowledge about PTSD and its original conceptual basis contributed to the acceptance of neurological changes following exposure to a trauma. These changes are particularly associated with the symptoms of PTSD and do not appear to be present as a result of exposure to trauma, per se (Yehuda and McFarlane, 1995). Nevertheless, an acute stress disorder is a reliable predictor of PTSD (Classen et al., 1998). To be diagnosed as suffering from an acute stress disorder, the patient must exhibit at least three dissociative symptoms in addition to at least one of the following: intrusive recollections, avoidance of stimuli associated with the trauma, and/or hyperarousal symptoms. The symptoms should persist 2–28 days and not be due to the ingestion of a substance, general medical condition, a brief psychotic disorder, or a pre-existing paramorbitity disorder (DSM-IV, American Psychiatric Association, 1994).

Since loss and grief are often associated with numerous physiological symptoms (e.g., impaired sleep, appetite and libido, decreased physical endurance, etc.) the presenting symptoms of PTSD must be evaluated with considerable caution. The following constructs are derived from several studies (Shalev et al., 1998). The forensic expert could significantly substantiate his/her findings by utilizing these four constructs:

1. Stress, as well as any significant experience to which the individual is exposed, alters neuro-biological systems.
2. Stress that occurs prior to the identified trauma, manifested in neuro-biological changes, modifies a variety of behavioral and physiological responses to subsequent experiences.
3. Neurological responses that allow short-term survival of acute stress situations may have detrimental consequences.
4. Traumatic experiences can cause neuro-biological changes that result in pathology. However, it is possible that other experiences may result in neuro-biological alterations that may alleviate or compensate for those induced by stress.

The forensic expert should be familiar with the various criteria for the diagnosis of PTSD, presented in Table 4.6.

The conglomerate of symptoms associated with PTSD places additional burdens on the forensic psychologist's ability to distinguish the presence of loss and/or grief from PTSD, depression, or TBI. Of the 17 symptoms, 13 (e.g., more than 70%) outlined in Table 4.6 are overlapping (indicated by the symbol of **) and could possibly be due to any one of 3 diagnostic criteria mentioned previously. Thus, the study of the relationship between acute stress disorder and PTSD consequent to mild TBI is pertinent. When adult patients who suffered a mild TBI were evaluated with the Acute Disorder Interview (Bryant et al., 1997, in Bryant, Allison, and Harvey, 1998) significant predictive utility was found for PTSD. Acute stress disorder was diagnosed in 14% of patients, and at follow-up 24% satisfied criteria for PTSD. Six months after the trauma, PTSD was diagnosed in 82% of patients who had been diagnosed with acute stress disorder, and in 11% of those who had not been diagnosed with acute stress disorder. The criteria for acute stress disorder were useful in identifying those patients who were at risk for developing chronic PTSD. Nevertheless, Bryant and Harvey (1998) opined that prevalent criteria require alteration in order to optimally predict PTSD following a mild TBI. Noteworthy is that among the 19 items included in Bryant and Harvey's list of symptoms, at least 5 symptoms

TABLE 4.6
Diagnostic Criteria for PTSD According to DSM-IV

A. Experiencing, witnessing, or being confronted by event(s) that threaten
     physical integrity (e.g., death or serious injury of self or others)   **
     1. response of intense fear, helplessness, or horror   **
B. Re-experiencing criteria (one required)
     2. recurrent, intensive, distressing recollections
     3. recurrent, distressing dreams   **
     4. flashbacks   **
     5. intense psychological distress or exposure to events that
     symbolize or resemble the traumatic event
C. Avoidance criteria (three required)
     6. avoidance of associated thoughts and feelings   **
     7. avoidance of associated activities or situations   **
     8. inability to recall an important aspect of the trauma   **
     9. markedly diminished interest in significant activities   **
     10. feelings of detachment or estrangement from others
     11. restricted range of affect   **
     12. sense of foreshortened future   **
D. Arousal criteria (two required)
     13. insomnia
     14. irritability or outbursts of anger   **
     15. difficulty concentrating   **
     16. hypervigilence   **
     17. exaggerated startle response
E. Duration of at least one month
F. Clinically significant distress or impairment.

** See explanations below.

Source: Adopted from Pitman 1997.

are attributable to TBI, regardless of any emotional concomitants. These are: reduced awareness, insomnia, irritability, poor concentration, and motor restlessness. Indeed, the onset, overlap, and course of PTSD and major depression following traumatic events were examined in a recent study which revealed that comorbid depression occurred in close to one half (44.5%) of PTSD patients at one month and in 43.2% at 4 months (Shalev et al., 1998). However, survivors with PTSD had higher heart rate levels at the emergency rooms and described more intrusive symptoms, exaggerated startle, and dissociation when compared with those with major depression.

Neuropsychological impairments were found to be prevalent among patients with PTSD. Short-term, explicit verbal memory dysfunction, excessive retroactive interference, and reduced MRI-derived right hemisphere hippocampal volume were also associated with PTSD (Bremner et al., 1993). The previous findings mentioned might seem confounding and to further complicate the assessment of the loss and grief issues which are concurrent with TBI due to functional and anatomical correlates reported. However, the problem of concurrent diagnosis of PTSD and TBI producing amnesia is the outcome of a unitary memory theory. Moreover, the cognitive and emotional correlates of TBI are not totally differentiated from those of PTSD. These dysfunctions include: impaired concentration; anxiety and apprehension due to the patient's experience of his/her cognitive dysfunctions; and feelings of grief and loss resulting from perceived impaired abilities, neurological dysfunctions, or both. These incongruities and questionable diagnoses could be resolved by adhering to the distinction between declarative and implicit memory systems (Squire, 1992). This concept of dual recall acknowledges that the same stimulus or event may have both declarative and non-declarative attributes and could be stored independently in both systems (Mishkin and Appenzeller, 1987). A refined proposal was constructed for the explanation of PTSD with concomitant amnestic symptoms (Layton and Wardi-Zonna, 1995). The basic hypothesis is that declarative memory for a traumatic event is not a necessary condition for the development of PTSD. Layton et al. (1995), suggested that operation of a non-declarative memory system is a sufficient condition for the development of this emotional condition and substantiated their construct with a prior study (Horton, 1993) which provided a similar construct for the occurrence of PTSD in patients with mild TBI. Consequently, Layton et al.'s (1995), proposition is consistent with the multiple system theory of memory which asserts that not all experience need be accessible to consciousness in order to affect future experience.

The emotional responses of depression, anxiety, and apprehension consequent to TBI have been addressed in Section 4.2 of this chapter. The general consensus is that depression, hypomania, or emotional blunting are the correlates of feelings of loss and grief resulting from most traumatic experiences. Sorrow, sadness, despondency, and pessimism are the main indicators of the depressive state. Moreover, decreased initiative and motivation are exacerbated by self-blame, shame, and remorse for past behavior.

4.2.10 EFFECT ON RELATIONSHIPS

The temporal impact of the multiple dysfunctions associated with TBI on the various relationships between the injured patient and family members, caregivers, and employers may range from several months (Macciocchi and Barth, 1993) to several years (Lezak, 1978). The factors which significantly contribute to this consequence of TBI include: severity of the injury (Lezak, 1978); impact of daily stress and level of perceived stress (Machuloa et al., 1998); and the grief experienced by family members (Lezak, 1986; Romano, 1974; Del Orto and Power, 1994). Independent of the frequency of the stressful events, the non-injured individual's perception of stress is most significantly related to the level of symptom complaint by the patient. In contrast, there is no significant relationship between the frequency of stressful events and level of symptom complaint by the patient (Machuloa et al., 1998).

The cognitive, emotional, and behavioral dysfunctions associated with TBI include aggressive behavior and agitation, which usually present the most complex problems for caregivers and family members with which to deal. Interestingly, very simple cognitive dysfunctions (e.g., disorientation to place and time) were the most significant predictors of aggressive behaviors (Galski et al., 1994). Hence, the forensic neuropsychologist should utilize this information, which is easily recognizable during the clinical interview, to provide intervention guidelines for caregivers and family members. When considering the finding that approximately one third of even those patients with mild TBI have serious cognitive and emotional sequelae (Frankowski, 1986), the clinical utilization of the findings by Galski et al. (1994) is of utmost importance.

The various dysfunctions manifested by patients with TBI cause profound alteration of functioning for the injured patient, and marked distress for family members, often triggering grief reactions for these significant others. Indeed, an early study (Panting and Merry, 1972) noted that a significant number of relatives reported stress-related symptoms (e.g., impaired sleep) and that TBI had a more adverse and distressing impact on spouses than parents. An elevated level of stress, manifested in anxiety and depression, was apparent in the spouses of patients who sustained a TBI with resulting symptomatology lasting approximately six years (Linn, Allen, and Willer, 1994). The finding reported by Linn, Allen, and Willer (1994) was substantiated by quantitative data derived from the utilization of the Symptoms Checklist-90 (SCL-90; Derogatis, 1983). They found that 73% of spouses acknowledged symptoms of depression and 55% demonstrated symptoms of anxiety. There is, however, a methodological flaw in the design of the study by Linn, Allen, and Willer (1994); the participants' selection was not random, creating a biasing factor. Nevertheless, Linn, Allen, and Willer's study yielded relevant data regarding the comparison of levels of distress in patients and their spouses: 70% of patients with TBI evidenced increased levels of depression and 50% manifested symptoms of anxiety.

The forensic expert should consider the following more intricate and informative study of the impact of TBI on parents and spouses of patients. Kreutzer, Gervasio, and Camplair (1994) studied the intra-familial situations and psychological distress of 62 primary caregivers. In total, 34 parents (6 fathers, 28 mothers) and 28 spouses (3 husbands, 25 wives) were assessed via the Brief Symptoms Inventory (BSI; Derogatis, 1995) and the Family Assessment Device (FAD; Epstein, Baldwin, and Bishop, 1983). Kruntzer, Gervasio, and Camplair determined that 47% of the relatives in the study sample either met or surpassed the criteria for emotional "caseness." Yet, when the criteria for caseness were examined, only 32% of caregivers' functioning matched the level of severity score above the 90th percentile for 2 criteria and 13% of relatives met only 1 criterion.

A recent review of the literature regarding the emotional consequences of TBI on relationships was provided by Perlesz, Kinsella, and Crowe (1999). The forensic psychologist might utilize this publication as a guideline regarding the issues explored in the present section, with one cautionary note: several relevant publications were not included in Perlesz, Kinsella, and Crowe's (1999) article. The grief reactions of mothers of adolescents and young adults with TBI (Zinner et al., 1997) utilized a modified version of the Grief Experience Inventory (Sanders, Mauger, and Strong, 1985); mothers rated their child's functioning on a modified Neurobehavioral Rating Scale (Levin et al., 1987). Zinner et al. (1997) reported more severe grief by mothers who rated their children as having poor neurobehavioral functioning and by mothers of young adults, rather than adolescent patients. The experience of the guilt component of grief varied significantly across the 3-year, post-injury interval measured in the study. Moreover, historical comparisons of those respondents with different bereaved populations demonstrated that mothers of adolescents and young adults with head injury described more severe grief than parents who experienced other significant non-death traumata or losses. Sleep disturbance and loss of vigor were higher among mothers of TBI patients, while despair and despondency were lower when compared to the parental bereavement group. Yet, contrary to theoretical constructs that propose gradual progress toward a decreased grief response, no significant differences were found by Zinner et al. (1997) as time progressed, up to 3-years post-injury. Family members of patients with TBI experience long-term suffering due to financial difficulties and complex changes in required caretaking. While some denial is experienced during the early stages of recovery from the TBI, this is not sustained over time. The family members' depressive phase of response to the injury usually occurs 3–12 months post-injury, but there is uncertainty about the duration and sequence of subsequent stages of adjustment to the TBI (Kreutzer, Marwitz, and Kepler, 1992). Noteworthy, is that family functioning and children's academic performance and behavioral dysfunctions in the year following TBI were associated with injury severity and, to a lesser extent, poor pre-injury family and child functioning (Rivara et al.,1994). Hence, pre-injury emotional and behavioral functioning must be appraised by the forensic expert in order to obtain a valid and reliable appraisal of the effect of TBI on relationships.

The neurobehavioral symptoms in adults with TBI can result in a myriad of dysfunctions which tend to be most distressing for family members. Depression, inappropriate behavior, prognosis, and indifference emerge as most significantly associated with family functioning and caregiver stress. Interestingly, the severity of injury has less of an impact on family functioning than the neurobehavioral symptoms that result from the injury (Groom et al., 1998). Therefore, Barrer's (1988) paradigm of family involvement in facilitating the injured patient's recovery from TBI is an essential construct for dealing with the overwhelming effect of TBI on various relationships (McNeill, Schuyler, and Ezrachi, 1997).

4.3 CONCLUDING REMARKS

This chapter has explored in detail the complexity of the forensic psychological/neuropsychological evaluation by reviewing the cognitive, emotional, and behavioral consequences of TBI on patients and their families. It described the complex process of the differential diagnosis of organic vs. emotional disorders by reviewing the predominant symptoms, research studies, and theoretical constructs that pertain to this issue. As we have seen, there are various approaches in the literature to the differential diagnostic process. However, it is hoped that the construct of the *convergent neuropsychological assessment* presented by the author of this chapter will offer the forensic expert a truly comprehensive, integrated, and thoroughly substantiated approach to the challenging process of differential diagnosis.

REFERENCES

Adams, R.D. and Victor, M., (1989). *Principles of Neurology* (4th ed.). McGraw-Hill, New York.

Al-Adawi, S., Powell, J.H. and Greenwood, R.J., (1998). Motivational deficits after brain injury: a neuropsychological approach using new assessment techniques. *Neuropsychology,* 12, 115-124.

American Psychiatric Association, (1994). *Diagnostic and Statistical Manual of Mental Disorders* (4th ed.). Washington, D.C.

Anderson-Parente, J.K., Dicesare, A. and Parente, R., (1990). Spouses who stayed. *Cognitive Rehabilitation,* 8, 22-25.

Ardilla, A., Rosselli, M., and Ostrosky, F., (1992). Sociocultural factors in neuropsychological assessment, in *Handbook of Neuropsychological Assessment: A Biopsychosocial Perspective,* Puente, A.E. and McCaffrey, R.J., Eds., Academic Press, New York, p. 181-192.

Armstrong, C., (1997). Selective versus sustained attention: a continuous performance test revisited. *The Clinical Neuropsychologist,* 11, 18-33.

Axelrod, B.N. and Goldman, R.S., (1996). Use of demographic corrections in neuropsychological interpretation: how standard are test scores? *The Clinical Neuropsychologist,* 10, 1-11.

Baddeley, A., (1998). The central executive: a concept and some misconceptions. *Journal of the International Neuropsychological Society,* 4, 523-526.

Banich, M.T. and Belger, A., (1990). Interhemispheric interactions. How do the hemispheres divide and conquer tasks? *Cortex,* 26, 77-94.

Barona, A., Reynolds, C.R. and Chastain, R., (1984). A demographically based index of premorbid intelligence for the WAIS-R. *Journal of Consulting and Clinical Psychology,* 52, 885-887.

Barona, A. and Chastain, R.L., (1986). An improved estimate of pre-morbid I.Q. for blacks and whites on the WAIS-R. *International Journal of Clinical Neuropsychology,* 8, 169-173.

Barrer, A.E., (1988). Systems approach to working with families of the traumatically brain injured. *American Psychological Association Presentation,* August 12.

Barth, J.T., Ryan, V.T., and Hawk, G.L., (1992). Forensic neuropsychology: A reply to the method skeptics. *Neuropsychology Review,* 251-266.

Basso, M.R., and Bornstein, R.A., (1999). Neuropsychological deficits in psychotic vs. non-psychotic unipolar depression. *Neuropsychology,* 13, 69-75.

Beck, A.T., (1967). *Depression: Clinical Experimental and Theoretical Aspects.* Hoeber, New York.

Benton, A.L., (1989). Historical notes on the post-concussion syndrome, in *Mild Head Injury,* Levine, M.S., Eisenberg, H.M., and Benton, A.L., Eds., Oxford University Press, New York, p. 3-7.

Berenstein, J.G., (1988) *Handbook of Drug Therapy in Psychiatry* (2nd ed.). PSG Publishing, Littleton, MA.

Bieliauskas, L.A., (1993). Depressed or not depressed? That is the question. *Journal of Clinical and Experimental Neuropsychology,* 15, 119-134.

Binder, L.M., (1997). A review of mild head trauma. Part II: clinical implications. *Journal of Clinical and Experimental Neuropsychology,* 19, 432-457.

Binder, L.M., (1986). Persisting symptoms after mild head injury: a review of the post-concussive syndrome. *Journal of Clinical and Experimental Neuropsychology,* 8, 323-346.

Birrer, R.B., (1998). Depression and aging too often do mix. *Postgraduate Medicine,* 104, 143-164.

Bishop, D.S. and Miller, I.W., (1988). Traumatic brain injury: empirical family assessment techniques. *Journal of Head Trauma Rehabilitation,* 3, 16-30.

Black, F.W., (1974). The utility of the Shipley-Hartford as predictor of WAIS full scale IQ for patients with traumatic brain injuries. *Journal of Clinical Psychology,* 30, 168-170.

Blair, J.R. and Spreen, O., (1989). Predicting pre-morbid I.Q.: a revision of the National Adult Reading Test. *The Clinical Psychologist,* 3, 129-136.

Boles, D.B., (1992). Factor analysis and the cerebral hemispheres: temporal, occipital and frontal functions. *Neuropsychologia,* 30, 963-988.

Boll, T. and Bryant, B.K., Eds., (1988). *Clinical Neuropsychology and Brain Function: Research, Measurement and Practice.* American Psychological Association.

Boone, K.B., Ponton, M.D., Gorsuch, R.L., Gonzalez, J.J., and Miller, B.L., (1998). Factor analysis of four measures of prefrontal lobe functioning. *Archives of Clinical Neuropsychology,* 13, 585-595.

Bornstein, R.A. and Suga, L.J., (1988). Educational level and neuropsychological performance in healthy elderly subjects. *Developmental Neuropsychology,* 4, 17-22.

Bowman, M.L., (1996). Ecological validity of neuropsychological and other predictors following head injury. *The Clinical Neuropsychologist,* 10, 382-396.

Bremner, J.D., Steinberg, M., Southwick, S.M., Johnson, D.R. and Charney, D.S., (1993). Use of structured clinical interview for DSM-IV dissociative disorders of systematic assessment of dissociative symptoms in post traumatic stress disorder. *American Journal of Psychiatry,* 150, 1011-1014.

Bremner, J.D., Scott, T.M., Delaney, R.C., Southwick, S.M., Mason, J.W., Johnson, D.R., Innis, R.B., McCarthy, G., and Charney, D.S., (1993). Deficits in short-term memory in post traumatic stress disorder. *American Journal of Psychiatry,* 150, 1015-1019.

Bremner, J.D., Randall, P., Scott, C.M., Bronen, R.A., Seibyl, J.P., Southwick, S.M., Delaney, R.C., McCarthy, G., Charney, D.S., and Innis, R.B., (1995). MRI-based measurement of hippocampal volume in combat-related post traumatic stress disorder. *American Journal of Psychiatry,* 152, 973-981.

Brooks, N., Campsie, L., Symington, C., Beattie, A. and McKinlay, W., (1987). The effects of severe head injury on patient and relative within seven years of injury. *Journal of Head Trauma Rehabilitation,* 2, 1-13.

Brouwer, W.H. and Van Wolffelar, P.C., (1985). Sustained attention and sustained efforts after closed-head injury: Detection and 0.10 H_z heart rate variability in a low event rate vigilance task. *Cortex,* 21, 111-119.

Bryant, R.A. and Harvey, A., (1998). Relationship between acute stress disorder and post traumatic stress disorder following mild traumatic brain injury. *American Journal of Psychiatry,* 155, 625-629.

Burgess, P.W., Alderman, N., Wilson, B.A., Evans, J.J., and Emslie, H., (1996). The dysexecutive questionnaire, in *Behavioral Assessment of the Dys-executive Syndrome,* Wilson, B.A., Alderman, N., Burgess, P.W., Emslie, H., and Evans, J.J., Eds., Thames Valley Test Company, Bury St. Edmunds, U.K.

Busch, C.R. and Alpern, H.P., (1998). Depression after mild traumatic brain injury: a review of current research. *Neuropsychology Review,* 8, 95-108.

Butler, Retzlaff, and VanDerPloeg (1991). Neuropsychological test usage. *Professional Psychology: Research and Practice,* 22, 510-512.

Cavallo, M.M., Kay, T., and Ezrachi, O., (1992). Problems and changes after traumatic brain injury: differing perceptions, within and between families. *Brain Injury,* 6, 327-335.

Chervinsky, A.B., Ommaya, A.K., De Jonge, M., Spector, J., Schwab, K., and Salazar, A.M., (1998). Motivation for traumatic brain injury rehabilitation Questionnaire (MOT-Q): reliability, factor analysis, and relationship to MMPI-2. *Archives of Clinical Neuropsychology,* 13, 433-446.

Classen, C., Koopman, C., Hales, R., and Spiegel, D., (1998). Acute stress disorder as a predictor of post traumatic stress disorder. *American Journal of Psychiatry*, 155, 620-624.

Cohen, B.M., Renshaw, P.F. and Yurgelun-Todd, D., (1995). Imaging the mind: magnetic resonance spectroscopy and functional brain imaging. *American Journal of Psychiatry*, 152, 655-658.

Crawford, J.R., (1989). Estimation of pre-morbid intelligence: a review of recent developments, in *Development in Clinical and Experimental Neuropsychology*, Crawford, J.R. and Parker, D., Eds., Plenum Press, New York, p. 55-74.

Crawford, J.R. and Allan, K.M., (1997). Estimating pre-morbid WAIS-R I.Q. with demographic variables: Regression equation derived from a UK sample. *The Clinical Neuropsychologist*, 11, 192-197.

Cullum, C.M., Heaton, R.K., and Grant, I., (1991). Psychogenic factors influencing neuropsychological performance: somatoform disorders, factitious disorders and malingering, in *Forensic Neuropsychology: Legal and Scientific Bases*, Doerr, H.D. and Carlin, A.S., Eds., Guilford, New York.

Del Orto, A. and Power, P.W., (1994). *Head Injury and The Family: A life and Living Perspective*, PMD Publishers Group, Winter Park, FL.

Deptula, D., Singh, R., and Pomara, N., (1993). Aging, continuous state, and memory. *American Journal of Psychiatry*, 150, 429-434.

Derogatis, L.R., (1983). *SCL-90-R Administration, Scoring and Procedures Manual — II for the Revised Version and Other Instruments of the Psychopathology Rating Scale Series*. Clinical Psychometric Research, Towson, MD.

Derogatis, L.R., (1975). *Brief Symptom Inventory*. Clinical Psychometric Research, Baltimore, MD.

Devanand, D.P., Nobler, M.S., Singer, T., Kiersky, J.E., Turret, N., Roose, S.P., and Sackeim, H.A., (1994). Is Dysthymia a different disorder in the elderly? *American Journal of Psychiatry*, 151, 1592-1599.

Eames, P., (1988). Behavior disorders after severe head injury: their nature and causes and strategies for management. *Journal of Head Trauma Rehabilitation*, 3, 1-6.

Eckardt, M.J., Stapleton, J.M., Rawlings, R.R., Davis, E.Z., and Grodin, D.M., (1995). Neuropsychological functioning in detoxified alcoholics between 18 and 35 years of age. *American Journal of Psychiatry*, 152, 53-59.

Eker, C., Asgeissor, B., Grande, P.O., Schalen, W., and Nordstrom, C.H., (1998). Improved outcome after severe head injury with a new therapy based on principles for brain volume regulation and preserved microcirculation. *Critical Care Medicine*, 126, 1881-1886.

Emery, O., (1988). *Pseudodementia: A Theoretical and Empirical Discussion: Interdisciplinary Monograph Series*. Western Reserve Geriatric Education Carter, Cleveland, OH.

Emery, V.O. and Oxman, T.E., (1992). Update on the dementia spectrum of depression. *The American Journal of Psychiatry*, 149, 305-317.

Epstein, J.N., Conners, C.K., Sitareniss, G., and Erhardt, D., (1988). Continuous performance test results of adults with attention deficit hyperactivity disorder. *The Clinical Neuropsychologist*, 12, 155-168.

Epstein, N.B., Baldwin, L.M., and Bishop, D.S., (1983). The MacMaster Family Assessment Device. *Journal of Marital and Family Therapy*, 9, 171-180.

Evans, D.A., Funkenstein, H.H., Albert, M.S., Scherr, P.A., Cook, N.R., Chown, M.J., Herbert, L.E., Hennekens, C.H., and Taylor, J.O., (1989). Prevalence of Alzheimer's disease in a community population of older persons. *Journal of the American Medical Association*, 262, 2551-2556.

Eviatar, Z., Hellige, J.B., and Zaidel, E., (1997). Individual differences in lateralization: effects of gender and handedness. *Neuropsychology*, 11, 562-572.

Faust, D., (1991). Forensic neuropsychology: the art of practicing a science that does not yet exist. *Neuropsychology Review,* 2, 205-231.

Ficks, D.S., (1995). Management of concussion in collision sports. *Postgraduate Medicine,* 97, 53-60.

Folstein, M. and McHugh, P., (1978). Dementia syndrome of depression, in Alzheimer's Disease. Senile Dementia and Related Disorders, in *Aging.* Katzman, R., Terry, R.D., and Bick, K.L., Raven Press, New York.

Fowler, K.S., Saling, M.M., Conway, E.L., Semple, J.S., and Louis, W.J., (1997). Computerized neuropsychological tests in the early detection of dementia: prospective findings. *Journal of the International Neuropsychological Society,* 3, 139-146.

Fox, D.D., Lees-Haley, P.R., Earnest, K., and Dolexal-Wood, S., (1995). Base-rates of post-concussive symptoms in health maintenance organization patients and control. *Neuropsychology,* 9, 606-611.

Frankowski, R.F., (1986). Descriptive epidemiologic studies of head injury in the United States: 1974-1984., in *Psychiatric Aspects of Trauma,* Peterson, L.G. and O'Shanick, G.J., Eds., Karger, New York.

Franzen, M.D., Burgess, E.J., and Smith-Seemiller, L., (1997). Methods of estimating premorbid functioning. *Archives of Clinical Neuropsychology,* 12, 711-738.

Fristoe, N.M., Salthouse, T.A., and Woodard, J. (1997). Examination on age-related deficits on the Wisconsin Card Sorting Test. *Neuropsychology,* 11, 428-436.

FrommAusch, D. and Yeudall, L., (1983). Normative data for the Halstead-Reitan Neuropsychological tests. *Journal of Clinical Neuropsychology,* 5, 221-238.

Galski, T., Palasz, J., Bruno, R.L., and Walker, J.E., (1994). Predicting physical and verbal aggression on a brain trauma unit. *Archives of Physical Medicine and Rehabilitation,* 75, 380-383.

Gasquoine, P.G., (1998). Historical perspective on post-concussion symptoms. *The Clinical Neuropsychologist,* 12, 315-324.

Gasquoine, P.G., (1997). Post-concussion symptoms. *Neuropsychology Review,* 7, 77-85.

Gasquoine, P.G., and Gibbons, T.A., (1994). Lack of awareness of impairment in institutionalized severely and chronically disabled survivors of traumatic brain injury: a preliminary investigation. *Journal of Head Trauma Rehabilitation,* 9, 16-24.

Gelenberg, A.J., Bassuck, E.L and Schooner, S.C., Eds., (1991). *The Practitioner's Guide to Psychoactive Drugs* (3rd ed.). Plenum Publishing Corp., New York.

Geschwind, N., (1965). Disconnection syndromes in animals and men. *Brain,* 88, 237-294.

Geschwind, N., (1970). The organization of language and the brain. *Science,* 170, 940-294.

Geschwind, N., (1985). Brain disease and the mechanisms of mind, in *Functions of the Brain,* Cohen, C.W., Ed., Clarendon Press, Oxford.

Geschwind, N. and Galaburda, A.M., (1987). *Cerebral Lateralization. Biological Mechanisms, Associations and Pathology.* MIT Press, Cambridge, MA.

Gewirtz, G., Squires-Wheeler, E., Sharif, Z, and Honer, W.G., (1994). Results of computerized tomography during first admission for psychosis. *British Journal of Psychiatry,* 164, 789-795.

Gierz, M., Sewell, D.D., Kramer, R., Gillin, J.C., and Jeste, D.V., (1995). Psychotic versus non-psychotic depression in older patients. *American Journal of Geriatric Psychiatry,* 164, 789-795.

Golden, C.J. and Van Den Broek, A., (1998). Potential impact of age- and education-corrected scores on HRNB score patterns in participants with focal brain injury. *Archives of Clinical Neuropsychology,* 13, 683-694.

Goldstein, G., and McCue, M., (1995). Differences between patient and informant functional outcome ratings in head-injured individuals. *International Journal of Rehabilitation and Health,* 1, 25-35.

Goldstein, F.C., Gary, H.E., and Levin, H.S., (1986). Assessment of the accuracy of regression equations proposed for estimating pre-morbid intellectual functioning on the Wechsler Adult Intelligence Scale. *Journal of Clinical and Experimental Neuropsychology*, 8, 405-412.

Goldstein, F.C., Levin, H.S., Roberts, V.J., Goldman, W.P., Kalechstein, A.S., Winslow, M., and Goldstein, G., (1996). Neuropsychological effects of closed head injury in older adults: a comparison with Alzheimer's Disease, *Neuropsychology*, 10, 147-154.

Goldstein, G., and Incagnoli, T.M., Eds., (1997). *Contemporary Approaches to Neuropsychological Assessment*. Plenum Publishing House, New York.

Goran, D.A., Fabiano, R.J., and Crewe, N., (1997). Employment following severe traumatic brain injury: The utility of the Individual Ability Profile System. *Archives of Clinical Neuropsychology*, 12, 691-698.

Groom, K.N., Shaw, T.G., O'Conner, M.E., Howard, N.I., and Pickens, A., (1998). Neurobehavioral symptoms and family functioning in traumatically brain-injured adults. *Archives of Clinical Neuropsychology*, 13, 695-711.

Guidelines for the evaluation of dementia and age-related cognitive decline, (1998). *American Psychology*, 53, 1298-1303.

Hall, S., Pinkston, S.L., Szalda-Petree, A.C., and Coronis, A.R., (1996). The performance of healthy older adults on the Continuous Visual Memory Test and the Visual-Motor Integration Test: preliminary findings. *Journal of Clinical Psychology*, 52, 449-454.

Hall, K.M., Karzmark, P., Stephens, M., Englander, J., O'Hare, P., and Wright, J., (1994). Family stressors in traumatic brain injury: A two year follow-up. *Archives of Physical Medicine and Rehabilitation*, 75, 876-883.

Hammarberg, M., (1992). Penn Inventory for post traumatic stress disorder: psychometric properties. *Psychological Assessment*, 4, 67-76.

Hartlage L.C., (1990). *Neuropsychological Evaluation of Head Injury*. Professional Resource Exchange, Sarasota, FL.

Hartlage, L.C., (1997). Clinical aspects and issues in assessing pre-morbid IQ and cognitive function. *Archives of Clinical Neuropsychology*, 12, 763-768.

Hartman, D.E., (1995). *Neuropsychological Toxicology: Identification and Assessment of Human Neurotoxic Syndromes* (2nd ed.),. Pergamon Press, New York.

Heaton, R.K., Grant, I., and Matthews, C.G., (1986). Differences in test performance associated with age, education and sex, in *Neuropsychological Assessment in Neuropsychiatric Disorders: Clinical Methods and Empirical Findings*, Grant, I. and Adams, K., Eds., Oxford University Press, New York.

Heaton, R.K., Grant, I., and Matthews, C.G., (1991). *Comprehensive Norms for an Expanded Halstead-Reitan Battery*, Psychological Assessment Resources, Odessa, FL.

Hellige, J.B., (1995). Coordinating the different processing biases of the left and right cerebral hemispheres, in *Hemispheric Communication: Mechanisms and Models*, Kitterle, F.L., Ed., Erlaum, Hillsdale, NJ, p. 347-362.

Hellige, J.B., (1993). *Hemispheric Asymmetry: What's Right and What's Left*. Harvard University Press, Cambridge, MA.

Hellige, J.B., Block, M.I., Cowin, E.L., Eng, T.L., Eviatar, Z., and Sergent, V., (1994). Individual variation in hemispheric asymmetry: multitask study of effects related to handedness and sex. *Journal of Experimental Psychology: General*, 123, 235-256.

Higgins, K. and Sherman, M., (1978). The effect of motivation on loose thinking in schizophrenics as measured by the Bermister-Fransella Grid Test. *Journal of Clinical Psychology*, 34, 624-628.

Hodges, J.R., Gerrard, P., Perry, R., Patterson, K, Ward, R., Bak, T., and Gregory, C., (1999). The differentiation of semantic dementia and frontal lobe dementia (temporal and frontal variants of frontotemporal dementia) from early Alzheimer's Disease: a comparative neuropsychological study. *Neuropsychology,* 13, 31-40.

Hoffman, R.E., (1986). Verbal hallucinations and language production process in schizophrenia. *Behavioral and Brain Sciences,* 9, 503-548.

Hom, J., (1992). General and specific cognitive dysfunctions in patients with Alzheimer's disease. *Archives of Clinical Neuropsychology,* 7, 121-133.

Horton, M., (1993). Post-traumatic stress disorder and mild head trauma: follow-up of a case study. *Perceptual and Motor Skills,* 76, 243-246.

Ivnik, R.J., Smith, G.E., Lucas, J.A., Peterson, R.C., Boeve, B.F., Kokmen, E., and Tangalos, E.G., (1999). Testing normal older people three or four times at 1-2 year intervals: defining normal variance. *Neuropsychology,* 13, 121-127.

Johnson, S.C., Bigtler, G.D., Burr, R.B., and Blatter, D.D., (1994). White matter atrophy, ventricular, and intellectual functioning following traumatic brain injury. *Neuropsychology,* 8, 307-315

Jordan, B.D., (1997). Emergic concepts in sports neurology. *Annals of the New York Academy of Sciences.*

Julien, R.M., (1995). *A primer of Drug Action: A Concise, Non-technical Guide to the Actions, Woes and Side Effects of Psychoactive Drugs* (7th Ed.). W.H. Freeman and Company, New York.

Kalechstein, A.D., Van Gorp, W.G., and Rapport, L.J., (1998). Variability in clinical classification of raw test scores across normative data sets. *The Clinical Neuropsychologist,* 12, 339-347.

Kaplan, P.C. and Corrigan, J.D., (1994). The relationship between cognition and functional independence in adults with traumatic brain injury. *Archives of Physical Medicine and Rehabilitation,* 75, 643-647.

Karaken, D., (1997). Judgement pitfalls in estimating pre-morbid intellectual function. *Archives of Clinical Neuropsychology,* 12, 701-709.

Karzmark, P., (1992). Prediction of long-term cognitive outcome of brain injury with neuropsychological, severity of injury, and demographic data. *Brain Injury,* 6, 213-217.

Katz, L.J., Wood, D.S., Goldstein, G., Auchenbach, R.C., and Geckle, M., (1998). The utility of neuropsychological tests in evaluation of attention-deficit/hyperactivity disorder (ADHD) vs. depression in adults. *Assessment,* 5, 45-51.

Katzung, B.G., Ed., (1995) *Basic and Clinical Pharmacology* (6th ed.). Appleton and Lange, Norwalk, CT.

Kaufman, A.S., Reynolds, C.R., and McLean, J.E., (1989). Age and WAIS-R intelligence in a national sample of adults in the 20- to 74- year age range: a cross-sectional analysis with education level controlled. *Intelligence,* 13, 235-253.

Keefe, R.S.E., (1995). The contribution of neuropsychology to psychiatry. *American Journal of Psychiatry,* 152, 6-15.

Keefe, R.S.E. and Harvey, P.D., (1994). *Understanding Schizophrenia.* Free Press, New York.

Kent, D.L., Haynor, D.R., Longstreth, W.T., and Larson, E.G., (1994). The clinical efficiency of magnetic resonance imaging in neuroimaging. *Annals of Internal Medicine,* 856-875.

Kerns, A.K. Mateer, C.A., and Brousseau, S., (1998). Computerizing the clinician: internet resources for neuropsychology. *The Clinical Neuropsychologist,* 12, 217-230.

King, D.A., Cox, C., Lyness, J.M., Conwell, Y., and Caine, E.D., (1998). Quantitative and qualitative differences in the verbal learning performance of elderly depressives and healthy controls. *Journal of the International Neuropsychological Society,* 4, 115-116.

Klein, S.H., (1996). Cognitive dysfunction in patients with silicone gel breast implants. *Archives of Clinical Neuropsychology,* 11, 409-410.

Klein, S.H., (1998). Regarding neuropsychological findings in silicone gel breast implant complainants: a comment on Youngjohn, Spector and Mapou (1998). *The Clinical Neuropsychologist,* 12, 231-232.

Kotrla, K.J., Chacko, R.C., Harper, R.G., and Doody, R., (1995). Clinical variables associated with psychosis in Alzheimer's disease. *American Journal of Psychiatry,* 152, 1377-1379.

Kraus, M.F., (1995). Neuropsychiatric sequelae of stroke and traumatic brain injury: the role of psycho-stimulants. *Interactive Journal of Psychiatry in Medicine,* 25, 39-51.

Kreutzer, J.S., Gervasio, A.M., and Camplair, P.S., (1994). Primary caregiver's psychological status and family functioning after traumatic brain injury. *Brain Injury,* 8, 197-210.

Kreutzer, J.S., Marwitz, J.H., and Kepler, K., (1992). Traumatic brain injury: family response and outcome. *Archives of Physical Medicine and Rehabilitation,* 73, 771-778.

Kwasnica, C.M., and Heinemann, A., (1994). Coping with traumatic brain injury: representative case studies. *Archives of Physical Medicine and Rehabilitation,* 75, 384-389.

Lanson-Kerr, K., Smith, P., and Beck, D., (1991). Behavioral neuropsychology. Past, present, and future direction with organically based affect/mood disorders. *Neuropsychology Review,* 12, 65-107.

Larrabee, G.J. and Curtiss, G., (1995). Construct validity of various verbal and visual memory tests. *Journal of Clinical and Experimental Neuropsychology,* 17, 536-547.

Layton, B.S. and Wardi-Zona, K., (1995). Post traumatic stress disorder with neurogenic amnesia for the traumatic event. *Clinical Neuropsychologist,* 9, 2-10.

Le Bihan, D., Jezzard, P., Haxby, J., Sadato, N., Rueckert, L., and Mattay, V., (1995). Functional magnetic resonance imaging of the brain. *Annals of Internal Medicine,* 122, 296-303.

Levin, B., Stuss, D.T., Milberg, W.P., Alexander, M.P., Schwartz, M., and MacDonald, R., (1998). The effects of focal and diffuse brain damage on strategy application: evidence from focal lesions, traumatic brain injury and normal aging. *Journal of the International Neuropsychological Society,* 4, 247-264.

Levin, H.S., Williams, D.H., Eisenberg, H.M., High, W.M., and Guinto, F.C., (1992). Serial MRI and neurobehavioral findings after mild to moderate closed head injury. *Journal of Neurology, Neurosurgery and Psychiatry,* 55, 255-262.

Levin, H.S., High, W.M., Goethe, K.E., Sisson, R.A., Overall, J.E., Rhoae, H.M., Eisenberg, H.M., Kalisky, Z., and Gary, H.E., (1987). The Neurobehavioral Rating Scale: assessment of the behavioral sequelae of head injury by the clinician. *Journal of Neurology, Neurosurgery, and Psychiatry,* 50, 183-193.

Levine, S.C., Banich, M.T., and Koch-Weser, M., (1984). Variations in patterns of lateral asymmetry among dextrals. *Brain and Cognition,* 3, 317-344.

Lezak, M., (1978). Living with the characterologically altered brain injured patient. *Journal of Clinical Psychiatry,* 39, 592-598.

Lezak, M.D., (1995). *Neuropsychological Assessment* (3rd ed.). Oxford University Press, New York.

Lezak, M.D., (1986). Psychological implications of traumatic brain damage for the patient's family. *Rehabilitation Psychology,* 31, 241-250.

Linn, R.T., Allen, K., and Willer, B.S., (1994). Affective symptoms in the chronic stage of traumatic brain injury: a study of married couples. *Brain Injury,* 8, 135-147.

Livingston, M.G., Brooks, D.N., and Bond, M.R., (1985). Three months after severe head injury: psychiatric and social impact on relatives. *Journal of Neurology, Neurosurgery and Psychiatry,* 48, 870-875.

Luria, R.A., (1973). *The Working Brain.* Basic Book, New York.

Luria, R.A., (1980). *Higher Cortical Functions in Man* (2nd ed.). Basic Books, New York.

Luria, R.A., Simernitskaya, E.G., and Tubylevich, B., (1970). The structure of psychological procession relation to cerebral organization. *Neuropsychologia*, 8, 13-19.

Machuloa, M.M., Berquist, Ito, V., and Chew, S., (1998). Relationship between stress coping, and post-concussion symptoms in a healthy adult population. *Archives of Clinical Neuropsychology*, 13, 415-424.

McGlynn, S.M., and Schacter, D.L., (1989). Unawareness of deficits in neuropsychological syndromes. *Journal of Clinical and Experimental Neuropsychology*, 11, 143-205.

McNeill, D.E., Schuyler, B.A., and Ezrachi, O., (1997). Assessing family involvement in traumatic brain injury rehabilitation. The development of a new instrument. *Archives of Clinical Neuropsychology*, 12, 645-660.

Melamed, S. Rahamani, L., Greenstein, Y, Groswasser, Z and Najenson, T., (1985). Divided attention in brain injured patients. *Scandinavian Journal of Rehabilitation Medicine*, 12, 16-20.

Mesulam, M.M., (1985). *Principles of Behavioral Neurology*, F.A. Davis Company, Philadelphia, PA.

Migliorelli, R., Tesón, A., Sabe, L., Petrachi, M., Leiguarda, R., and Starkstein, S., (1995). Prevalence and correlates of dysthymia and major depression among patients with Alzheimer disease. *American Journal of Psychiatry*, 152, 37-44.

Mishkin, M. and Appenzeller, T., (1987). The anatomy of memory. *Scientific American*, 256, 80-89.

Moses, J.A., Pritchard, D.A., and Adams, R.L., (1999). Normative corrections for the Halstead Reitan Neuropsychological Battery. *Archives of Clinical Neuropsychology*, 14, 445-454.

Nelson, L.D., Drebing, C., Satz, P, and Uchimaya, C., (1998). Personality change in head trauma: a validity study of the Neuropsychology Behavior and Affect Profile. *Archives of Clinical Neuropsychology*, 13, 549-560.

Nemiah, J.C., (1995). A few intrusive thoughts on post traumatic stress disorder. *American Journal of Psychiatry*, 152, 501-503.

Nemiah, J.C., (1995). Post traumatic stress disorder: psychology, biology and the manichaean warfare between false dichotomies. *American Journal of Psychiatry*, 152, 963-965.

Newman, R., (1992). The role of the psychologist expert witness: provider of perspective and input. *Neuropsychology Review*, 2, 241-249.

Niemann, H. Ruff, R.M., and Kramer, J.H., (1996). An attempt towards differentiating attentional deficits in traumatic brain injury. *Neuropsychology Review*, 6, 11-46.

Nolan, K. and Burton, L.A., (1998). Incidence of the FULD WAIS-R profile in traumatic brain injury and Parkinson's disease. *Archives of Clinical Neuropsychology*, 13, 425-432.

Novak, T.A. and Johnstone, B., (1998). Addressing a continuum of recovery after acquired brain injury. *Journal of the International Neuropsychological Society*, 4, 409.

Novak, T.A., Daniel, M.S., and Long, C.J., (1984). Factors relating to emotional adjustment following head injury. *International Journal of Clinical Neuropsychology*, 6, 139-142.

O'Boyle, M., Amadeo, M., and Salf, D., (1990). Cognitive complaints in elderly depressed and pseudo-demented patients. *Psychology and Aging*, 5, 467-468.

Oldfield, R.C., (1971). The assessment and analysis of handedness. The Edenburg Inventory. *Neuropsychologia*, 9, 97-113.

Ostrosky-Solis, F., Ardilla, A., Rosselli, M., Lopez-Arango, G., and Uriel-Mendoza, V., (1998). Neuropsychological test performance in illiterate subjects. *Archives in Clinical Neuropsychology*, 13, 645-660.

Panting, A. and Merry, P.M., (1972). Long term rehabilitation of severe head injuries with particular reference to the need for social and medical support for the patient's family. *Rehabilitation*, 38, 33-37.

Paolo, A.M., Troster, A.I., and Ryan, J.J., (1998). Continuous Visual Memory Test performance in healthy persons 60–94 years of age. *Archives of Clinical Neuropsychology*, 333-337.

Paolo, A.M. and Ryan, J.J., (1992). Generalizability of two methods of estimating pre-morbid intelligence in the elderly. *Archives of Clinical Neuropsychology*, 7, 135-143.

Parasuraman, R., Mutter, S.A., and Malloy, R., (1991). Sustained attention following mild closed-head injury. *Journal of Clinical and Experimental Neuropsychology*, 13, 789-711.

Parkin, A.J., (1998). The central executive does not exist. *Journal of the International Neuropsychological Society*, 4, 518-522.

Penry, J.K., (Ed.) (1991). *Epilepsy and Life Performance*. Raven Press, New York.

Perlesz, A., Kinsella, G., and Crowe, S., (1999). Impact of traumatic brain injury on the family: a critical review. *Rehabilitation Psychology*, 44, 6-35.

Peters, L.C., Stambrook, M., Moore, A.D., and Esse, L. (1990). Psychosocial sequelae of closed head injury: Effects on the marital relationship. *Brain Injury*, 4, 39-47.

Posner, M.I. and Rafal, R.D. (1987). Cognitive theories of attention and the rehabilitation of attentional deficits, in *Neuropsychological Rehabilitation*, Meier, M., Benton, A., and Diller, L., Eds., The Guilford Press, New York, p. 182-201.

Potter, S.M. and Graves, R.E., (1988). Is inter-hemispheric transfer related to handedness and gender? *Neuropsychologia*, 26, 319-325.

Pribram, K.M. and McGuinness, D., (1975). Arousal, activation and effort in the control of attention. *Psychological Review*, 82, 176-179.

Prigatano, G.P., Altman, I.M., and O'Brien, K.P., (1990). Behavioral limitations that traumatic-brain-injured patients tend to underestimate. *The Clinical Neuropsychologist*, 4, 163-176.

Prigatano, G.P. and Altman, I.M., (1990). Impaired awareness of behavioral limitations after traumatic brain injury. *Archives of Physical Medicine and Rehabilitation*, 71, 1058-1069.

Prigatano, G.P., (1999). Impaired awareness, finger tapping, rehabilitation outcome after brain injury. *Rehabilitation Psychology*, 44, 145-159

Puente, A.E., (1991). Introduction to the special issue on forensic clinical neuropsychology. *Neuropsychology Review*, 2, 203-204.

Putnam, S.H. and Millis, S.R., (1994). Psychosocial factors in the development and maintenance of chronic somatic and functional symptoms following mild traumatic brain injury. *Advances in Medical Psychotherapy*, 7, 1-22.

Raz, N., Gunning-Dixon, F.M., Head, D., Dupuis, J.H., and Acker, J.D., (1998). Neuroanatomical correlates of cognitive aging: evidence from structural magnetic resonance imaging. *Neuropsychology*, 12, 95-114.

Reitan, R.M. and Wolfson, D., (1995). Influence of age and education on neuropsychological test results. *Clinical Neuropsychologist*, 9, 151-158.

Reitan, R.M. and Wolfson, D., (1998). *Mild Head Injury: Intellectual, Cognitive and Emotional Consequences*. Neuropsychology Press, Tucson, AZ.

Reitan, R.M. and Wolfson, D., (1999). The two faces of mild head injury. *Archives of Clinical Neuropsychology*, 12, 191-202.

Reynolds, C.R., (1997). Postscripts on premorbid ability estimation: conceptual addenda and a few words on alternative and conditional approaches. *Archives of Clinical Neuropsychology*, 12, 769-778.

Reynolds, C.F., Dew, M.A., Frank, E., Begley, A.E., Miller, M.D., Cornes, C., Mazumdar, S., Perel, J.A., and Kupfer, D.J., (1998). Effects of age at onset of first lifetime episode of recurrent major depression on treatment response and illness course in elderly patients. *American Journal of Psychiatry*, 6, 795-799.

Riccio, D.C., Rabinowitz, V.C., and Axelrod, S., (1994). Memory: When less is more. *American Psychologist*, 49, 917-926.

Richards, P.M. and Ruff, R.M., (1989). Motiviational effects on neuropsychological functioning: comparison of depressed versus nondepressed individuals. *Journal of Consulting and Clinical Psychology,* 57, 396-402.

Richardson, E.D. and Marottoli, R.A., (1996). Education — specific normative data on common neuropsychological indices for individuals older than 75 years. *The Clinical Neuropsychologist,* 10, 375-381.

Rivara, J.B., Jaffe, K.M., Polissar, N.L., Fay, G.C., Martin, K.M., Shurtleff, H.A., and Liao, S., (1994). Family functioning and children's academic performance and behavior problems in the year following traumatic brain injury. *Archives of Physical Medicine and Rehabilitation,* 75, 369-379.

Robinson, R.G. and Szetta, B., (1981). Mood change following left hemisphere brain injury. *Annals of Neurology,* 9, 447-453.

Rogaeva, E., Premkumar, S., Song, Y., Sorbi, S., Brindle, N., Paterson, A., Duara, R., levesque, G., Yu, G., Nishimura, M., Ideda, M., O'Toole, C., Kawarai, T., Jorge, R., Vilarino, D., Bruni, A.C., Farrer, L.A., and George-Hyslop, P.H., (1988). Evidence for an Alzheimer disease susceptibility locus on chromosome 12 and for further locus heterogeneity. *Journal of the American Medical Association,* 280, 614-618.

Romano, M.D., (1974). Family responses to traumatic brain injury. *Scandinavian Journal of Rehabilitation Medicine,* 6, 1-4.

Rosseli, M., Ardilla, A., and Rosas, P., (1990). Neuropsychological assessment in illiterates II: language and praxic abilities. *Brain and Cognition,* 12, 281-296.

Russell, E.W., Neuringer, C., and Goldstein, E., (1970). *Assessment of Brain Damage: A Neuropsychological Key Approach.* John Wiley and Sons, New York.

Sakow, D., (1963). Psychological deficit in schizophrenia. *Behavioral Science,* 8, 275-305.

Sala, S.D., Logie, R.H., Trivelli, C., Cubelli, R., and Marchetti, C., (1998). Dissociation between recency and span: neuropsychological and experimental evidence. *Neuropsychology,* 12, 533-545.

Sala, S.D., Gray, C., Spinnler, H., and Trivelli, C., (1998). Frontal lobe functioning in man. The riddle revisited. *Archives of Clinical Neuropsychology,* 13, 663-682.

Sanders, C.M., Mauger, P.A., and Strong, P.N., (1985). *A Manual for the Grief Experience Inventory.* Consulting Psychologists Press, Palo Alto, CA.

Sbordone, R.J., (1991). *The side effects of neuro-pharmacological medications on neuropsychological test performance in the traumatically brain injured patient.* Abstract. Annual Meeting of the American Psychological Association, San Francisco.

Schlegel, S., Maier, W., Philipp, M., Aldenhoff, J.B., Heuser, I., Kretzschmar, K., and Benkert, O., (1989). Computed tomography in depression: association between ventricular size and psychopathology. *Psychiatry Research,* 29, 221-230.

Segalowitz, S.J., Dywan, J., and Unsal, A., (1997). Attentional factors in response time variability after traumatic brain injury: An ERP study. *Journal of the International Neuropsychological Society,* 3, 95-107.

Selnes, O.A., Jacobsen, L., Machado, A.M., Becker, J.T., Wesch, J., Miller, E.M., Visscher, B., and McArthur, J., (1991). Normative data for a brief neuropsychological screening battery. Multi-center AIDS Cohort Study. *Perceptual and Motor Skills,* 73, 539-550.

Shalev, A.Y., Freedman, S., Peri, T., Brandes, D., Sahar, T., Orr, S.P., and Pitman, R.K., (1998). Perspective study of post traumatic stress disorder and depression following trauma. *American Journal of Psychiatry,* 155, 630-637.

Shallice, T. and Burgess, P., (1991). Deficits in strategy application following frontal lobe damage in man. *Brain,* 114, 727-741.

Shallice, T. and Burgess, P., (1993). Supervisory control of action and thought selection, in *Attention: Selection, Awareness and Control: A Tribute to Donald Broadbent,* Baddeley, A. and Weistrantz, L., Eds., Clarendon Press, Oxford, U.K., p. 171-187.

Sherer, M., Boake, C., Levin, E., Silver, B.V., Ringholz, G., and High, W.M., (1998). Characteristics of impaired awareness after traumatic brain injury. *Journal of the International Neuropsychological Society,* 4, 380-387.

Sherman, A.G., Shaw, T.G., and Glidden, H., (1994). Emotional behavior as an agenda in neuropsychological evaluation. *Neuropsychological Review,* 4, 45-69.

Small, G.W., La Rue, A., Komo, S., Kaplan, A., and Mandelkern, M.A., (1995). Predictors of cognitive change in middle-aged and older adults with memory loss. *American Journal of Psychiatry,* 152, 1757-1764.

Speedie, L. Rabins, P., Pearlson, G., and McBerg, P., (1978). Confrontation naming deficit in dementia of depression. *Journal of Neuropsychiatry and Clinical Neurosciences,* 2, 59-63.

Squire, L.R., (1992). Declarative and non-declarative memory: multiple brain systems supporting learning and memory. *Journal of Cognitive Neuroscience,* 4, 232-243.

Stein, R.A. and Strickland, T.L., (1998). A review of the neuropsychological effects of commonly used prescription medications. *Archives of Clinical Neuropsychology,* 13, 259-284.

Stern, Y., Gurland, B., Tatemichi, T.K., Tang, M.X., Wilder, D., and Mayeux, R., (1994). Influence of education and occupation on the incidence of Alzheimer disease. *Journal of the American Medical Association,* 271, 1004-1010.

Storandt, M., and Van Den Bos, G.R., Eds., (1994). *Neuropsychological Assessment of dementia and depression.* American Psychological Association, Washington D.C.

Stuss, D.T., and Benson, D.F., (1986). *The Frontal Lobes.* Raven Press, New York.

Suchy, Y., Blint, A., and Osmon, D.C., (1997). Behavioral dyscontrol scale: criterion and predictive validity in on inpatient rehabilitation unit population. *The Clinical Neurologist,* 11, 258-265.

Sweet, J., (1983). Confounding effects of depression on neuropsychologist testing. Five illustrative cases. *Clinical Neuropsychology,* 5, 103-109.

Symonds, C.P., (1987). Mental disorder following head injury. *Proceedings of the Royal Society of Medicine,* 30, 1081-1094.

Tromp, E. and Mulder, T., (1991). Slowness of information processing after traumatic head injury. *Journal of Clinical and Experimental Neuropsychology,* 13, 821-830.

Tucker, D.M., (1981). Lateral brain function, emotion and conceptualization. *Psychological Bulletin,* 89, 19-46.

Uchiyama, C.L., Mitrushina, M., Satz, P., and Schall, M., (1996). Direct and indirect effects of demographic medical and psychological variables on neuropsychological performance in normal geriatric persons. A structural equation model. *Journal of the International Neuropsycholgical Society,* 2, 299-305.

Vakil, E., Openheim, M., Falck, D., Aberbuch, S., and Groswasser, Z., (1997). Indirect influence of modality on direct memory of words and their modality: closed-head-injured and control participants. *Neuropsychology,* 11, 545-551.

Van Gorp, W.G. and McMullen, W., (1997). Courting the Clinician: potential sources of bias in forensic neuropsychological evaluations. *The Clinical Neuropsychologist,* 11, 180-187.

Van Zomeren, A.M., Brouwer, U.H., and Deelman, B.G., (1984). Attentional deficits: the riddles of selectivity, speed and alertness, in *Closed Head Injury: Psychological, Social and Family Consequences,* Brooks, N., Ed., New York, Oxford University Press, p. 74-107.

Vasterling, J.J., Brailey, K., Constans, J.I., and Sutker, P.B., (1998). Attention and memory dysfunction in post-traumatic stress disorder. *Neuropsychology,* 12, 125-133.

Watson, C.G., Davis, W., and Gaser, B., (1978). The separation of organics from depressives with ability and personality-based tests. *Journal of Clinical Psychology,* 34, 393-397.

Watts, F.N., (1995). Depression and Anxiety, in *Handbook of Memory Disorders,* Baddeley, A.D., Wilson, B.A., and Watts, F.N., Eds., John Wiley & Sons, Chichester, U.K., p. 293-317.

Wedding, D., (1991). Clinical judgement in forensic neuropsychology: a comment on the risks of claiming more than can be delivered. *Neuropsychology Review,* 2, 233-239.

Weinstein, G.A. and Kahn, R.L., (1955). *Denial of Illness.* Charles Thomas, Springfield, IL.

Wilson, R.S., Rosenbaum, G., Brown, G., Rourke, D., Whitman, R.D., and Griselli, J., (1978). An index of pre-morbid intelligence. *Journal of Consulting and Clinical Psychology,* 46, 1554-1555.

Yates, A., (1956). The use of vocabulary in the measurement of intellectual deterioration: a review. *Journal of Mental Science,* 102, 409-440.

Yedid, J., (2000). The neuropsychological evaluation, in *The Forensic Evaluation of Traumatic Brain Injury: A Handbook for Clinicians and Attorneys,* Murrey, G., Ed., CRC Press LLC, Boca Raton, FL.

Yehuda, R. and McFarlane, A.C., (1995). Conflict between current knowledge about post-traumatic stress disorder and its original conceptual basis. *American Journal of Psychiatry, 152,* 1705.

Youngjohn, J.R., Spector, J., and Mapou, R.L., (1998). *The Clinical Neuropsychologist, 12,* 233-236.

Youngjohn, J.R., Burrows, L., and Erdal, K., (1995). Brain damage or compensation neurosis? The controversial post-concussive syndrome. *The Clinical Neuropsychologist,* 9, 112-123.

Zaidel, E., Aboitiz, F., Clarke, J., Kaiser, D., and Matteson, R., (1995). Sex differences in inter-hemispheric language relations, in *Hemispheric Communication: Mechanisms and Models,* Kitterle, F., Ed., Erlbaum, Hillsdale, NJ, p. 85-175.

Zinner, E.S., Ball, J.D., Stutts, M.L., and Philput, C., (1997). Grief reactions of mothers and adolescents and young adults with traumatic brain injury. *Archives of Clinical Neuropsychology, 12,* 435-449.

5 The Forensic Examiner as an Expert Witness: What You Need to Know to Be a Credible Witness in an Adversarial Setting

Joseph A. Davis and Gregory J. Murrey

CONTENTS

5.1 INTRODUCTION

Due to advances in research, science, and medicine over the past 75 years, courts, "fact finders," and "triers of fact" have looked for standards of acceptability. In the scientific and medical community, a standard is usually agreed upon by practicing professionals, researchers, and academics from which evidence can be compared or examined. For example, a specific procedure, technique, and method (or lack thereof) used to perform some operation can be agreed upon as a standard method of operation in examining a patient. Any unusual deviation of such a method can be questioned, particularly if harm or negligence to a patient becomes the legal question to be argued.

Expert testimony is not a new phenomenon that has recently entered county, state, or federal criminal cases. "Ever since 1946 there has been a comprehensive federal procedure for court-appointed experts and many states have similar procedures" (Kaplan, Waltz, and Roger, 1992). Expert witnesses have gained recent notoriety by television exposure of many sensationalized murder cases. With the advent of Court-TV-related viewing, and programs involving "trial watch," viewers can monitor, track, and listen in, right in the comfort of their homes or offices.

Due to the advances in forensic science, such as more sensitive neuroimaging technology, psychological analysis, and evidence collection, expert testimony is becoming increasingly important in today's legal system and in personal injury litigations. Most lay people today may not understand the legal aspects of expert testimony beyond what they have viewed on television. When it comes to the battle of the experts, the evidence can be lost due to confusion over the two conflicting sides. An easy solution is the use of court appointed experts — however, they are rarely used, even in high profile cases. When a trial involves technical or scientific issues of fact, expert witnesses may become very important. "An attorney will use great care in choosing his expert and in preparing for trial" (Kraft, 1982, p. 53). He or she will not necessarily seek one who is most qualified; instead, he will probably choose the expert who will best support his client's cause, and, perhaps, conceal its weaknesses. The strategy he or she employs may be used with equal skill by his adversary. "The result is a "battle of experts," the performance often baffles jurors and judges alike, leaving them unable to detect the truth or to pass upon the underlying questions of competency and honesty between the contenders" (Kraft, 1982, p. 53).

"The present mode of doing battle by experts has been condemned by various commentators" (Cecil and Willging, 1993). The extreme partisanship of expert witnesses is perceived as its chief evil. The practice of shopping for experts, as stated by the Advisory Committee on the Federal Rules of Evidence, is a matter of deep concern in the administration of justice. More than a century ago, the problem was described by the United States Supreme Court, in *Winans v. New York & Eric R. R.*, 1858: "Experience has shown that opposite opinions of persons professing to be experts may be obtained to any amount; and what often occurs is that not only many days, but often weeks are consumed in cross examinations to test the skill or knowledge of such witnesses and the correctness of their opinions, (wasting the time and wearying the patience of both court and jury, and perplexing, instead of elucidating, the questions involved in the issue)".

The problem of the "battle of the experts" seems to be of great importance in our judicial system. Then why are court-appointed experts not used to diffuse this problem? The courts have the power to appoint an impartial expert witness, however, this is done very rarely and only in certain situations.

5.2 THE MEDICAL PROFESSIONAL AND THE NEUROPSYCHOLOGIST AS FORENSIC EXPERT

"The importance of expert testimony, often crucial to the outcome of a trial, has long been known to lawyers and judges" (Kraft, 1982, p. 23). There are literally hundreds, even thousands, of subjects of expert testimony: neuropsychology, medicine, surgery, automobiles, ballistics, blood, accounting, property valuation, genealogy, safety, and others too numerous to mention.

By definition, "an expert is a person skilled in some art, trade, or science to the extent that he or she possesses information not within the common knowledge of people" (O'Hara and O'Hara 1994). The skills or knowledge of an expert may be acquired through experience, study, observation, or education. To be an expert witness, one need not necessarily have a formal education. "The expert witness is permitted to interpret facts and give opinions about their significance; the lay witness may only present facts which are a matter of first hand knowledge" (Swanson, Chamelin, and Territo, 1988).

"The expert witness is called on to assist the jurors in understanding facts which they are ordinarily not sufficiently trained to understand, such as the results of medical examinations, chemical analysis, ballistics reports, and findings from questioned documents" (Anderson, 1987). Expert testimony is not proof, but evidence that can be accorded its own credibility and weight by each member of the court.

5.2.1 LEGAL TESTS OF ADMISSIBILITY AND EXPERT TESTIMONY

"An expert may not testify as such until they have satisfied the court that they have the proper skill, knowledge, and background of experience or education" (O'Hara and O'Hara, 1994). In other words, he or she must possess the proper qualifications. Experts must also testify on a subject in which expert testimony should be received. The facts relating to the opinion must be of such a technical nature that the judge and jury may not be expected to have sufficient knowledge, skill, and understanding of such matters.

Frye v. United States (1923), dealt with evidence derived from newly introduced scientific theories. "Frye requires expert opinion testimony to be based on an established body of scientific, technical, or particularized knowledge, information, or study sufficiently established to have gained general acceptance in the particular field" (Feder, 1991). An expert witness must be prepared to show that the professional, scientific, or technical premise on which they rely has been sufficiently well established to have gained general acceptance in the specific field to which it belongs. "However, the Federal Rules of Evidence probably represents the mainstream of current legal thinking about admissibility of expert testimony" (Feder, 1991).

As has always been the case, the presiding judge in any case has the ultimate authority to rule on the admissibility of expert testimony. However, the presiding judge in any given case typically applies existing standards such as the Federal Rules of Evidence (specifically Rule 702 addressing testimony by experts) or the standards set in landmark court decisions such as those in *Frye, Daubert* and more recently, the *Joiner* case. The Federal Rules of Evidence that may be applicable to expert testimony in traumatic brain injury (TBI) cases include the following:

Rule 104a	Preliminary Questions
Rule 401	Definition of Relevant Evidence
Rule 402	Relevant Evidence is Generally Admissible; Irrelevant Evidence is Inadmissible
Rule 403	Exclusion of Relevant Evidence on Grounds of Prejudice, Confusion or Waste of Time
Rule 701	Opinion Testimony by Lay Witnesses
Rule 702	Testimony of Experts
Rule 703	Bases of Opinion Testimony by Experts
Rule 705	Disclosure Facts or Data Underlying Expert Opinion
Rule 706	Court Appointed Experts

In Rule 702, The Testimony of Experts specifically states that if scientific, technical, or otherwise specialized knowledge will assist the trier of fact to understand the evidence or to determine a fact an issue, a witness qualified as an expert by knowledge, skill, experience, training, or education may testify thereto in the form of an opinion or otherwise.

The recent Supreme Court Decision in *Joiner* (*General Electric v. Joiner*, 1997), gives the judge the freedom to "conclude that there is simply too great an analytical gap between the data and the opinion proffered" by the expert witness. Thus, "the trial judge may require that expert conclusions be substantiated and not speculative" (Reed, 1999). Thus, the Supreme Court has now granted a much greater discretion to lower court judges on ruling on the admissibility of expert witness testimony. Appendix C provides a listing of state courts using Federal Rule 702 and those using the Daubert standard. Considering the historical as well as newer standards on the admissibility standards being applied by judges on the admissibility of expert witness testimony, it behooves forensic examiners to support their professional opinions on the given case with sound scientific data.

Generally, a fact witness stipulates to events based upon their direct observation of an event or occurrence that they happened to see. From that direct observation, they simply provide information to the court on what event actually took place. To be a fact witness only requires direct firsthand knowledge regarding information that is before the court as part of a matter that is central or key to the legal debate or argument. Typically, the scientific vs. the legal truth lies somewhere between the presented theory, the evidence of each case, the court, and the trier of fact. What is important as fact to the neuropsychologist or medical professional as a forensic scientist may not be important to the attorney. For a variety of reasons, unless argued and agreed upon during a pretrial hearing, the judge decides what is admissible in terms of evidence and testimony before and during the trial process. In all cases, the judge, based upon legal argument, decides what (if any) evidence the jury will be exposed to.

Certain types of evidence can or cannot be admitted depending upon its educational, demonstrative, or probative value to assist the trier of fact in rendering a final decision or verdict. However, some evidence can have potential "inflammatory and prejudicial" qualities in terms of admissibility if it serves more to influence the jury's emotions and sympathy vs. having a probative and demonstrative value to inform and educate the fact finder and trier of fact. Other evidence can often have irrelevant legal qualities in terms of referencing information that may potentially mislead the trier of fact. Such an occurrence can often lead to a mistrial as this type of information can certainly affect jury emotion and testimony.

Other types of evidence, such as unimportant and legally irrelevant but factual evidence, finds its way into court such as the portrayal of a victim as an upstanding citizen vs. a frail nobody seeking a monetary award from a successful, deep-pocketed insurance company. Voir dire is yet another type of evidence where by the court may want to further question an expert to determine if certain facts of the argued case are important or not. A voir dire (examination) is conducted where a side-bar conversation between the judge and attorneys is conducted outside the jury's listening range typically to discuss issues of admissibility and relevance.

The judge has the discretion over the court to dismiss or release the jury momentarily so that the attorneys and judge can question the expert outside the jury's presence on the relevance of the facts pertaining to the issues being argued in the case. If the testimony is relevant, the question is repeated for the jury's appreciation and understanding. Also, the "type and form of evidence" is important as all evidence must conform and be admitted based on tightly prescribed rules of evidence allowable and admissible to the forum (court). These rules of evidence vary depending on whether is it a criminal, civil, or non-adversarial situation. Other evidence such as "hearsay evidence" allows the expert witness to testify to information other than "firsthand" data — that is, from direct individual observation.

Typically, one is precluded from testifying to or about the observations from others, however, an exception is made for "hearsay" evidence. The medical professional as a scientist is afforded tremendous latitude in this area because of their expertise and is permitted to testify to matters such as interpreting the importance of or accuracy/inaccuracy of medical records, reports, tests, or charts written or prepared by others. Furthermore, physicians and other such medical "scientists" (such as neuropsychologists) can also testify to certain methods, protocols, or procedures used, performed, or conducted by others as well.

Degrees of certainty are also matters that arise in the forum (courtroom) when such information as scientific technology, neuropsychology, science, and medicine clash and require the expert witness to provide "a reasonable degree of scientific or medical certainty" (opinion) as to an outcome or the probability of an outcome. In such cases, the expert witness needs to be careful of semantics. In court (especially in tort, wrongful death, or personal injury cases), attorneys like to take qualifiable issues and quantify them into facts in the form of numbers. As a caveat, it is recommended here that the neuropsychologist or forensic expert approach this issue or matter with extreme precaution and surgical precision as almost anything is possible in the world of medical science since events can happen that can not be explained away by conventional and traditional technique, method, or skill. Furthermore, since attorneys enjoy quantifying data, be careful of the "within a certain degree of medical or scientific certainty question" designed to solicit your opinion based upon percentages and probabilities. Oftentimes, these percentages and probabilities in the real world of mathematical equation and formula cause problems for the physician or other forensic examiner because such numbers can be arbitrary and very difficult to support.

The "hypothetical question" is another scenario in which the attorney paints a picture involving some piece of evidence already admitted into the forum. The hypothetical question is designed to solicit an opinion carefully constructed as to stipulate that it is typically "consistent with one's observations." If from the record and your experience, your impression is consistent, say so. If not, don't. Often, experts will testify to both sides of the argument or debate when proffered. Ultimately, it is up to the jury to decide if the "hypothetical" story or scenario in this case, is believable.

5.2.2 COURT APPOINTED FORENSIC EXPERTS

The court may, on its own motion or on the motion of any party, enter an order to show cause why expert witnesses should not be appointed, and may request the parties to submit nominations. "The judge can either appoint experts agreed upon by the parties or can appoint experts of his own selection" (Kaplan, Waltz, and Roger, 1992). A court appointed expert is informed of his or her duties by the judge, either in writing or at a conference where both parties have an opportunity to take part. A court appointed expert will inform the parties of his or her findings and can thereafter be called to the stand by the trial judge or any party to give testimony. Court appointed experts are subject to full examination by all parties. "Experts appointed by the trial court are most commonly encountered in cases in which it is suggested either that the accused was legally insane at the time of the offense (NGRI) charged or that the accused is presently incompetent to stand trial (ICST) because of his inability to comprehend the proceedings and cooperate with his defense counsel" (Haddad et al. 1992). When this situation occurs the court may appoint one or more psychiatrists to examine the accused and to report the results.

"The use of a court appointed expert is a means for improving the truth finding process through competence and objectivity" (Kraft, 1982). The expert's lack of personal interest in the outcome of the case should enhance his or her contribution. If the expert testifies, cross examination is likely to be limited to the technical issues rather than collateral matters. "Avenues for impeaching the adversary expert by showing that he was hired by a party and is being paid for his opinion, that he is a professional expert witness and the like, will be unavailing" (Kraft, 1982, p. 57). Even before trial, the influence of objective scrutiny is especially valuable in preventing or overcoming exaggerated positions. The report on the operation of the Medical Expert Testimony project between 1952 and 1954 concluded that it seems highly probable that the very existence of the project tends to deter doctors and lawyers from making consciously false or grossly exaggerated medical claims.

The adoption of *Rule 706 of Federal Rules of Evidence Code* and corresponding provisions in many states may stimulate the use of court appointed experts. According to Kraft (1982), litigators should be aware of the following potential benefits offered by court appointed impartial experts:

1. To assist the triers of fact in reaching a correct result.
2. To improve the predictability of the outcome.
3. To help in evaluating the case.
4. To cast a prophylactic influence on partisan expert reports and testimony, tending to curb excesses.
5. To provide qualified, reliable experts who might otherwise refuse to testify.
6. To stimulate settlement negotiations by impartial reports on the influence of the above factors.
7. To supply testimony that will help shorten the trial.

According to Kraft (1982), there is a risk that appointed experts may not, in fact, be impartial. Conscious or unconscious motives may affect their opinions. On cross-examination they may identify with their own opinions and, as a result, introduce a degree of bias. "One antagonist asserts that no one is impartial; therefore, court appointed experts are likely to have biases and prejudices just as other people do" (Kraft, 1982, p. 29). In addition, the existence of bias on other levels is also possible. For example, it has been suggested that the appointment of a local expert will not work in malpractice cases because he may be reluctant to testify against a defendant from the same community. This may explain why medical and dental malpractice cases are excluded from the local court rule applicable to personal injury, disability, and death actions in Bronx and New York counties as adopted by the Appellate Division for the First Judicial Department.

The possibility of bias, thus, cannot be ignored as there is no guarantee that an appointee will have no bias or predilections. This is a factor that must be measured since it adds an element of uncertainty in predicting the ultimate result in the case. "The court's appointment of the expert, his high competence, and the selection of cases which are amenable to objective, technical analysis should reduce or supplant bias that might otherwise exert its influence" (Kraft, 1982). Another safeguard is the joint selection of an expert by the parties rather than by the court when the parties are able to agree. It is important that care in the selection of the appointed expert is a key factor in his or her value.

5.2.3 IMPEACHMENT OF THE EXPERT: DISCREDITING THE FORENSIC EXAMINER

The impeachment of the neuropsychologist or other medical professional as an expert witness in TBI cases is nothing more than an attempt of an opposing attorney during inquiry to show contradictory testimony and disclosure. This often happens when what was said by the expert under oath and "on the record" during deposition contradicts or is different than what is said in court. Remember, attorneys work from many pretrial records and documents and typically never ask a question unless they know the answer in advance from that record. In court, semantics play a integral role in cross-examination and re-cross examination (done by opposing legal counsel). A "re-wording" of a question can elicit a sometimes surprise response from the expert which can lead to disastrous consequences. The forensic examiner should be on the look out for any questions prefaced with "do you remember me taking your statement during deposition"? Such statements should remind the witness that he or she is being impeached and will need to explain the apparent differences in the testimony to the attorney and to the trier of fact. In cases in which the contradiction cannot be (or in which the opposing attorney does not allow the witness to explain that contradiction) explained, the attorney who has engaged that professional as a designated forensic expert will have to attempt to maneuver a clinical strategy to repair or rehabilitate the expert on the stand. If not, the attorney of record can bring another expert to repair or rehabilitate the contradictory (and sometimes damaging) testimony. In all cases, to avoid impeachment and discrediting which invites the need for rehabilitation, the forensic expert should always remain consistent throughout the deposition and courtroom testimony and know every fact and detail of the case. The forensic expert should always remember that he or she is the expert witness in the case and not the attorney.

5.2.4 COMPENSATION FOR THE FORENSIC EXPERT

If the forensic expert is an employee of a medical clinic or facility, fees and compensation are routine and a fee structure has typically already been established. If the expert is engaged in private practice, compensation should be set forth in an "engagement letter" (Fisher, 1993). Expert fees vary as arrangements can be made on a per hour, per day, or even by retainer agreement. Fees expert witnesses today charge also can vary depending on who is doing the engaging for services such as a public service agency, i.e., District Attorney, Public Defender, or a private civil defense law firm. Witness fees may be determined by experience, complexity of the assignment, or time constraints placed on the expert. Both forensic examiners and legal professionals should be aware that cross examination of an expert directed at establishing bias through financial interest is allowed (Strong, 1992). According to Strong, the cross examiner may seek to establish financial interest in the case at hand by reason of remuneration for services, including services performed which enable him to testify, continued employment by a party, or the fact of prior testimony for the same party or the same attorney. Other inquiries allowed by cross examination of an expert include the amount of previous compensation from the same party and the relation between the expert's income from testifying for this one party and the total income of the expert. As shown, compensation amounts can raise a new line of questioning regarding the expert witness that do not relate to his or her expert knowledge.

5.2.5 RESEARCH ON FORENSIC EXPERTS

In a review of expert profiles, Feder (1991) surveyed 160 forensic experts from 7 major speciality categories (see Table 5.1 for a summary of the number of respondents by specialty) regarding various issues relative to the expert and forensic cases. Of these experts, 54 responded to the survey. Table 5.2 shows the results of the survey — note that the averages shown were obtained by totaling the number of responses to each question and then dividing by the number of response to the particular question. There are a number of findings that have been derived from this and other

TABLE 5.1
Survey Results of Forensic Experts:
Number of Respondents by Specialty Category

Specialty Category	Number of Respondents
Medicine and psychiatry	9
Economics, sociology, and psychology	9
Accident investigation and reconstruction	6
Construction and engineering	10
Accounting	4
Appraisal	13
Document-text interpretation	13
Demonstrative evidence or miscellaneous	13

TOTAL = 54

Source: Adapted from Feder (1991).

TABLE 5.2
Survey of Forensic Examiners: Average Responses to Specific Survey
Questions

Information	Average Responses
Years serving as forensic expert	14.6 years
Total number of cases investigated	442.0 cases
Depositions given	79.0 depositions
Trials which required testimony	55.5 trials
Administrative hearings requiring testimony	18.9 hearings
Depositions conducted by experts without attorney	36.0 depositions
Attorney assisted depositions or testimony (without attorney)	15.4 trials
Cases where attorney would have been helpful	58.8 cases
Cases where attorney would not have been helpful	17.4 cases
Cases for which a written fee and letter was used	33.9 assignments
Cases involving fee disputes with client or attorney	2.3 situations

Source: Adapted from Feder (1991).

studies which may have practical implications for forensic professionals. For example, if a pretrial procedure fails to reveal information necessary to permit a reasonable resolution of the disputed issues, the judge may wish to appoint an expert. However, the Federal Judicial Center's case study and this author's own research suggest that such cases will be infrequent and will be typically characterized by evidence that is particularly difficult to comprehend (particularly when credible forensic experts find little basis for agreement resulting in profound failure of the adversarial system which cannot, in such cases, provide information necessary to sort through the conflicting claims and interpretations). Judges who had appointed experts emphasized the extraordinary nature of such a procedure and showed no willingness to abandon the adversarial process before it had failed to provide the information necessary to understand the issues and resolve the dispute.

Appointment of an expert by the court thus represents a striking departure from the process of presenting information for the resolution of disputes. Such an appointment, however, should not be regarded as a lack of faith in the adversarial system.

This author has learned that judges who appointed experts appear to be as devoted to the adversarial system as those who made no such appointments. Most appointments of experts were made after extensive efforts failed to find a means within the adversarial system to gain the information necessary for a reasoned resolution of the dispute.

5.2.6 QUALITIES OF THE EFFECTIVE EXPERT

Davis (1996) and Feder (1991) give eight qualities that identify the effective, credible expert witness:

- The expert must perform a thorough investigation.
- The expert must be personable, genuine, and natural.
- The expert must have an ability to teach.
- The expert must be generally competent.
- The expert must be believable.
- The expert must persuade without advocacy.
- The expert must be prepared.
- The expert must demonstrate enthusiasm.

Visual aids, such as large charts or overheads that can be presented by the attorney and/or forensic witness for the jurors and/or judge to refer to, can also be invaluable in TBI cases. Such aids help the jurors and judge to remain attentive and to better understand sometimes complex or even technical information and data. The following is a list of visual aids that could be used by the forensic examiner and/or legal professional during deposition or testimony:

1. Medical or legal definitions and/or criteria for TBI particularly mild TBI (see Table 1.2 in Chapter 1).
2. Brief definitions of specific medical terms associated with TBI (e.g., closed head injury, concussion, post-concussional syndrome, amnestic disorder, etc.).
3. A list of common chronic symptoms following TBI (see Table 1.6 in Chapter 1).
4. A checklist of the examinee's documented symptoms, injuries, and/or medical problems post-injury.
5. A chart showing the examinee's medical, psychological/emotional, cognitive, and functional status and abilities, pre- and post-injury (listing pre- and post-injury status side-by-side for comparison).
6. A list of examinee performance and impairment level (mild, moderate, severe) by specific neuropsychological or cognitive function (see Appendix A).
7. Chronological history of evaluations and diagnoses of the examinee.
8. A comparison of findings between two or more examiners (e.g., neurologist, psychologist, neuropsychologist, etc.).

9. Enlarged, simplified illustration of the brain and skull designating site(s) of injury.
10. List of neuroimaging studies or technology (e.g., CT, MRI, EEG, PET, etc.) with brief definitions of each and/or findings specific to the TBI case.

Visual aids should be clear and concise, preferably in bullet format with large print or design. The visual aids should not overload the jury with too much information. Also, when a jury is present, the expert should always make an effort to maintain eye contact with and face towards the jurors.

If the forensic examiner can become knowledgeable and experienced in the use of such aids and approaches, the more effective he or she will be as an expert witness.

5.2.7 THE NEUROPSYCHOLOGIST AS EXPERT WITNESS

The expert witness is typically an individual specifically recognized by the court as having education, experience, training, and knowledge beyond that of the trier of fact, i.e., the jury and the court, to assist in rendering an opinion on a particular subject, topic, or issue. To be an expert does not necessarily mean that you have more knowledge in the real world than anyone. What it does mean is that you are recognized as having special knowledge to explain complicated methods and procedures, technical matters and data, as well as the ability to interpret and render an objective opinion about certain set of facts or information to the court.

Often, the practicing neuropsychologist as forensic scientist will be called upon to render an opinion as to medical procedure, protocol, diagnosis, and treatment (or lack of as in malpractice), as well as to specific degrees of medical certainty as it relates to a clinical trials, and the application of a procedure as it relates to rehabilitation and recovery outcomes.

In our American judicial system, the adversarial process means that an attorney represents his or her viewpoint of a legal issue while the other attorney argues and represents the opposing side of that issue. In addition to opposing arguments, the adversarial system also includes procedures involving deposition and, of course, trials to include pretrial evidentiary hearings and post-trial hearings involving sentencing.

Typically, when opposing attorneys call and examine experts for their proffered opinions, there are oftentimes conflicts between legal counsel and the medical practitioner or forensic scientist. These conflicts can be avoided by remembering to be a neutral party and always an objective scientist who is, for all practical purposes, genuinely disinterested in the outcome of the case, regardless of who calls you to the stand to testify. And, regardless of the situation, issue, or case, always remain an objective scientist.

The neuropsychologist as a forensic examiner is not an advocate or a legal adversary (that is the function of the attorneys). To testify as a matter of course in a deposition or a trial is to always render your opinion with integrity and truthfulness regardless of the negative or positive impact it may have.

An important issue for a neuropsychologist in forensic cases is the clarification of the difference between a "neurologist" and a "neuropsychologist." A clinical neuropsychologist is a licensed doctoral level trained clinical psychologist, who has received extensive speciality training in brain behavior relationships in the assessment of cognitive or higher cortical brain functions such as attention, memory, and learning, visual spatial abilities, and planning and problem solving. A neuropsychologist is trained in neuroanatomy, neurophysiology, and behavioral neurology. Although neither a medical doctor nor able to prescribe medications, the neuropsychologist is trained in determining clinical diagnoses of psychological and cognitive disorders (secondary to or associated with central nervous system disorders). The neuropsychologist is also trained in the assessment of TBI and other neurological disorders through the use of standardized neuropsychological test batteries. There are currently two primary organizations that provide "board certification" to clinical neuropsychologists: the American Board of Professional Psychology (Clinical Neuropsychology) and The American Board of Professional Neuropsychology. Both organizations conduct a thorough review of the professional's training, experience, and credentials as well as in-depth testing of the potential diplomate (see Table 5.3 for the standard background and qualifications for a forensic neuropsychologist).

Although "board certification" is not required of nor obtained by all qualified clinical neuropsychologists, it is of particular importance in the forensic setting by which the clinician is able to establish his or her credibility and qualification as an expert witness in this speciality area. The attorney initially questioning the forensic neuropsychologist during deposition or trial will almost always ask the professional to define what is a "neuropsychologist" and how that profession differs from neurology. The following statement is an appropriate response by the neuropsychologist to such questions:

> As a neuropsychologist, I am trained in the use of standardized tests and measures to assess functioning in such areas as memory, concentration, attention, planning, problem solving, speech, language, and other brain functions; whereas the neurologist holds a medical degree, I am a licensed psychologist with a doctoral degree in clinical psychology and specialty training in neuropsychology.

One example the author uses to personally illustrate the difference between neurology and neuropsychology to the jury is that of an auto mechanic.

> When your car is not functioning properly, you take it to an auto mechanic who first conducts a computerized analysis of the engine. At this point, the auto mechanic may or may not find something diagnostically wrong with your car. This is very similar to what a neurologist does. He, the neurologist, will often use highly technical diagnostic equipment such as CT scans or MRI's to see if there are any visible lesions or damage to the brain. The neurologist may or may not find structural damage to the brain. In either case, the person, like the car, needs to be taken out for a test drive to see if there are any functional problems. This is where I come in as a neuropsychologist. I, like a mechanic, now takes the subject out for a test drive - that is I assess how the person

---

TABLE 5.3
Standard Background, Training, and Qualifications of a Forensic Neuropsychologist

1. Doctoral degree in clinical psychology.
2. State licensure as a psychologist at the independent practitioner level.
3. Specialized course work and training in the following areas:
   a. Neuroanatomy and neurophysiology
   b. Behavioral neurology
   c. Neuropathology
   d. Neuropsychological assessment
4. Minimum of two years (one year of which may include the pre-doctoral internship training) clinical experience in neuropsychology under the direct supervision of a "qualified" clinical neuropsychologist.
5. The majority of the clinician's time must be spent in the practice of neuropsychology (including neuropsychological assessment, consultation, rehabilitation, and therapy of persons with neurological, medical, and/or neuropsychological disorders).
6. Diplomate (board certification) status through the American Board of Clinical Neuropsychology or the American Board of Professional Neuropsychology — which demonstrates the highest level of expertise in the field of neuropsychology.

Source: Adapted from the Guidelines for Training of Division 40 of the American Psychological Association, and Guidelines for "board certification" from the American Board of Professional Neuropsychology and the American Board of Clinical Neuropsychology.

---

is functioning, something that the neurodiagnostic studies such as the computer CT scan or MRI, cannot tell you.

5.3 PRACTICAL ISSUES FOR THE EXPERT WITNESS IN TBI CASES

5.3.1 THE INITIAL FORENSIC CASE CONSULTATION: DUTIES, RESPONSIBILITIES, AND BEING PAID AS AN EXPERT WITNESS

In all matters pertaining to the engagement of the expert witness physician or medical scientist, a request for any and all material relating to the case is imperative to your understanding and proffered objective opinion of the case. Attorneys typically work in nature to design questions that can be answered in a "yes" or "no" response pattern. If a question cannot be answered in that manner, the expert should tell the attorney that the question cannot be answered with a "yes" or "no" response. If the expert cannot answer the question, he or she should state such as opposed to looking for an answer that sounds pseudo-professional, and appears plausible or feasible. The expert should never testify outside the boundaries of the well-defined area of expertise established by the forensic examiner's specific profession. The expert's well-defined area of expertise is limited to knowing a tremendous amount of information about something very, very small in terms of subject matter or content applicable to the particular case. If not, anyone and everyone could potentially offer an opinion and give testimony about TBI, neuropsychology examination, medical treatment, or neurorehabilitation.

In regards to the initial attorney-expert consultation, it is the responsibility of the medical professional to request the material needed during that initial contact (provided the attorney has agreed to engage the professional as a designated expert). The expert should not let the attorney tell him or her what is needed. If the professional in the field of medicine or neuropsychology is unsure of what exactly is needed, the expert should listen to the attorney's theory of the case and ask precise questions in terms of how the case involves the expert opinion. The expert should refrain from giving an opinion based on his or her own theory. The forensic expert should request the needed materials from the attorney and meticulously review the record for key data and facts. Before the close of the initial attorney-expert phone consultation, the expert should discuss matters pertaining to fee structure (for research, record review, travel, on-call or standby, deposition, and trial), and procedures for submitting an invoice of billable hours. Some experts charge based on the demands of the case on their professional time. Although it varies from expert to expert, some charge per hour, while others charge by day or half day. Some forensic examiners charge by being placed on a "retainer" which is based on a projected dollar estimate from the time one will spend on the case. The expert must keep the attorney informed of the status of the initial retainer as it will eventually run out. When the retainer is depleted, the forensic expert should inform the attorney and a new estimate for a revised retainer should be submitted. As a matter of choice, this author recommends that an expert never take a case on a contingency fee basis as the expert should have no invested interest in the case other than to provide an expert, scientifically or medically grounded opinion. Finally, charging for phone calls, postage, envelopes, paper, pencils, copy services, and supplies are, at best, discretionary on the part of the expert.

Invariably, one can only estimate how much time it will take in any case. However, the expert should be as precise and practical as possible when it comes to your travel, research, reading, and pre-trial preparation time of the case. However, the expert's time is valuable. Typically, no one spends one hour in court. In most TBI cases, the expert will spend the majority of the day away from the hospital or practice setting. The expert should charge for time while on the phone discussing the case with the attorney or paralegal, for pre-trial preparation, travel time, and court time (including time spent waiting to be called and while on the stand). Often the opposing attorney will request the expert's presence for a deposition. In such cases, the opposing counsel pays for the expert's time at the end of the deposition. It is good practice to ensure that payment is made before leaving the deposition unless other arrangements have been made in advance. Typically experts are only paid for the time in deposition and not for travel or pre-deposition preparation which is typically billed to the attorney who has engaged the expert in the first place. In any case, keep a precise record of your time and bill the attorney for your pre-trial research, phone consultation, and trial time.

5.3.2 THE FORENSIC EXPERT AS WITNESS AND THE AD HOMINEM
ATTACK

The "ad hominem" legal attack often times involves the attack of the credibility of an expert witness. Many witnesses, including this author, interpret this as an assault on the personal and professional integrity of the expert. In fact, that is exactly the design, intent, and purpose of an ad hominem attack. The attack, in scope, is an attempt by those cross examining (opposing) to upset the expert witness when the expert's opinion on a particular point appears weak or in some cases, unpenetrable. Such attacks are often made when a case is impossible to defend and the attorney needs to develop new avenues or approaches to litigating the personal injury case. There are four things the expert needs to know in regard to the ad hominem attack: (1) the ad hominem attack is typically not a personal attack on you per se; rather, it is just a clinical strategy designed to annoy, emote, distract, and even change the demeanor and court "professional face" (trial disposition) of the expert; (2) the expert should *always* remain calm and in control despite the seemingly unruly character of the attorney; (3) complete all sentences and answers from the questions asked by the attorney (unless directed by the judge or the attorney who has retained you) not to; and (4) the expert should refuse to submit to any ploys such as game playing that involve estimates, formulas, numbers, or percentages.

Throughout the attack, the expert should always remain consistent in his or her opinion, particularly when citing technical books and respected treatises or medical doctrines which may have been quoted out of context by the attorney. Maintaining a professional demeanor is critical. The expert has the advantage when an ad hominem attack is launched by the attorney. Hostile attorneys can and will be confronted by the court (judge) if they are out of line.

5.3.3 ADVICE FOR THE EXPERT WITNESS IN FORENSIC LITIGATION
AND CONSULTING CASES

When an expert is engaged or retained as a forensic expert, the following are some practical points, tips, and business guidelines that the author has found to be effective:

- Make sure you have a letter of engagement from the attorney or firm on their letterhead requesting your mental health opinion regarding the case.
- Provide the firm or agency with a follow-up letter on your letterhead to confirm the engagement to include a disclaimer that you can not guarantee the outcome of any trial regardless your opinion, expertise, credentials, and experience.
- Provide the engaging attorney or agency with your curriculum vitae and biographical statement. Be very brief (even if you are greatly accomplished) as a lengthy CV in court can make you appear as a "hired gun."
- Let the attorney present your credentials in court. The opposing attorney can object as to the necessity of your appearance and try to disqualify you. Ultimately, the judge (the court) decides if you meet the definition

of an expert in your field which is generally based upon the Federal Rules of Evidence (FRE) Code (Federal Judicial Center, 1994).

- Make sure from the beginning that you are clear as to what party, i.e., attorney, agency, firm, etc., is underwriting your expenses.
- Set and establish the fee structure up front, i.e., across the board, door-to-door, as fees are generally different for evidence review, pre-trial work, deposition and trial, report writing, etc.
- Never be inconsistent about your fee structure. Once establishing a fee for expert services, honor it. The matter of fees for services can be problematic so keep them simple. Fee structures can be staggered depending on the task and level of involvement or straight across the board.
- Get your fee up front if possible, unless you are retained by a large reputable agency or firm.
- If your involvement in the case is limited, i.e., record review, set an equitable time for your involvement and bill for only that time. If you are required to appear at deposition, clarify who is making the request (most often opposing counsel), and be sure to be paid immediately after the deposition is completed.
- If you are needed again, such as to appear during trial, establish this early with the attorney who has hired you as the fee for trial-related work is generally higher.
- Ask for a reasonable retainer from the attorney or firm and bill from there if you feel more comfortable having expenses paid for up front.
- Always ask for a retainer. If that is not possible, then ask the firm, agency, attorney, or fiscal officer if they provide "itemized billing sheets" and when you should appropriately submit them, i.e., ever two weeks, monthly, etc.
- If itemized billing sheets are not used, regardless of the firm or attorney, **always** keep meticulous records of your time and involvement in the case and submit your billing in accordance with what has been arranged between you, the firm, or the attorney of record engaging your services.
- With inexperienced trial attorneys or new attorneys, be polite and give professional guidance related to your area of expertise (neuropsychology, psychology, neurology, rehabilitation medicine, etc.).
- You do not have to work pro bono. At the time of deposition, get your work on record and stop when it is time to stop.
- Do not be inconsistent on your expert opinion. If you must change your opinion, tell the attorney as soon as possible and substantiate why you feel your impression or opinion has changed.
- Do not place notes in the case file regarding conversations you have had with your attorney. Keep only those notes that pertain to the case itself. These notes can be used by the opposing attorney during the process of "discovery."
- **Never** expose or disclose cases on which have been consulted in the past six months especially if you have not been designated or retained as the expert in that case.

- Form a solid clinical and forensic opinion and stay with it. Do not be pressured to change it for whatever reason. If for whatever reason you **must** change your opinion, inform the attorney of record immediately and stipulate as to why this is grounded in scientific basis or fact.
- Keep the legal firm or attorney who retained you aware of your time involving billing hours. Problems may arise with very large bills, especially with public service offices (i.e., district attorney, public defender, etc.).
- Never give your opinions to other experts. Remember, you never know who may be listening with great interest. Your opinion is confidential and should ONLY be disclosed under certain prescribed conditions (i.e., pre-trial counsel, deposition, or during the actual trial).
- When you make a promise to the legal firm, agency, or attorney, try to keep that commitment if possible. The attorney may have made promises to the other agencies, attorneys, judges, and trial court.
- When preparing for deposition, know your case and file well. Review it frequently and as often as possible. Your additional review for your own comfort zone and confidence level must not be confused with your initial review of the record for purposes of payment. Always remember that a review of the scientific evidence or record is to get information, provide clarification, and provide foundation for your opinion. Additional review of the record might serve to decrease your own anxiety over the case but is not a basis for additional billing. Use common sense and be practical. Read the case thoroughly the first time for background and information and record your involvement. Then, as a matter of course, you may wish to re-read the case as necessary to glean specific facts that might involve foundation for your forensic opinion. However, that is your time and a second review is standard practice right before deposition and trial. Remember, any notes you make on the actual record or on paper can be used in deposition and trial.
- During the trial, always remember that the judge and jury are your audience. Direct your attention, eye contact, voice projection, body language, and responses in their direction. In general, they do not like experts per se, but experts are an understood part of the adversarial system.
- At trial, remain calm. Try to talk and project your voice moderately in a rate that is coherent and relaxed. Practice and cognitively visualize (*in vitro*) your appearance before you go to court which can desensitize you and minimize the anxiety response in actual (*in vivo*) situation when the court date arrives.
- Use "lay person" terminology (nomenclature), especially when discussing diagnostic procedures, techniques, and methods, etc. Coach the attorney when a medical/scientific term must be used. In all cases, strive to always explain difficult material in a simple way so no one in court feels alienated in a way that only you know what you are talking about. That is the art of testifying as an expert which can not be overemphasized here.
- Do not try to impress or overwhelm the jury or judge with your clinical knowledge and intuition. Keep it simple. In the end, "psychobabble"

and technical ICD-9 or DSM-type nomenclature can work against you and the case. If a clinical or medicolegal term must be introduced, do so but with considerable judgement, academic wisdom, clarification, and the understanding that you are not talking to jurors with Ph.D.s or MDs.

- Have a pre-trial case consultation with your attorney before court so you are on the same page.
- If the attorney of record does not ask you the questions you would like, assist him or her during this phase of the trial during direct or re-direct testimony.
- When you put a note in your record, always think how the opposing attorney could us it to confront or cross-examine you as a means to damage your position in trial. If your testimony is "damaged," rehabilitation by counsel is certain which generally calls for another expert to provide "damage control" around your testimony. In general, keep all your clinical notes (impressions) in your head. Remember, your thoughts cannot be subpoenaed or sequestered.
- Dress and look conservatively and always act in a professional manner.
- Do not purge your case file immediately. Keep a file of the forensic examination for approximately one to two years. Remember, a legal appeal might be forthcoming. If you are concerned about the life of the case file, contact the attorney or agency who engaged you.
- Do not surrender the file to anyone. Similar to patient records, shred the original record to insure protection of yourself and the client (i.e., agency, firm, etc.).

5.4 CONCLUSION

Research findings show that the appointment of an expert is a very complicated issue. Various factors must be taken into account before we understand why an expert is or is not selected or appointed. As the expert witness and the technology concerning the expert witness grows and improves, it is important for the judicial system to keep pace. In the near future, court appointed experts may be needed in a greater number of cases and judges will need to be aware of the issues and rules concerning the appointment of a court expert.

In summary, the best advice the author can give to a forensic expert involved in a personal injury case is to be thoroughly knowledgeable of the case, the facts of the case, and your preparation around those facts. The expert needs to stay in close contact with the attorney that has engaged him or her during the case and as new developments surface, the expert needs to review the case and new documents. Points between conversations, depositions, and trial can often become unclear and confusing. Ultimately, however, it is the responsibility of the attorney to prepare the forensic expert for trial and it is the expert's duty to inform the attorney if the opinion has changed based on new evidence or from the facts surrounding the case. Finally, the expert needs only be honest, neutral, disinterested, and above all, objective in his or her opinion as a scientist and practitioner.

SUGGESTED READINGS

Moenssens, A.A., Starrs, J.E., Henderson, C.E., and Inbau, F.E., (1995). *Scientific Evidence and Expert Testimony (Fourth Edition)*. Foundation Press, Inc., Westbury, NY.

Waltz, J.R. and Park, R.C., (1995). *Evidence: Cases and Materials (Eighth Edition)*. University Casebook Series. Foundation Press, Inc., Westbury, NY.

Ziskin, J. and Foust, D., (1988). *Coping with Psychiatric and Psychological Testimony: Vol. I*, Law and Psychiatry Press, Inc., Marina del Rey, CA.

Ziskin, J. and Foust, D., (1988). *Coping with Psychiatric and Psychological Testimony: Vol. II*, Law and Psychiatry Press, Inc., Marina del Rey, CA.

Ziskin, J. and Foust, D.,(1988). *Coping with Psychiatric and Psychological Testimony: Vol. III*, Law and Psychiatry Press, Inc., Marina del Rey, CA.

REFERENCES

Anderson, P.R., (1987). *Expert Witnesses*. State University of New York Press, Albany, NY.

Cecil, J.S. and Willging, T.E., (1993). *Court Appointed Experts. Defining the role of experts appointed under Federal Rule of Evidence 706*. Federal Judicial Center.

Cooke, G., (1980). *The Role of the Forensic Psychologist*. Charles C. Thomas, Springfield, IL.

Davis, J.A., (1996a). On the stand: the expert witness. Part - II. *Journal of the Forensic Examiner,* 5(9,10), September/October, Springfield, MO.

Davis, J.A., (1996b). On the stand: the expert witness. Part - I. *Journal of the Forensic Examiner,* 5(7,8), July/August, Springfield, MO.

Davis, J.A., (1996c). On the stand: the expert witness. An Introduction. *Journal of the Forensic Examiner,* 5(5,6), May/June, Springfield, MO.

Davis, J.H., (1986). Peer review in the courtroom. *Journal of Forensic Sciences,* 31, 803-804.

Dorran, P.B., (1982). *The Expert Witness*. Planners Press, Chicago, IL.

Eckert, W.G., (1984). Medicolegal (Forensic) examination: don't go beyond your competence. *American Journal of Medical Pathology,* 5, 5-6.

Ewing, C.P., (1985). *Psychology, Psychiatry, and the Law.* (pp. 389-410). Professional Resource Exchange, Inc., Sarasota, FL, p. 389-410.

Feder, H. A. (1991). *Succeeding as an Expert Witness*. Van Nostrand Reinhold, New York.

Federal Judicial Center, (1994). *Reference Manual on Scientific Evidence*. Federal Judicial Center, Washington, D.C.

Fisher, B.A., (1993). *Techniques of Crime Scene Investigation*. CRC Press LLC, Boca Raton, FL, p. 22-24.

Fox, G.D., (1986). Compelling expert testimony: can (and should) you do it? *Florida Bar Journal,* 60, 69-71.

French, A.P., (1984). The expert witness. *Journal of the American Medical Association (JAMA),* 245, 361.

Haddad, J.B., Zagel, J.B., Starkman G.L., and Bauer, W.J., (1992). *Criminal Procedure.* The Foundation Press, Inc., Westbury, NY, p. 338-350.

General Electric v. Joyner. 117, S. Ct. 1243 (1997); *Fine Law,* No 96-188 (Dec. 18, 1997).

Howard, L.B., (1986). The dichotomy of the expert witness. *Journal of Forensic Sciences,* 31, 337-341.

Kaplan, J., Waltz, J.R., and Roger, C.P., (1992). *Evidence.* The Foundation Press, Inc., Westbury, NY, p. 764-775.

Kraft, M.D., (1982). *Using Experts in Civil Cases*. Practicing Law Institute, New York.

Labowitz, D.I., (1988). Getting involved in the legal system: choice or chance? *Clinical Chemistry,* 34, 460-463.

Lewis, A.A., (1984). *The Evidence Never Lies.* Holt, Rinehart, and Winston, New York.

Lundberg, G.D., (1984). Expert witness for whom? *Journal of the American Medical Association (JAMA),* 252, 251.

McKracken, D.D., (1971). *Public Policy and the Expert. Ethical Problems of the Witness.* The Council on Religion and International Affairs, New York.

O'Hara, C.E. and O'Hara, G.L., (1994). *Fundamentals of Criminal Investigation.* Charles C. Thomas, Springfield, IL, p. 649-670.

Peterson, J.L., (1975). *Scientific Investigation in Criminal Justice.* New York, NY: AMS Press, Inc.

Reed, J., (1999). Current status of the admissibility of expert testimony after Daubert and Joiner. *Journal of Forensic Neuropsychology.* 1(1), 49-69.

Shapiro, D. L. (1984). *Psychological Evaluation and Expert Testimony.* Van Nostrand Reinhold, New York.

Sperber, N.D., (1981). Forensic odontology. *Scientific and Expert Evidence.* Practising Law Institute, p. 721-754.

Spitz, W.U. and Fisher, R.S., (1993). *Guidelines for the Application of Pathology to Crime Investigation.* Medicolegal investigation of death. Charles C. Thomas, Springfield, IL.

Strong, J.W., (1992). *McCormick on Evidence.* West Publishing Co., St. Paul, MN, p. 19-30.

Swanson, C.R., Chamelin, N.C., Territo, L., (1988). *Criminal Investigation.* Random House, New York, p. 581-583.

Wentworth, P, and Carson, J. (1988). Remember one main rule when called to testify: Be prepared. *Journal of the Canadian Medical Association,* 138, 843-845.

Wetli, C.V. (1988). On being an expert witness. *Laboratory Medicine,* 545-550.

Appendix A: Model Outline for the Assessment of Mild Traumatic Brain Injury

The following is a model outline for assessment of mild traumatic brain injury (TBI) cases by a forensic examiner to determine if the examinee meets the criteria for mild TBI:

Review of post-injury documents and reports:

1. Police report at scene of accident.
2. Ambulance report.
3. Emergency room and hospital record.
4. Inpatient or outpatient physician consultation/evaluation or follow-up notes.
5. Chiropractor evaluation and treatment notes.
6. Professional (physical, occupational, and speech therapies and nursing progress) evaluation and treatment reports.
7. Psychological evaluation and treatment reports.
8. Neuropsychological consultation and testing result reports.
9. Clinical interview.

Assessment Issues:
- ☐ Date of injury
- ☐ Age at time of injury
- ☐ Reports from spouse/significant others
- ☐ Documented loss or change in level of consciousness
- ☐ Glasgow Coma Scale Score (GCS):
  - ☐ Date(s): _____
  - ☐ Reporter(s): _____
- ☐ Galveston Orientation and Amnesia Test Score (GOAT):
  - ☐ Date(s): _____
  - ☐ Reporter(s): _____
- ☐ Report of alteration in mental state: _____Yes   _____No
  - ☐ Date(s): _____
  - ☐ Reporter(s): _____
  - ☐ Length of time: _____
- ☐ Post-traumatic amnesia:
  - ☐ Date(s): _____
  - ☐ Reporter(s): _____

0-8493-2035-6/00/$0.00+$.50
© 2000 by CRC Press LLC

☐   Anterograde amnesia/length of time: _____
☐   Retrograde amnesia/length of time: _____

☐   Neuroimaging studies:
   ☐   Head CT
      ☐   Date(s):   _____Normal   _____Abnormal
   ☐   Head MRI
      ☐   Date(s):   _____Normal   _____Abnormal
   ☐   EEG
      ☐   Date(s):   _____Normal   _____Abnormal

☐   Current medications   ☐   Date started

   ☐   _____   ☐   _____

   ☐   _____   ☐   _____

   ☐   _____   ☐   _____

   ☐   _____   ☐   _____

   ☐   _____   ☐   _____

☐   Post-injury seizures   _____Yes   _____No
☐   Other neurological findings:
   ☐   Concussion   _____Yes   _____No
      ☐   Date(s): _____
      ☐   Reporter(s): _____
   ☐   Hematoma   _____Yes   _____No
      ☐   Date(s): _____
      ☐   Reporter(s): _____
   ☐   Closed head injury
   ☐   List of other neurological diagnoses: _____
_____
      ☐   Date(s): _____
      ☐   Reporter(s): _____
☐   Symptom complaints: _____
_____
_____

☐   Neuropsychological test results/date: _____

	Significantly Impaired	Mildly Impaired	Low-Normal	Normal	High-Normal
☐ Attention and concentration	_____	_____	_____	_____	_____
☐ Working memory	_____	_____	_____	_____	_____
☐ Verbal memory	_____	_____	_____	_____	_____
☐ Visual memory	_____	_____	_____	_____	_____
☐ Mental flexibility	_____	_____	_____	_____	_____
☐ Speech-language abilities	_____	_____	_____	_____	_____
☐ Psychomotor functioning	_____	_____	_____	_____	_____
☐ Visual spatial abilities	_____	_____	_____	_____	_____
☐ Executive functioning	_____	_____	_____	_____	_____

□   Premorbid IQ estimate:
- □   Below average
- □   Low average
- □   Average
- □   High average plus

□   **PHYSICAL SYMPTOMS**   **DATE FIRST REPORTED**
- □   Headache   _____
- □   Dizziness   _____
- □   Visual difficulties   _____
- □   Sleep disturbance   _____
- □   Fatigue   _____
- □   Other   _____

COGNITIVE SYMPTOMS
- □   Short-term memory loss   _____
- □   Forgetfulness   _____
- □   Slow mental speed   _____
- □   Decreased impulse control   _____
- □   High distractibility   _____
- □   Poor attention   _____
- □   Problem solving and planning difficulties   _____
- □   Word finding difficulties   _____
- □   Poor judgement   _____
- □   Other   _____

EMOTIONAL/PSYCHOLOGICAL SYMPTOMS
- □   Mood swings   _____
- □   Irritability   _____
- □   Suicidal thoughts   _____
- □   Anxious mood   _____
- □   Decreased libido   _____
- □   Other   _____

□   Review of pre-injury history and reports:
    Documents to be reviewed:
- □   Developmental history
- □   School records and transcripts
- □   Standardized test scores
- □   Military history (standardized tests or training)
- □   Vocational history
- □   Medical history
- □   Psychological/psychiatric history
- □   Family medical and psychiatric history

□   Assessment issues:
    Academic achievement:
- □   Developmental learning disability
  - □   Type: _____   Date Documented: —————
  - □   Completed high school/GPA —————

- ☐ College training/years: _____ /GPA _____
- ☐ Pre-injury IQ test/date: _____
  - FSIQ Score: _____
- ☐ Standardized Achievement Test (SAT)
  - ☐ Type: _____
  - ☐ Date: _____
  - ☐ Scores: _____
- ☐ Vocational history
  - ☐ Current position/title
    - ☐ Laborer
    - ☐ Technical
    - ☐ Professional
- ☐ History of pre-existing medical conditions.
- ☐ History of TBI:
  - ☐ Date(s): _____
  - ☐ Severity: _____
- ☐ Seizure disorder:
  - ☐ Date(s): _____
- ☐ Other neurologic condition
- ☐ Medical problems/diagnoses:
  - ☐ Date(s): _____
- ☐ Psychiatric diagnoses:
  - ☐ Date(s): _____
- ☐ Psychopharmacological treatment/type:
  - ☐ Date(s): _____
- ☐ Psychotherapy/counseling:
  - ☐ Date(s): _____
- ☐ Examinee meets American Congress of Rehabilitation Medicine definition for mild TBI (meets at least one of the following criteria):
  - ☐ Any period of loss of consciousness of less than 30 minutes and Glasgow Coma Scale of 13–15
  - ☐ Retrograde and/or anterograde amnesia with PTA of less than 24 hours
  - ☐ Alteration in mental state at time of accident (dazed, disoriented, confused)
  - ☐ Focal and neurological deficits, transient or permanent
- ☐ Examinee meets criteria for the following DSM-IV criteria:
  - ☐ Amnestic disorder due to TBI
  - ☐ Cognitive disorder, not otherwise specified
  - ☐ Personality change due to TBI
  - ☐ Mood disorder due to TBI
  - ☐ Anxiety disorder due to TBI
  - ☐ Adjustment disorder
  - ☐ Other: _____

Appendix B: Select Issues in the Forensic Assessment of Traumatic Brain Injury with Key References from the Research Literature

A. Definitions of and criteria for traumatic brain injury (TBI):

American Congress of Rehabilitation Medicine, (1993). Definition of mild traumatic brain injury. *Journal of Head Trauma Rehabilitation,* 8(3), 86-87.

Evans, R.W., (1992). Mild traumatic brain injury. *Physical Medicine and Rehabilitation Clinics of North American,* 3(2), 427-439.

Esselman, P.C. and Uomoto, J.M., (1995). Classification of the spectrum of mild traumatic brain injury. *Brain Injury,* 9, 417-424.

American Psychiatric Association, (1994). *Diagnostic and Statistical Manual of Mental Disorders — Fourth Edition.* American Psychiatric Association, Washington, D.C.

Teasdale, G. and Jennett, B., (1974). Assessment of coma and impaired consciousness: a practical scale. *Lancet,* 2, 81-84.

Medicode, Inc., (1998). *International Classification of Disease — 9th Revision.* Medicode, Inc., Salt Lake City, UT, Section 850.

B. Neuropsychological impairment and neuroimaging studies:

Gale, S.D., Johnson, S.C., Bigler, E.D., and Blatter, D.D., (1995). Trauma-induced degenerative changes in brain injury: a morphometric analysis of three patients with pre-injury and post-injury MR scans. *Journal of Neurotrauma,* 12(12), 151-8.

Wilson, J. and Wyper, D., (1992). Neuroimaging and neuropsychological functioning following closed head injury: CT, MRI and SPECT. *Journal of Head Trauma Rehabilitation,* 7(2), 29-39.

Eslinger, P.J., Damasio, H., Radford, N.D., and Damasio, A.R., (1984). Examining the relationship between computer tomography and neuropsychological measures in normal and demented elderly. *Journal of Neurology, Neurosurgery and Psychiatry,* (12), 1319-1325.

0-8493-2035-6/00/$0.00+$.50
© 2000 by CRC Press LLC

Thatcher, R.W., Camacho, M., Salazar, A., Linden, C., Biver, C., and Clarke, I., (1997). Quantitative MRI of the gray-white matter distribution in traumatic brain injury. *Journal of Neurotrauma,* 14(1), 1-14.

Anderson, C.V., Wood, D.M., Bigler, E.D., and Blatter, D.D., (1996). Lesion volume, injury severity, and thalamic integrity following head injury. *Journal of Neurotrauma,* 12, (1) 35-40.

C. Neuropsychological base rates and TBI:

Dikman, S., Machamer, J., Winn, H.R., and Temkin, N., (1995). Neuropsychological outcome at one year post head injury. *Neuropsychology,* 9(1) 80-90.

Lees-Haley, P.R. and Brown, R.S., (1993). Neuropsychological complaint base rates of 170 personal injury claimants. *Archives of Clinical Neuropsychology,* 8, 203-209.

Nemeth, A.J., (1996). Behavior-descriptive data on cognitive, personality and somatic residua after relatively mild brain trauma: studying the syndrome as a whole. *Archives of Clinical Neuropsychology,* 11(8), 677-695.

Palmer, B., Boone, K., Lesser, I., and Wohl, M., (1998). Base rates of "impaired" neuropsychological test performance among healthy older adults. *Archives of Clinical Neuropsychology,* 13(6), 503-511.

D. Neuropsychological recovery and outcome post-TBI:

Dikman, S., Machamer, J., Winn, H.R., and Temkin, N., (1995). Neuropsychological outcome at one year post head injury. *Neuropsychology,* 9(1) 80-90.

Dikman, S. and Levin, H., (1993). Methodological issues in the study of mild head injury. *Journal of Head Trauma Rehabilitation,* 8(3), 30-37.

Gale, S.D., Johnson, S.C., Bigler, E.D., and Blatter, D.D., (1995). Trauma-induced degenerative changes in brain injury: a morphometric analysis of three patients with pre-injury and post-injury MR scans. *Journal of Neurotrauma,* 12(12) 151-8.

Nemeth, A.J., (1996). Behavior-descriptive data on cognitive, personality and somatic residua after relatively mild brain trauma: studying the syndrome as a whole. *Archives of Clinical Neuropsychology,* 11(8), 677-695.

Prigatano, G.P. and Fordyce, D.J., (1986). Cognitive dysfunction and psychosocial adjustment after brain injury, in *Neuropsychological Rehabilitation After Brain Injury,* Prigatano, G.P., Fordyce, D.J., and Zeiner, H.K., Eds., Johns Hopkins University Press, Baltimore, MD.

Prigatano, G.P. and Altman, I.M., (1990). Impaired awareness of behavioral limitations after traumatic brain injury. *Archives of Physical Medicine and Rehabilitations,* 71, 1058-1064.

Willer, B., Rosenthal, M., Kreutzer, J.S., Gordon, W.A., and Rempel, R., (1993). Assessment of community integration following rehabilitation for traumatic brain injury. *Journal of Head Trauma Rehabilitation,* 8(2), 75-87.

E. TBI and the MMPI-2:

Youngjohn, J., Davis, D., and Wolfe, I., (1997). Head injury and the MMPI-II: paradoxical severity effects and the influence of litigation. *Psychological Assessment,* 9(3) 177-184.

Scott, J., Emick, M., and Adams, R., (1999). The MMPI-II and closed head injury: effects of litigation and head injury severity. *Journal of Forensic Neuropsychology,* 1(2) 3-13.

Peck, E., Mitchell, S., Burke, E., Baber, C., and Schwartz, S., (1993). *Normative data for 463 head injury patients for the MMPI, BDI, and SCL-90 tests across three time periods post-injury.* Poster presented at the 21st Annual Meeting of the International Neuropsychological Society, February 24, 1993, Galveston, TX.

Paniak, C.E. and Miller, H.B., (1993). *Utility of MMPI-2 validity scales with brain injury survivors.* Paper presented at the meeting of the National Academy of Neuropsychology, October 28–30, 1993, Phoenix, AZ.

Levin, H.S., Gass, C., and Wold, H., (1997). MMPI-II interpretation in closed-head trauma. Crossed validation of a correction factor. *Archives of Clinical Neuropsychology,* 12(3), 199-205.

Lees-Haley, P.R., (1991). MMPI-II F and F-K. Scores of personal injury malingerers in vocational neuropsychological and emotional distress claims. *American Journal of Forensic Psychology,* 9(3), 5-14.

Alphona, D.P, Finlayson, A.J., Stearns, G.M., and Elison, P.M., (1990). The MMPI in neurologic dysfunction: profile configuration and analysis. *The Clinical Neuropsychologist,* 4, 69-79.

F. The forensic assessment of malingering:

Binder, L.M., (1993). Assessment of malingering after mild head trauma with the Portland Digit Recognition Test. *Journal of Clinical and Experimental Neuropsychology,* 15, 170-182.

Franzen, M.D., Iverson, G.L., and McCracken, L.M., (1990). Detection of malingering in neuropsychological assessment. *Neuropsychology Review,* 1(3), 247-279.

Frederick, R.I., Carter, M., Powel, J., (1995). Adapting symptom validity testing to evaluate suspicious complaints of amnesia in medicolegal evaluations. *The Bulletin of American Academy of Psychiatry and the Law,* 23(2), 227-233.

Lees-Haley, P.R., (1989). Litigation response syndrome: how the stress of litigation confuses the issues or personal injury: family and criminal litigation. *Defense Counsel Journal,* 56(1), 110-114.

Mittenberg, W., Azrin, R., Millsaps, C., and Agilbronner, R., (1993). Identification of malingered head injury on the Wechsler Memory Scale — Revised. *Psychological Assessment,* 5(1), 34-40.

G. Post-TBI depression:

American Psychiatric Association, (1994). *Diagnostic and Statistical Manual of Mental Disorders — Fourth Edition.* American Psychiatric Association, Washington, D.C.

Busch, C.R. and Alpern, H.P., (1998). Depression after mild traumatic brain injury: a review of current research. *Neuropsychology Review,* 8 (2), 95-108.

Putnam, S.H. and Millis, S.R., (1994). Psychosocial factors in the development and maintenance of chronic somatic and functional symptoms following mild traumatic brain injury. *Advances in Medical Psychotherapy,* 7, 1-22.

Rosenthal, M., Christenson, B.K., and Ross, T.P., (1998). Depression following traumatic brain injury. *Archives of Physical Medicine and Rehabilitation,* 79, 90-103.

H. Estimation of pre-morbid (pre-injury) functioning:

Barona, A., Reynolds, C.R., and Chastani, R., (1994): A demographically based index of premorbid intelligence for the WAIS-R. *Journal of Consulting in Clinical Psychology,* 52, 885-887.

Barry, D.T., Carpenter, G.S., Campbell, D.A., Schmitt, F.A., Helton, K., and Lipka-Molby, J.N., (1994). The New Adult Reading Test — Revised: accuracy in estimating WAIS-R IQ scores obtained 3.5 years earlier from normal older persons. *Archives of Clinical Neuropsychology,* 9, 239-250.

Blair, J.R. and Spreen, O., (1989). Predicting premorbid IQ: A revision of the national adult reading test. *The Clinical Neuropsychologist,* 3, 129-136.

Crawford, J., (1992). Current and premorbid intelligence measures in neuropsychological assessment, in *A Handbook of Neuropsychological Assessment,* Crawford, J.R., Parker, D.M., and McKinlay, W.W., Eds., Lawrence Erblom Associates, Englewood Cliffs, NJ.

Johnstone, B., Callahan, C.D., Kapila, C., and Bounan, D., (1996). The comparability of the WRAT-R reading test and NAART as estimates of premorbid intelligence in neurologically impaired patients. *Archives of Clinical Neuropsychology,* 11(6), 513-519.

Karaken, D.A., Gur, R.C. and Saykain, A.J., (1995). Reading on the Wide Range Achievement Test-Revised and Parental education as predictors of IQ: Comparison with the Barona Equation. *Archives of Clinical Neuropsychology,* 10, 147-157.

Wines, A.N., Bryan, J.E., and Crossen, J.R., (1993). Estimating WAIS-R FS IQ from The National Adult Reading Test-Revised in normal subjects. *The Clinical Neuropsychologist,* 7, 70-84.

Appendix C: Listing of State Courts Using Federal Rule 702 and/or Daubert Standard

Rule 702	Daubert Standard
Alabama	Arkansas
Alaska	Connecticut
Arizona	Delaware
Arkansas	District of Columbia
California	Georgia
Colorado	Hawaii
Delaware	Idaho
District of Columbia	Indiana
Florida	Iowa
Georgia	Kentucky
Hawaii	Louisiana
Idaho	Maine
Illinois	Massachusetts
Indiana	Montana
Iowa	Nevada
Kansas	New Hampshire
Kentucky	New Jersey
Louisiana	New Mexico
Maine	North Carolina
Maryland	North Dakota
Michigan	Ohio
Minnesota	Oklahoma
Mississippi	Oregon
Missouri	Rhode Island
Montana	South Carolina
Nebraska	South Dakota
Nevada	Tennessee
New Hampshire	Texas
New Jersey	Utah
New Mexico	Vermont
North Carolina	Virginia
North Dakota	West Virginia
Ohio	Wisconsin
Oklahoma	Wyoming
Oregon	
Rhode Island	
South Carolina	
South Dakota	
Tennessee	
Texas	
Utah	
Vermont	
Virginia	
Washington	
West Virginia	
Wisconsin	
Wyoming	

Index